Managing M Teams: MS-700 Exam Guide

Configure and manage Microsoft Teams workloads and achieve Microsoft 365 certification with ease

Peter Rising

Nate Chamberlain

BIRMINGHAM—MUMBAI

Managing Microsoft Teams: MS-700 Exam Guide

Group Product Manager: Wilson D'suoza

Publishing Product Manager: Shrilekha Inani

Senior Editor: Rahul Dsouza

Content Development Editor: Sayali Pingale

Technical Editor: Sarvesh Jaywant

Copy Editor: Safis Editing

Project Coordinator: Neil Dmello

Proofreader: Safis Editing

Indexer: Pratik Shirodkar

Production Designer: Shankar Kalbhor

First published: February 2021

Production reference: 1090221

Published by Packt Publishing Ltd.
Livery Place
35 Livery Street
Birmingham
B3 2PB, UK.

ISBN 978-1-80107-100-0

www.packt.com

To my amazing wife, Louise, and my incredible sons, George and Oliver. I'm so proud of you all and grateful for the strength you give me in very uncertain times in the world. I love you all dearly.

– Peter Rising

To my parents, Pam and Calvin Chamberlain, for their examples of bravery, love, and determination that have inspired me to rise to any challenge life brings. I'm proud to be their son.

– Nate Chamberlain

Foreword

Microsoft Teams is important

As the fastest-growing app in Microsoft history, Microsoft considers Teams so important that in a recent interview with the Financial Times, Satya Nadella said that Teams will become a "digital platform as significant as the internet browser." It's yet another accolade in an incredible story for an app that – by the time this book is published – will only be 4 years old. Having entered general availability in the spring of 2017 after it was developed in an internal hackathon, Teams is a converged application, bringing together communication and collaboration workloads such as chats, meetings, calling, and apps. It has won Enterprise Connect twice. It is now used by over 90% of the Fortune 100. It is available in over 180 markets and supports over 50 languages. Today, we know that the global **Daily Active Usage** (**DAU**) is somewhere north of 115 million. Back in July 2019 when Microsoft announced that Teams had overtaken Slack in terms of usage at Microsoft Inspire, the DAU stood at only 13 million.

So, this raises the million-dollar question: what has fueled the growth of Microsoft Teams since the latter half of 2019? What has caused this explosion in usage? All things considered, the principal factor driving its usage has undoubtedly been Covid-19. As the pandemic has spread across borders and over continents, organizations of every type in every vertical in every country have needed to adapt to a new way of working to survive or function. Life as we know it has changed. With the shift of many organizations to operating remotely, Teams has been key in helping them achieve continuity and resilience while allowing people to stay in touch. Students can still go to school and both learn and interact with their teachers. Patients can still see their doctors for a consult. By bringing together the tools we need to work effectively and the means to communicate seamlessly with others, Teams has helped many of us be just as productive as before – or sometimes even more productive.

Yet even though Covid brought what Microsoft considered to be "2 years of digital transformation in 2 months," it hasn't been the only reason for Teams' growth. Firstly, the rapid rate of innovation in Teams, where Microsoft has listened extensively to users and loaded its development assets into the product, has led to a continuous stream of new features that has refined Teams at an amazing pace.

Private channels, custom backgrounds, shared system audio, Together mode, Large Gallery view, policy packages, tighter integration with SharePoint, tighter integration with the Power Platform, the introduction of Teams on Linux, and Skype consumer interop are just some of these features. Even the small additions that backfill Skype for Business functionality, such as Longest Idle, Busy on Busy, and Simultaneous Ring, keep on increasing Teams' value. Secondly, Microsoft has worked hard the last few years on the extensibility of Teams.

Now supporting an ecosystem of over 800 store applications, any organization can build upon the out-of-the-box functionality and customize Teams to suit their needs. Having broadened the extensibility surface to include channels, chat, UI components, and even meetings, organizations can develop their own apps, bots, or messaging extensions, or even connect Teams to third-party apps they have already invested in via connectors and webhooks. They can do so using a full-code approach with their own tools or SPFX, or they can do so using a low-code or no-code approach with the Power Platform.

When organizations begin to use Teams as a base upon which other applications are developed, accessed, and surfaced, it is what we call "Teams as a Platform." This is the digital platform to which Satya refers: bringing what you need into one space, enabling continuity of workflow across apps, and enabling the accessing of apps from anywhere on any device, benefitting all workers, including those in frontline roles. It is a new phase for Teams that will see it go beyond simply being a communications and collaboration app to being an app that looks more like an operating system such as Windows.

Finally, the growth of Teams has happened because overall, Teams is very user-friendly. In addition to resonating with and appealing to how users aspire to work in the modern age, it is a great way to access and adopt the rest of the Microsoft 365 stack, increasing the return for organizations that have chosen to invest in it. When you have a conversation on Teams, you are leveraging Exchange Online. When you upload a file to Teams, you are using OneDrive or SharePoint. The point is, by bringing collaboration and communication workloads together, by bringing apps into Teams and using Teams as a platform, users are getting a great user experience, organizations have a single place where users can easily access and use the apps they need to do their best work, and Microsoft knows that their customers are more likely to begin using apps that they may never have used previously, such as Stream, Yammer, and even core apps such as SharePoint. This explains why Teams isn't an additional cost and why it's included within every Microsoft 365 subscription. It's no coincidence that with the DAU of Teams now being 115 million, SharePoint's **Monthly Average Usage** (**MAU**) has grown to 200 million.

Our look at the importance of Teams and why it has grown sets us up to look at the importance of the Teams administrator. It is the Teams administrator who is at the very center of the organization, driving digital transformation. They are accountable for how Teams is configured and administered, and they may also play a large part in how users adopt Teams, wherever they may be in the world. It is a role that will be increasingly seen as critical in terms of administration and the user experience of Microsoft 365. The Teams administrator will work with most, if not all, other administrators in the team, and they may get hands-on with some really cool devices. They will be expected to keep up with all the latest innovations to harness new functionality and make Teams work better.

Typical projects in which a Teams administrator may be involved could include migrating on-premises legacy file servers to the cloud so that each team in the organization can access and co-author files in Teams with other users inside and outside of the organization. The role could include setting up audio conferencing, the phone system, and calling plans so users can use Teams as a fully fledged phone and conferencing system, including building auto attendants and call queues, deploying common area phones, and procuring certified devices for each user. The role could also include applying advanced compliance features such as **Data Loss Prevention** (**DLP**) and communications compliance to ensure that sensitive data and PII isn't disclosed within Teams chats and channel conversations to adhere to regulatory standards.

What is critical and what makes for a great Teams administrator is putting users at the center of everything. How can you help make their day better? How can the latest innovations help make their lives easier given what your organization also needs you to achieve? Does this app improve what members of the team need to do, within the bounds of compliance? Is this team optimally configured? Do we have too many teams and need to introduce a life cycle policy to make sure we aren't weighed down with a sprawl of teams? Have we configured, and do employees know about, all the accessibility features, so that Teams can be as inclusive as possible for the benefit of all?

Getting to the business end, passing the *MS-700 Managing Microsoft Teams* exam will earn you the Teams Administrator Associate certification. Whether you sit the exam because you need to sit it for your role, to advance, or if it is part of your journey to Enterprise Administrator, or even if you simply have a passion for Teams or certifications, each of these reasons is equally valid. I sat the exam myself when it was in beta and did so simply because I wanted to validate my own experience and see how much I knew.

Now, to really understand MS-700, it's recommended to have a read through and deconstruct the skills outline. There is one word that crops up time and time again. It's also in the title of the exam. This word is *manage*. MS-700 is an exam designed for the all-up administrator. It's not one aimed at the developer, nor the voice or endpoint specialist. It is for the administrator who manages Teams in a typical midmarket to enterprise-size organization on a day-to-day basis. These administrators are fluent in the **Teams Admin Centre** (**TAC**); may have performed a migration from Skype for Business to Teams; have configured and maintained core workloads; have configured security and compliance features within Microsoft 365; have digested the weekly usage reports; have built policies; and understand the Teams life cycle, the architecture, how to configure a Teams room system, and how and when to use Powershell.

The exam does not, for example, go deep into graph or direct routing, or the ins and outs of App Studio. Indeed, in my experience of all the Microsoft exams I have taken, this one is both fair and well designed. I always like to say so when an exam has been clearly authored by those who have experience in the field. It's not broad to the point of being unwieldy, nor is it ridiculously deep and granular. It doesn't contain excessive amounts of Powershell. If you have truly engaged with and managed Teams for a period of 12 months, you should be familiar with or should have at least touched upon 70% of what is in the exam, and with this book, you should be able to go on and give it your best.

However, it would be remiss of me as a **Microsoft Certified Trainer** (**MCT**) if I didn't give you two things to be aware of before sitting the exam, which are two reasons many candidates fail if they lack exposure to the functionality in their own Microsoft 365 environments. The first thing is to remember that this is an enterprise exam; that's stated explicitly in the exam description. In other words, if you haven't already been hands-on with E5 functionality such as retention for Teams chats and conversations, DLP, communications compliance, information barriers, and entitlement in Azure Active Directory, now is the time. Secondly, a significant proportion of MS-700 is devoted to the calling workload, maybe up to 30% when networking is factored in. If your management experience has been limited to a voice-less Teams instance, then this could very well be a struggle. If you are a Microsoft partner, then Microsoft's CDX platform at `demos.microsoft.com` is a must; otherwise, it is strongly recommended that you test drive Phone System, audio conferencing, and those domestic and international call plans and use them alongside this book to get up to speed in this area.

To close, I want to clearly articulate what I feel this book brings to studying for the exam; having recently read it, I certainly wish something like this existed when I took the beta. Firstly, the book is very thorough but economical. It gives you all of what you need to know in digestible and well-ordered chapters that align with the exam objective domains, and it provides a significant number of screenshots as visual aids for reference and for working through in your own Microsoft 365 environment. At the end of every chapter, you'll be asked several multiple-choice or scenario-based questions to test your knowledge and assess your understanding, and should you want to read more around the topic at hand, there is a handy list of links to further reading.

Secondly, the book provides a mock exam, which is excellent preparation for the real exam and excellent value, given the price of the official Microsoft practice test. Last but not least, the book is written by Nate Chamberlain and Peter Rising, who are not only established authors in the Microsoft 365 space but also both MVPs, Teams evangelists, and "learn it alls" who have both sat and passed the exam themselves. Having known Nate and Peter personally for some time, I know how passionate they both are about helping others, making technical content accessible and understandable for all, and raising the general level of understanding about Teams. Unlike authors who churn out books simply because they can, Nate and Peter have dedicated their own time to making this book the very best book it could be. When they asked, I was delighted to have the opportunity to write this foreword.

I wish you the very best of luck and every success in your studies.

Chris Hoard

Teams MVP and MCT Regional Lead

Contributors

About the authors

Peter Rising is a Microsoft 365 Enterprise Administrator Expert, MCT, and Microsoft MVP in Office apps and services. He has worked for several IT solutions providers and private organizations in a variety of technical roles focusing on Microsoft technologies. Since 2014, Peter has specialized in the Microsoft 365 platform. He holds a number of Microsoft certifications, including MCSE: Productivity, MCSA: Office 365, Microsoft 365 Certified: Enterprise Administrator Expert, Microsoft 365: Security Administrator Associate, and Microsoft 365 Certified: Teams Administrator Associate. He is also the author of another Packt book, which is an MS-500 exam guide.

Nate Chamberlain is a Microsoft 365 Enterprise Administrator Expert, MCT, and Microsoft MVP in Office apps and services. He has 6 years of experience in helping organizations deploy Microsoft 365 apps and services and promoting their usage, governance, and adoption. His work has included administrative, analyst, and trainer roles in the higher education, healthcare, corporate, and finance sectors. Nate is the author of several other books, including an MS-101 exam guide, an MS-500 exam guide, an Office 365 administration cookbook, and a handful of smaller publications on SharePoint, OneNote, and leading advocate groups. Nate speaks at user groups and conferences both in person and virtually throughout the year.

About the reviewers

Adam Deltinger has been in the IT industry for almost 15 years and has in the last 4 years been focusing on helping customers work more efficiently, productively, securely, and collaboratively using the Microsoft 365 platform. He has also been an Microsoft MVP for a couple of years, focusing on helping people increase value with Microsoft Teams and end-user adoption, doing talks all over the world, and being very active in the Microsoft community.

Amanda Sterner's favorite feeling in her job is when she can see that someone has actually understood how a new way of working can benefit them and be a gain instead of a pain. For the last few years, Amanda has been working with the modern workplace, collaboration, and productivity and has more recently been focusing on Microsoft Teams and how it can make daily work life better. When asked about what she does at work, Amanda usually replies, "Everything Microsoft 365 that isn't code," and that pretty much sums up her interest in being a part in all things that go on before, during, and after an implementation of Microsoft 365 and Microsoft Teams. Amanda's main goal is to help you start loving Microsoft Teams the same way she does!

Thanks to my husband, Luchi, for always letting me try new things and thrive in the Microsoft Teams community.

Mike Swantek is a solutions architect and seasoned business professional. Mike leverages his corporate experience, strategy, and vision to help add significant value to companies by utilizing Microsoft products and solutions. Mike has demonstrated achievements in SharePoint, SharePoint Online, business intelligence, process improvement, enterprise content management, information security, and project management in his 25+ year career in business and IT. Mike enjoys speaking at various events throughout the year and is also a musician in the local Detroit, Michigan area.

Linus Cansby has worked as a consultant with Unified Communication for many years now. With experience from LCS, OCS, Lync, Skype for Business, and Teams, he has a lot of experience with Microsoft meeting and voice solutions. He blogs at his personal blog (`lync.se`), hosts the podcast Teamspodden (Swedish only), and is an active member of the community. When not helping out in the community, he spends time with customers in his job as a consultant at Uclarity; he works with customers mainly in Teams implementation and improvement projects.

Thanks to my family (Emmelie, Tuva, and Frej), who bring me joy, and thanks to the wonderful community, which teaches me new stuff daily.

Packt is searching for authors like you

If you're interested in becoming an author for Packt, please visit `authors.packtpub.com` and apply today. We have worked with thousands of developers and tech professionals, just like you, to help them share their insight with the global tech community. You can make a general application, apply for a specific hot topic that we are recruiting an author for, or submit your own idea.

Table of Contents

2
Assessing Your Network Readiness for a Microsoft Teams Deployment

3
Planning and Implementing Governance and Life Cycle Settings in Microsoft Teams

4
Configuring Guest Access in Microsoft Teams

5
Managing the Security and Compliance Settings in Microsoft Teams

6

Managing Endpoint Devices in Microsoft Teams

7

Monitoring Usage within Microsoft Teams

Section 2: Administering the Meeting, Calling, and Chat Features within Microsoft Teams

8
Managing Collaboration and Chat within Microsoft Teams

9
Managing Meetings and Live Events in Microsoft Teams

10
Managing Phone Numbers in Microsoft Teams

11
Managing Phone System in Microsoft Teams

Section 3: Planning, Deploying, and Managing Policies for Microsoft Teams, and Apps within Teams

12
Creating and Managing Teams

13
Managing Team Membership Settings

14
Creating App Policies within Microsoft Teams

Section 4:
Mock Exams and Assessments

15
Mock Exam

16
Mock Exam Answers

17
Assessments

Other Books You May Enjoy

Index

Preface

Managing Microsoft Teams: MS-700 Exam Guide offers complete, up-to-date coverage of the MS-700 exam so that you can take it with confidence, fully equipped to pass the first time. With this book, you will learn the steps for planning a deployment of Microsoft Teams within a business environment and managing Teams administrative functions on a day-to-day basis.

Who this book is for

This book is for IT professionals who wish to attain the Microsoft 365 Certified: Teams Administrator Associate certification. Readers of this book should already be familiar and comfortable with the principles of establishing and administering the core features and services within a Microsoft 365 tenant. An understanding of other Microsoft 365 workloads, such as Security & Compliance, Identity and Device Management, and messaging, will also be advantageous. A basic understanding of the features of Microsoft Teams is also assumed.

What this book covers

Chapter 1, Planning Your Migration to Microsoft Teams, covers topics of consideration when planning to move partially or completely from Skype for Business to Microsoft Teams.

Chapter 2, Assessing Your Network Readiness for a Microsoft Teams Deployment, helps you prepare your network to adequately handle Microsoft Teams traffic.

Chapter 3, Planning and Implementing Governance and Life Cycle Settings in Microsoft Teams, includes team templating, Microsoft 365 group creation policies, team classifications and expiration policies, and more related to team life cycles.

Chapter 4, Configuring Guest Access in Microsoft Teams, dives into guest access for users outside your organization and their permissions and abilities in your organization's meetings, chats, and calls.

Chapter 5, Managing the Security and Compliance Settings in Microsoft Teams, covers Teams admin roles, retention and sensitivity policies, Security & Compliance alerts, and more related to securing your organization's users and data in Microsoft Teams.

Chapter 6, Managing Endpoint Devices in Microsoft Teams, explores Microsoft Teams on different devices as well as Microsoft Teams Rooms device options and configurations.

Chapter 7, Monitoring Usage within Microsoft Teams, is all about reports and analytics of Microsoft Teams usage and call quality.

Chapter 8, Managing Collaboration and Chat within Microsoft Teams, covers messaging policies, external access, channel management, and more in the collaboration and chat area of Microsoft Teams administration.

Chapter 9, Managing Meetings and Live Events in Microsoft Teams, covers meeting settings and policies, live event settings and policies, and conference bridge settings.

Chapter 10, Managing Phone Numbers in Microsoft Teams, explores obtaining and managing phone numbers for use in Microsoft Teams systems, configuring emergency details, and managing voice settings in your organization.

Chapter 11, Managing Phone System in Microsoft Teams, looks specifically at resource accounts for use with call queues and auto attendants, and will also cover call park, calling, and caller ID policies.

Chapter 12, Creating and Managing Teams, is dedicated to team creation in various ways as well as managing privacy settings and organization-wide teams.

Chapter 13, Managing Team Membership Settings, helps you manage users and dynamic team membership for your organization's teams and includes configuration of Azure Active Directory access reviews.

Chapter 14, Creating App Policies within Microsoft Teams, covers the definition and process of creating app policies and app setup policies.

Chapter 15, Mock Exam, includes a case study and multiple-choice questions (25 questions in total) similar to those you can expect on the MS-700 exam itself.

Chapter 16, Mock Exam Answers, includes the answers and explanations to the 25 mock exam questions from the previous chapter.

Chapter 17, Assessments, includes the answers and explanations to all of the chapters' review questions throughout the book.

To get the most out of this book

In order to get the most out of this book, it is highly recommended to create a test Microsoft 365 environment where you can follow along and recreate the steps that are covered in each chapter.

You may sign up for an Office 365 E3 trial at `https://www.microsoft.com/en-us/microsoft-365/enterprise/office-365-e3?activetab=pivot%3aoverviewtab` – other trial options are available but the E3 suite is the most commonly used Office 365 subscription and will provide all that you need to test Microsoft Teams effectively.

The preceding trial subscription will allow you to recreate the steps covered in the chapters of this book.

This book also has some example PowerShell commands that can be used instead of the Microsoft Teams and Microsoft 365 admin centers. Therefore, it is suggested to have a Windows 10 device available where you can run PowerShell and practice some of the commands included in the chapters.

A Windows 10 device will also be useful for the purposes of installing and using the Microsoft Teams desktop client, the Microsoft Teams web version, and many more of the features described in the book.

A mobile device such as an iOS or Android device will also be useful for testing Microsoft Teams from a mobile user's perspective.

Software/hardware covered in the book	OS requirements
The Microsoft 365 admin centers (web access)	Windows, macOS, and Linux (any)
Windows PowerShell	Windows, macOS, and Linux (any)

Download the color images

We also provide a PDF file that has color images of the screenshots/diagrams used in this book. You can download it here: `http://www.packtpub.com/sites/default/files/downloads/9781801071000_ColorImages.pdf`.

Conventions used

There are a number of text conventions used throughout this book.

`Code in text`: Indicates code words in text, database table names, folder names, filenames, file extensions, pathnames, dummy URLs, user input, and Twitter handles. Here is an example: "You learned that Meeting Migration Service will be automatically triggered in several situations, and that you can manually migrate your users' meetings using PowerShell and the `Start-CsExMeetingMigration` command."

Any command-line input or output is written as follows:

```
Get-CsMeetingMigrationStatus -Identity username@domain.com
```

Bold: Indicates a new term, an important word, or words that you see onscreen. For example, words in menus or dialog boxes appear in the text like this. Here is an example: "With the **View Breakpoint** option, we can see the breakpoint established in the script."

> **Tips or important notes**
> Appear like this.

Get in touch

Feedback from our readers is always welcome.

General feedback: If you have questions about any aspect of this book, mention the book title in the subject of your message and email us at `customercare@packtpub.com`.

Errata: Although we have taken every care to ensure the accuracy of our content, mistakes do happen. If you have found a mistake in this book, we would be grateful if you would report this to us. Please visit `www.packtpub.com/support/errata`, selecting your book, clicking on the Errata Submission Form link, and entering the details.

Piracy: If you come across any illegal copies of our works in any form on the Internet, we would be grateful if you would provide us with the location address or website name. Please contact us at `copyright@packt.com` with a link to the material.

If you are interested in becoming an author: If there is a topic that you have expertise in and you are interested in either writing or contributing to a book, please visit `authors.packtpub.com`.

Reviews

Please leave a review. Once you have read and used this book, why not leave a review on the site that you purchased it from? Potential readers can then see and use your unbiased opinion to make purchase decisions, we at Packt can understand what you think about our products, and our authors can see your feedback on their book. Thank you!

For more information about Packt, please visit `packt.com`.

Section 1: Planning and Designing Your Microsoft Teams Deployment

Here, you will learn how to plan and design your Microsoft Teams environment within Microsoft 365. Upon completion of this section, you will be able to describe the upgrade paths to Microsoft Teams and plan network, security, compliance, and governance settings. Additionally, you will understand the principles of service usage within Teams along with guest access settings and how to deploy and manage endpoint devices to use Teams.

This part of the book comprises the following chapters:

- *Chapter 1, Planning Your Migration to Microsoft Teams*
- *Chapter 2, Assessing Your Network Readiness for a Microsoft Teams Deployment*
- *Chapter 3, Planning and Implementing Governance and Life Cycle Settings in Microsoft Teams*
- *Chapter 4, Configuring Guest Access in Microsoft Teams*
- *Chapter 5, Managing the Security and Compliance Settings in Microsoft Teams*
- *Chapter 6, Managing Endpoint Devices in Microsoft Teams*
- *Chapter 7, Monitoring Usage within Microsoft Teams*

1
Planning Your Migration to Microsoft Teams

If you are planning to start using **Microsoft Teams** within your organization, there is a strong chance that you will be upgrading from **Skype for Business**. If this is the case, then it is critical to plan your upgrade to Teams in a diligent and thorough manner in order to ensure a seamless transition for your users. In this chapter, we will explain the principles of upgrading from Skype for Business to Microsoft Teams.

We will demonstrate the concepts of coexistence modes within Teams, and how to choose an appropriate upgrade path. This will include an explanation of the differences between coexistence mode at the organizational level and per-user level. We will also explain the process of migrating Skype for Business meetings to Teams using the **Meeting Migration service**, along with how to set Teams upgrade notifications and meeting application choices.

In this chapter, we're going to cover the following main topics:

- Planning an upgrade path and coexistence mode from Skype for Business
- Understanding coexistence mode at both the organization and per-user level

- Configuring the Meeting Migration Service to migrate Skype for Business meetings to Teams

- Setting the Microsoft Teams upgrade notifications and default apps while in coexistence mode

Technical requirements

In this chapter, you will need to have access to the **Microsoft Teams Admin Center**, which you can reach at `https://admin.teams.microsoft.com`. You will need to be either a **Global Administrator** or a **Teams Service Administrator** in order to have full access to the features and capabilities within the Teams admin center.

You will also need to be able to connect to the Skype for Business Online PowerShell in order to run the commands required to configure hybrid connectivity between **Skype for Business on-premises** (if you have one) and your **Microsoft 365** environment.

Planning an upgrade path and coexistence mode from Skype for Business

Skype for Business Online will reach its end of life on July 31, 2021. Because of this, many organizations will need to plan how they are going to introduce and transition to Microsoft Teams. There is the option to complete this journey gradually by running Skype for Business and Teams alongside each other for a time, or by moving fully to Teams.

In this section, we will help you to understand the methods and tools that are key to a successful transition, and the principles of coexistence between Skype for Business and Microsoft Teams.

Choosing your upgrade path

The steps required to complete your migration to Microsoft Teams are largely dependent on which version of Skype for Business you are currently running in your organization. If you are running Skype for Business Online, then you will need to complete a coexistence mode setup with Teams.

However, should you be running Skype for Business on-premises, the process is more complex and requires not only setting up coexistence, but first establishing hybrid connectivity with your Microsoft 365 environment. This is required because Skype for Business on-premises users must be moved to the cloud in order to function correctly during the subsequent coexistence mode setup.

Understanding hybrid connectivity

In order to configure hybrid connectivity between your Skype for Business on-premises environment and Microsoft Teams, there are three key steps that need to be completed. These are as follows:

1. Federate your on-premises Edge service with Microsoft 365. This will allow your on-premises users to communicate with your Microsoft 365 users. To enable federation, you need to run the following command from the **Skype for Business Server Management Shell**:

```
Set-CSAccessEdgeConfiguration -AllowOutsideUsers $True
-AllowFederatedUsers $True -EnablePartnerDiscovery $True
-UseDnsSrvRouting
```

2. Set your on-premises environment to trust Microsoft 365 and configure a shared **Session Initiation Protocol** (**SIP**) address space. This will allow Microsoft 365 to host users who have an SIP domain address from the on-premises environment. To achieve this, we need to set a hosting provider by running the following commands.

3. First, check to see whether there is an existing hosting provider, and if so, remove it:

```
Get-CsHostingProvider | ?{ $_.ProxyFqdn -eq "sipfed.
online.lync.com" } | Remove-CsHostingProvider
```

4. Then, create the new hosting provider as follows:

```
New-CsHostingProvider -Identity Office365
-ProxyFqdn "sipfed.online.lync.com" -Enabled $true
-EnabledSharedAddressSpace $true -HostsOCSUsers $true
-VerificationLevel UseSourceVerification -IsLocal
$false -AutodiscoverUrl https://webdir.online.lync.com/
Autodiscover/AutodiscoverService.svc/root
```

5. Finally, enable the shared SIP address space in your Microsoft 365 environment by connecting to Skype for Business Online PowerShell with the following commands:

```
$cred = Get-Credential
```

```
Import-PSSession (New-CsOnlineSession -Credential $cred)
-AllowClobber
```

6. Once connected, we need to run the following command:

```
Set-CsTenantFederationConfiguration
-SharedSipAddressSpace $true
```

> **Important note**
> You must not change the `SharedSipAddressSpace` `$true` value to `false` until there are no Skype for Business users on the premises.

Now that you understand how to configure hybrid connectivity, let's look at the coexistence modes for Skype for Business and Microsoft Teams.

Understanding organizational coexistence modes

Skype for Business and Microsoft Teams can interoperate during the upgrade process at an organizational level. This means that during the process, some users may be using only Teams, while others may be using a mixture of Teams and Skype for Business. There are several coexistence modes available and these may be applied by Teams Administrators by using the Microsoft Teams admin center, which you can access by performing the following steps:

1. From your internet browser, navigate to `https://admin.teams.microsoft.com`. You will be prompted to sign in with your Microsoft 365 credentials, as shown in the following screenshot:

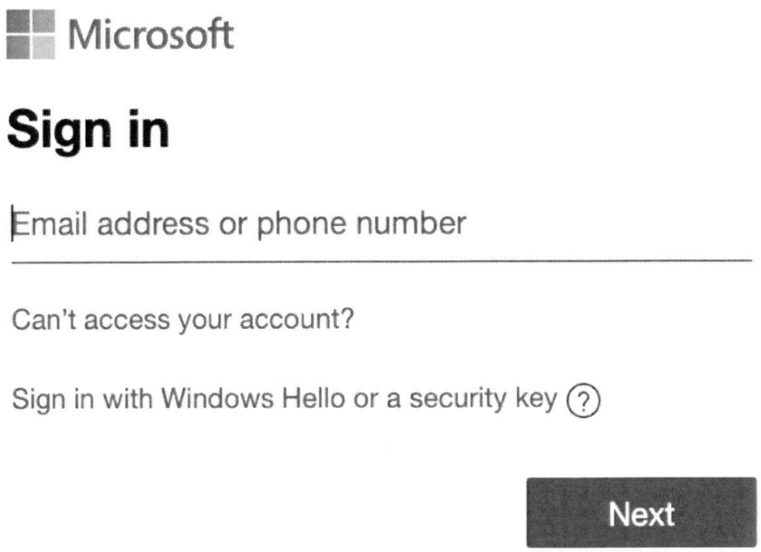

Sign in

Email address or phone number

Can't access your account?

Sign in with Windows Hello or a security key ⓘ

Figure 1.1 – Microsoft 365 Sign in screen

2. Enter your administrator credentials and then click **Next** to log in. The Teams admin center **Dashboard** screen is shown (*Figure 1.2*):

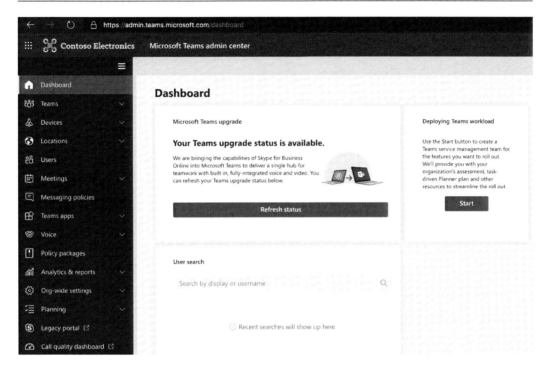

Figure 1.2 – Teams admin center

3.   From the left-hand navigation pane, select **Org-wide settings | Teams upgrade**, as shown in *Figure 1.3*:

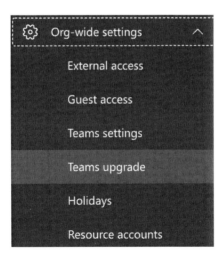

Figure 1.3 – Org-wide settings

4. You will now see the Teams upgrade options that are available to you. These are shown in *Figure 1.4*:

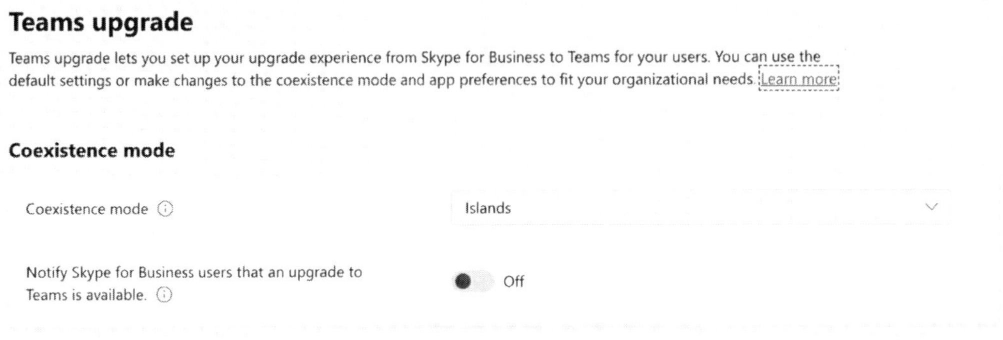

Teams upgrade

Teams upgrade lets you set up your upgrade experience from Skype for Business to Teams for your users. You can use the default settings or make changes to the coexistence mode and app preferences to fit your organizational needs. Learn more

Coexistence mode

Coexistence mode ⓘ   Islands   ⌄

Notify Skype for Business users that an upgrade to   ⚫ Off
Teams is available. ⓘ

Figure 1.4 – Teams upgrade settings

5. Under **Coexistence mode**, select the drop-down menu and you will see the following upgrade options (these will be explained in more detail in the following section of this chapter):

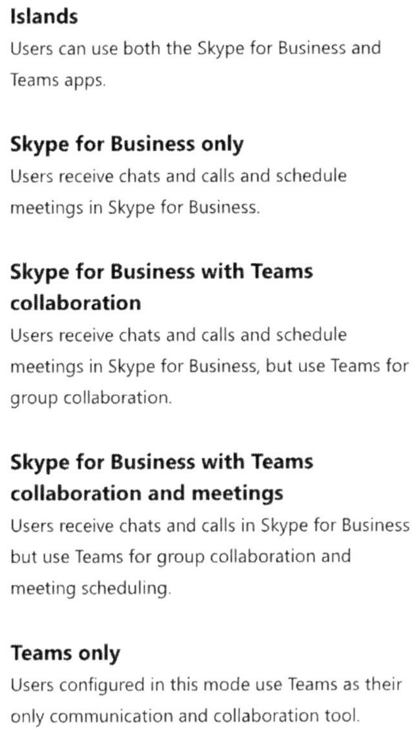

Islands

Users can use both the Skype for Business and Teams apps.

Skype for Business only

Users receive chats and calls and schedule meetings in Skype for Business.

Skype for Business with Teams collaboration

Users receive chats and calls and schedule meetings in Skype for Business, but use Teams for group collaboration.

Skype for Business with Teams collaboration and meetings

Users receive chats and calls in Skype for Business but use Teams for group collaboration and meeting scheduling.

Teams only

Users configured in this mode use Teams as their only communication and collaboration tool.

Figure 1.5 – Coexistence mode options

In the preceding example, the coexistence mode is set to **Islands** at the organizational level. This means that users may use a combination of both the Skype for Business and Teams apps. When planning a migration to Microsoft Teams, the ultimate objective is to enable **Teams only** mode across the entire organization.

However, we don't have to set all your users to **Teams only** mode at the same time, and any of the available coexistence modes may be used during the migration. The principles of per-user coexistence modes and how they differ from organizational coexistence modes are also important to understand. We will explain these differences in more detail in the *Understanding coexistence mode at both the organization and per-user level* section.

> **Tip**
> Make sure that you fully understand your hybrid connectivity and coexistence requirements when planning for your migration to Microsoft Teams from Skype for Business. It is important to engage with key stakeholders to understand how they will be affected by the transition, and this will help ensure that you plan correctly.

In this section, you learned about the upgrade paths available to Microsoft Teams. We showed you how to access the Microsoft Teams admin center and the Teams upgrade settings. We also examined the five coexistence options available while carrying out the migration to Teams.

Next, let's examine the differences of setting coexistence at both the organizational level and the per-user level.

Understanding coexistence mode at both the organization and per-user level

Now that you understand how to set coexistence mode for your organization from the Teams admin center, it is important to be aware that you also have the option to set coexistence for individual users or small sets of users as well.

In this section, we will look at the different options available in each of these methods, and some of the decisions that you will need to make.

> **Important note**
> Some older versions of Skype for Business clients may not respect some of the coexistence settings that you configure. Therefore, it is highly recommended to keep your Skype for Business versions up to date for all your users wherever possible.

We will start by taking a closer look at setting your upgrade options at the organizational level.

Setting the upgrade options for the whole organization in the Teams admin center

In the previous section, we showed you the five different upgrade options that are available from the *Org-wide settings* in the Teams admin center. In this section, we will explain when and why to choose each of these options.

In order to set the organization-wide upgrade options, we need to perform the following steps:

1. Log in to **Teams admin center**, as described in the previous section of this chapter, and navigate to **Org-wide settings | Teams upgrade**.

2. From the **Coexistence mode** drop-down menu, select from one of the following options:

    Islands: Choose this option to enable all your users to use both Skype for Business and Teams apps at the same time. There is no interoperability used when in Islands mode, and users will use Skype for Business to communicate only with other Skype for Business users, and Teams to communicate only with other Teams users. So, in effect, the two separate apps are, in fact, islands and completely independent of one another.

    Skype for Business only: Choose this option if you require all your users to use only Skype for Business. There will be no use of Teams at all with this method.

    Skype for Business with Teams collaboration: Choose this option if you require your users to use mainly Skype for Business, but also Teams, in order to collaborate in channels.

    Skype for Business with Teams collaboration and meetings: Choose this option if you require your users to use mainly Skype for Business, but also Teams in order to collaborate in channels, and to join and participate in Teams meetings. This mode also enables users to be able to create Teams meetings as well as join them. Skype meetings call also still be joined.

    Teams only: Choose this option if you require your users to only use Teams. In this scenario, users can still join Skype for Business meetings from Teams.

Saving your settings

Once you have chosen the required Teams upgrade settings for your organization, you may review your choices and then click to save them, as shown in the following screenshot:

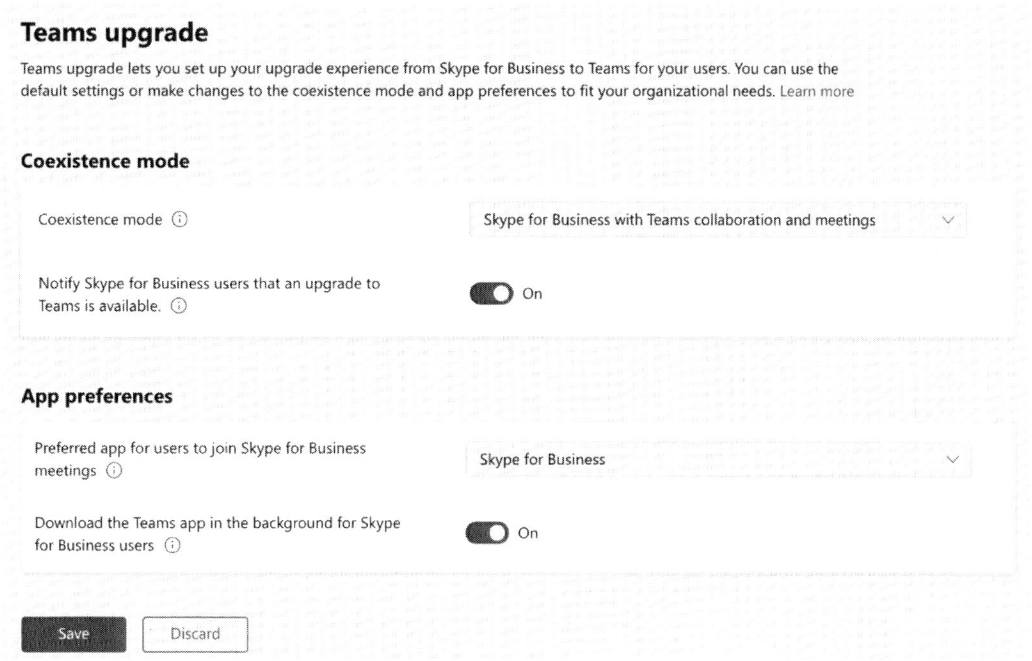

Figure 1.6 – Teams upgrade settings

> **Important note**
>
> Due to recent changes from Microsoft at the time of writing, it is not possible to set the org level to **Teams Only** unless all DNS records point to Skype Online. Therefore, unless you migrate all users to Skype only, and then point the DNS records to Skype Online, you will encounter errors.

Next, we will review the per-user upgrade options.

Setting the upgrade options for individual users in the Teams admin center

In this section, we will demonstrate how to set the upgrade options on a per-user basis. This can be achieved by performing the following steps:

1. Log in to the **Teams admin center**, as described in the previous section of this chapter and navigate to **Users**. You will see the list of your Teams users as shown in *Figure 1.7*:

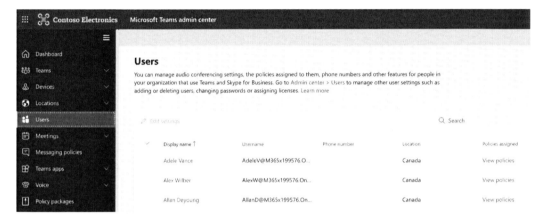

Figure 1.7 – Teams users

2. Select one of the users from the list. In this example, we will choose *Adele Vance*. Scroll down to the **Account** section for this user and, under **Teams upgrade**, you will see the options available for this user to set the coexistence mode:

Figure 1.8 – Teams upgrade options

3. Click on **Edit** as shown in *Figure 1.8* to change the upgrade setting and select from the following options:

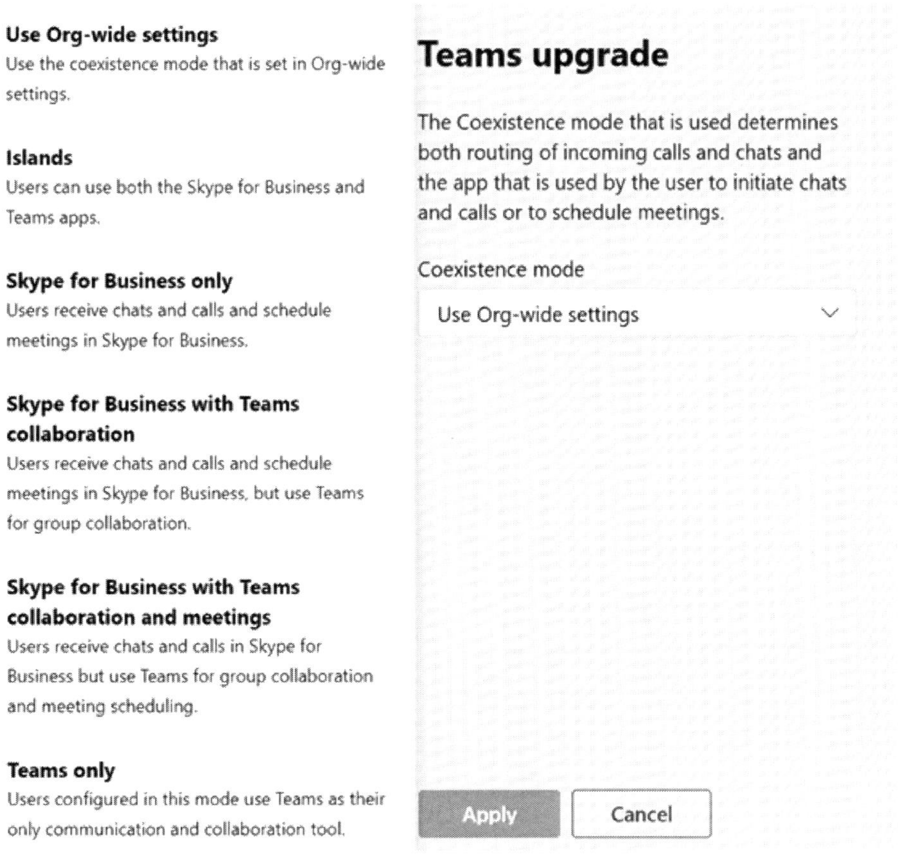

Use Org-wide settings

Use the coexistence mode that is set in Org-wide settings.

Islands

Users can use both the Skype for Business and Teams apps.

Skype for Business only

Users receive chats and calls and schedule meetings in Skype for Business.

Skype for Business with Teams collaboration

Users receive chats and calls and schedule meetings in Skype for Business, but use Teams for group collaboration.

Skype for Business with Teams collaboration and meetings

Users receive chats and calls in Skype for Business but use Teams for group collaboration and meeting scheduling.

Teams only

Users configured in this mode use Teams as their only communication and collaboration tool.

Teams upgrade

The Coexistence mode that is used determines both routing of incoming calls and chats and the app that is used by the user to initiate chats and calls or to schedule meetings.

Coexistence mode

| Use Org-wide settings   ⌄ |

[Apply]   [Cancel]

Figure 1.9 – Teams upgrade options

Use Org-wide settings: Choose this option if you would like the user to inherit the settings you configured in the Org-wide settings.

Islands: Choose this option to enable the user to use both Skype for Business and Teams apps at the same time.

Skype for Business only: Choose this option if you require the user to use only Skype for Business. There will be no use of Teams at all for the user with this method.

Skype for Business with Teams collaboration: Choose this option if you require the user to use mainly Skype for Business, but also Teams in order to collaborate in channels.

Skype for Business with Teams collaboration and meetings: Choose this option if you require the user to use mainly Skype for Business, but also Teams in order to collaborate in channels, and to join and participate in Teams meetings. This mode also enables users to be able to create Teams meetings.

Teams only: Choose this option if you require the user to only use Teams.

4. Once you have selected the desired upgrade setting for the user, click to save your changes.

In this section, we showed you the differences between setting your Teams upgrade options at the organization level, and at the per-user level. Next, we will explain how to migrate Skype for Business meetings to Microsoft Teams.

Configuring the Meeting Migration Service to migrate Skype for Business meetings to Teams

While completing your organizations upgrade to Microsoft Teams, you will need to understand the **Meeting Migration Service** (**MMS**) in certain situations. The MMS will be automatically triggered to update the meetings of your organization's users under the following circumstances:

- Users are migrated from Skype for Business on-premises to Skype for Business Online or Microsoft Teams (in Teams only mode).

- A user's audio-conferencing settings are modified.

- A user's coexistence mode is upgraded to **Teams only**.

- A user's coexistence mode is set to **Skype for Business with Teams collaboration and meetings**.

- Using the PowerShell command, `Start-CsExMeetingMigration`.

The automatic triggering of the MMS in any of the preceding conditions can be disabled by Teams administrators if required. In addition, it is also possible for the MMS to be triggered manually by Teams administrators by using PowerShell.

> **Important note**
> It is not possible to use the MMS if the user's mailbox resides on an Exchange on-premises environment, or if offboarding the user from the cloud back to on-premises.

So how does this work? Essentially, the MMS utilizes a queue system. When a user is set for migration, a search is performed against their mailbox for existing meeting events, and these are then converted to Skype for Business Online meetings, or Teams Meetings depending upon the upgrade and coexistence options, which are targeted to that user. The meeting block details are then all replaced, and the meeting invite is then updated for all invitees with the updated meeting details.

As an example, when a user is using Skype for Business on-premises, the meeting details within the invitation will appear as shown in the following screenshot:

Figure 1.10 – Skype meeting invite

However, once the user's migration has been migrated to Teams, the MMS will update the meeting invites in the user's calendar as follows:

Figure 1.11 – Teams meeting invite

Important note

If a user has edited the meeting invitation and added customized text, this will not be migrated. The updated meeting details will be the default content. In addition, content such as whiteboards and polls are not migrated with the MMS, and any such items will need to be manually recreated. Meetings with over 250 attendees may also not be migrated.

Of the five aforementioned criteria for when the MMS will be triggered, the first four will occur in a very automated fashion in most cases, so we will not focus on the processes that take place when these occur. If you would like to learn more about these, you may refer to the following Microsoft documentation:

```
https://docs.microsoft.com/en-us/skypeforbusiness/audio-
conferencing-in-office-365/setting-up-the-meeting-migration-
service-mms#updating-meetings-when-you-move-an-on-premises-
user-to-the-cloud
```

We will, however, spend some time looking at how meetings are migrated to Teams by using PowerShell commands.

Manually migrating meetings to Teams using PowerShell

By using PowerShell, Teams administrators may manually trigger meeting migrations for users with the `Start-CsExMeetingMigration` command.

An example of how this command could be applied to an individual user within your organization is shown here:

```
Start-CsExMeetingMigration -Identity username@domain.com
 -TargetMeetingType Teams
```

This command will create a migration request for the targeted user that will result in all the user's meetings being migrated to Teams.

While the migration is in progress, you may check on the status of the migration by running the following PowerShell command:

```
Get-CsMeetingMigrationStatus -Identity username@domain.com
```

Should you encounter any issues with migrating the meetings using PowerShell, individual users can use the per-user **Meeting Migration Tool** instead of migrating their own meetings. Details on how to use the Meeting Migration Tool can be found at the following link: `https://support.microsoft.com/en-gb/office/meeting-update-tool-for-skype-for-business-and-lync-2b525fe6-ed0f-4331-b533-c31546fcf4d4?ui=en-us&rs=en-gb&ad=gb`.

Should the Meeting Migration Tool also fail for any reason, users may need to manually create new meetings, or contact Microsoft for support.

In this section, we have explained the principles of the MMS and how it is used to update the meetings of your organization's users during your migration to Teams. You learned that the MMS will be automatically triggered in several situations, and that you can manually migrate your users' meetings using PowerShell and the `Start-CsExMeetingMigration` command.

Next, we will look at the options available to set Teams upgrade notifications and default apps while in coexistence mode.

Setting the Microsoft Teams upgrade notifications and default apps while in coexistence mode

When you are planning any significant change or upgrade process within your business IT environment, communication is a crucial part of the success or failure of your project. How you prepare your end users for an upcoming change will also impact their perception of any new technologies that you are planning to introduce.

This principle of effective communication is particularly applicable when planning your migration to Microsoft Teams.

Fortunately, the Microsoft Teams admin center contains some settings that can help you to ensure that your transition to Teams is accompanied by well-informed users.

To configure these settings, you will need to ensure that you have your Teams upgrade settings configured and ready, as described earlier in this chapter. You will then need to perform the following steps:

1. Log in to **Teams admin center** with your administrator account at `https://admin.teams.microsoft.com`:

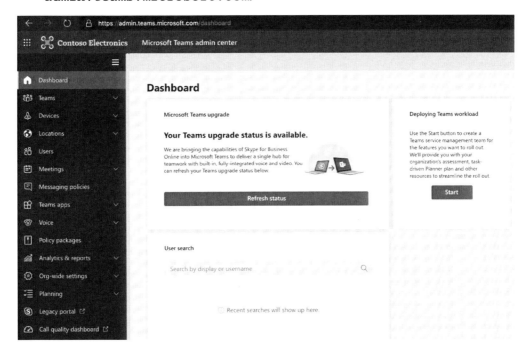

Figure 1.12 – Teams admin center

2. On the left-hand navigation pane, select **Org-wide settings**, and choose **Teams upgrade**:

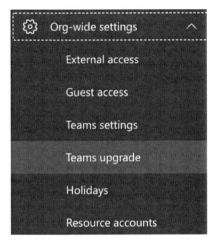

Figure 1.13 – Org-wide settings

3. Once again, this will take you to the **Teams upgrade** settings:

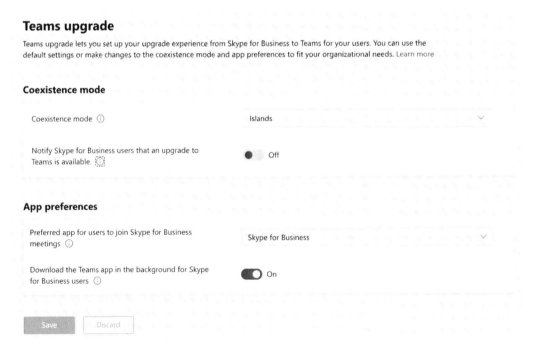

Figure 1.14 – Teams upgrade and App preferences

4. Under **Coexistence mode**, select **Notify Skype for Business users that an upgrade to Teams is available**. Note that this relates to Skype Online users only. Further reading on options for hybrid users moving to Teams is included at the end of the chapter in the *Further reading* section:

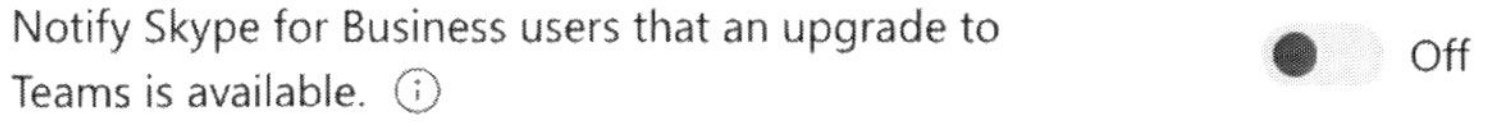

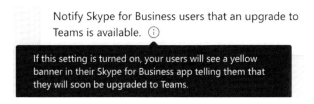

Figure 1.15 – Notifying Skype for Business users regarding the upgrade

5. Hovering over the information icon in this section will provide you with further information about what this setting will do once it is activated:

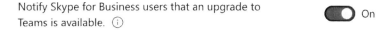

Figure 1.16 – Explanation of this setting

6. To enable user notifications, move the slider to **On**:

Figure 1.17 – Notifying Skype for Business users regarding the upgrade

The effect of this setting is that users will see a visual prompt within their Skype for Business app that informs them that the upgrade to Microsoft Teams is coming.

Next, we will illustrate how to set **App preferences**.

Setting app preferences

In addition to setting your upgrade options, you will also need to choose **App preferences** from the **Teams upgrade** section of **Teams admin center**:

Figure 1.18 – App preferences

The first of these settings allows you to select the **Preferred app for users to join Skype for Business meetings** option. The options for the preferred app may be configured as follows:

1. First, hover your cursor over the information icon and you will see that this setting is independent of the values chosen in the *Understanding coexistence mode at both the organization and per-user level* section:

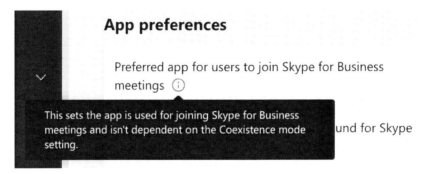

Figure 1.19 – App preferences

2. Next, click the dropdown next to **Preferred app for users to join Skype for Business meetings**. This will show you the options available for this setting. These options can be seen in *Figure 1.20*:

Figure 1.20 – App preferences

The first option is **Skype Meetings app**: This is the app for the consumer version of Skype.

The second option is **Skype for Business**: This is a limited features version of Skype for Business.

3. Once you have selected your preferred Skype app, move your cursor to hover over the option to **Download the Teams app in the background for Skype for Business users**. This will show you the impact of choosing this setting:

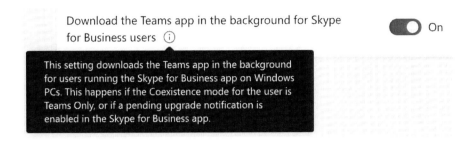

Figure 1.21 – Downloading the Teams app in the background

4. You should move the slider to the **On** position in order to activate this feature. This will cause the Teams app to be downloaded in the background on the Windows PCs of users who are running the Skype for Business app. For on-premises users, it is default behavior that when notifications are enabled, Win32 Skype for Business clients will silently download the Teams client so that the rich client is available prior to moving the user to Teams Only mode. However, you can also disable this behavior.

> **Important note**
>
> As highlighted in *Figure 1.20*, the setting to download the Teams app in the background for Skype for Business users will only be applied should the coexistence setting for the user be set to **Teams Only**, or if a pending upgrade notification is enabled in the Skype for Business app.

In this section, we have shown you how to set the Microsoft Teams upgrade notifications options and choose your default apps from the Microsoft Teams admin center. You learned that you can notify your users that a Teams upgrade is planned, that you can choose the preferred app for users to join Skype for Business meetings, and that the Teams app can be automatically downloaded in the background for users.

Summary

In this chapter, we explained the options that are available for planning a migration from Skype for Business on-premises, and Skype for Business Online to Microsoft Teams. You learned that in order to upgrade to Teams from Skype for Business on-premises, you need to configure hybrid connectivity to Microsoft Teams before choosing and configuring the appropriate coexistence mode. Additionally, we showed you how an upgrade to Teams from Skype for Business Online only requires coexistence settings to be configured.

We also explained how coexistence may be configured at both the organizational and per-user level, and how users' existing meetings may be migrated either automatically or triggered manually with PowerShell commands. Finally, we demonstrated how to configure Teams upgrade notifications and how to set your default apps while in coexistence mode.

In the next chapter, we will demonstrate how to assess your network readiness for a Microsoft Teams deployment. You will learn how to use the Teams Network planning tool, and the Network Testing Companion tool within the Teams admin center. We will also show you how to calculate the bandwidth you will require to successfully run Teams Meetings and Live Events, how the required network ports and protocols need to be configured, and how to optimize media configuration using **Quality of Service (QoS)**.

Questions

As we conclude, here is a list of questions for you to test your knowledge regarding this chapter's material. You will find the answers in the *Assessments* section of the *Appendix*:

1. When running Skype for Business on-premises, which of the following will be required to prepare for a migration to Microsoft Teams?

    a. Configure coexistence with Teams only

    b. Configure hybrid connectivity with Teams only

    c. Configure both hybrid connectivity and coexistence with Teams

    d. None of the above

2. What is the name of the service that can manually or automatically migrate users' Skype for Business meetings to teams?

    a. Skype for Business admin center

    b. Meeting Migration Tool

    c. Teams admin center

    d. Meeting Migration Service

3. True or false – Skype for Business internal users can communicate with Teams internal users when the coexistence mode is set to Islands mode?

    a. True

    b. False

4. Which of following is the correct URL for the Teams admin center?

    a. `https://teams.microsoft.com`

    b. `https://admin.teams.office.com`

    c. `https://admin.teams.microsoft.com`

    d. `https://teams.admin.microsoft.com`

5. True or false – With the Skype for Business with Teams Collaboration coexistence mode, users will use mainly Skype for Business, but can use Teams for collaborating in team channels?

    a. True

    b. False

6. Which of the following is not one of the coexistence options available within the Teams upgrade options?

    a. Lync with Teams Collaboration

    b. Teams only

    c. Skype for Business only

    d. Islands

    e. Skype for Business with Teams Collaboration

7. Which sections of the Teams admin center allow you to configure Teams coexistence settings? (Choose two).

    a. Org-wide settings | Teams settings

    b. Org-wide settings | Teams upgrade

    c. Users

    d. Teams | Manage Teams

8. True or false – The PowerShell command to trigger meeting migrations is `Start-CsExMeetingMigration`?

    a. True

    b. False

9. Which of the following is not one of the steps completed when configuring hybrid connectivity between Skype for Business on premises and Microsoft Teams?

    a. Federate your on-premises Edge service with Microsoft 365

    b. Set your on-premises environment to trust Microsoft 365 and configure a shared **Session Initiation Protocol (SIP)** address space

    c. Enable the shared SIP address space in your Microsoft 365 environment by using Skype for Business Online PowerShell

    d. Enable the shared SIP address space in your Microsoft 365 environment by using the Teams admin center

10. True or false – In coexistence mode, when selecting the option to Notify Skype for Business users that an upgrade to Teams is available, users will see a yellow banner in the Skype for Business app telling them that they will soon be upgraded to Teams?

    a. True

    b. False

Further reading

Here are links to more information on some of the topics that we have covered in this chapter:

- Upgrading from Skype for Business Online to Teams: `https://docs.microsoft.com/en-us/MicrosoftTeams/upgrade-to-teams-execute-skypeforbusinessonline`

- Skype for Business Online to be retired in 2021: `https://techcommunity.microsoft.com/t5/microsoft-teams-blog/skype-for-business-online-to-be-retired-in-2021/ba-p/777833`

- Planning your Teams upgrade: `https://docs.microsoft.com/en-gb/learn/modules/m365-teams-upgrade-plan-upgrade/`

- Getting started with your Microsoft Teams upgrade: `https://docs.microsoft.com/en-us/MicrosoftTeams/upgrade-start-here`

- About the upgrade framework: `https://docs.microsoft.com/en-us/MicrosoftTeams/upgrade-framework`

- Teams upgrade planning workshops: `https://docs.microsoft.com/en-us/MicrosoftTeams/upgrade-workshops-landing-page`

- Upgrading from a Skype for Business on-premises deployment to Teams: `https://docs.microsoft.com/en-us/microsoftteams/upgrade-to-teams-execute-skypeforbusinessonpremises`

- Configuring hybrid connectivity between Skype for Business Server and Microsoft Teams: `https://docs.microsoft.com/en-us/skypeforbusiness/hybrid/configure-hybrid-connectivity?toc=/SkypeForBusiness/toc.json&bc=/SkypeForBusiness/breadcrumb/toc.json`

- Configuring a Skype for Business hybrid: `https://docs.microsoft.com/en-us/skypeforbusiness/hybrid/configure-federation-with-skype-for-business-online`

- Managing Teams in the Microsoft Teams admin center: `https://docs.microsoft.com/en-us/microsoftteams/manage-teams-in-modern-portal`

- Using the **Meeting Migration Service** (**MMS**): `https://docs.microsoft.com/en-us/skypeforbusiness/audio-conferencing-in-office-365/setting-up-the-meeting-migration-service-mms`

- Moving users from on-premises to Teams: `https://docs.microsoft.com/en-us/skypeforbusiness/hybrid/move-users-from-on-premises-to-teams`

2
Assessing Your Network Readiness for a Microsoft Teams Deployment

When planning to introduce **Microsoft Teams** to your organization, it is important to ensure that your users will be able to use it effectively. Network and bandwidth issues will have a negative impact on your users' experience with **Microsoft Teams**. Therefore, assessing your network's ability to run Teams smoothly will be critical to the success of your Teams rollout.

In this chapter, you will learn how to assess and determine your network requirements for a successful **Microsoft Teams** deployment within your organization. We will demonstrate the Teams network planning and network testing companion tools in the **Microsoft Teams admin center**, show you how to calculate the bandwidth you will need for Teams meetings and live events, how to configure the required network ports and protocols that are required by the Teams client application, and how to optimize media configuration using **Quality of Service** (**QoS**).

In this chapter, we're going to cover the following main topics:

- Understanding the required network bandwidth for Microsoft Teams meetings and live events
- Using the Teams Network Planner and Network Testing Companion to assess readiness and determine your network requirements
- Configuring network ports and protocols to be used by the Teams client application
- Optimizing your Teams media configuration using QoS

Technical requirements

In this chapter, you will need to have access to the **Microsoft Teams admin center**, which you can reach at `https://admin.teams.microsoft.com`. You will need to be either a **global administrator,** a **Teams service administrator**, or a **Teams communications administrator** in order to carry out the steps covered in this chapter.

You will also need to be able to access Windows PowerShell in order to install the **Network Testing Companion module**.

Understanding the required network bandwidth for Microsoft Teams meetings and live events

In this chapter, we will show you some tools and processes that you can use to assess the state of your network and its readiness for a Microsoft Teams deployment. The tools we will be looking at include the **Network Planner** and **Network Testing Companion**.

However, before we look at how, we need to understand why and when you plan to deploy Teams into your organization. It's important to understand the way Teams prioritizes QoS in relation to the state of your network.

An example of how this works is that when Teams detects limited bandwidth, then audio quality will be given priority over video quality. Teams will always attempt to maximize both audio and video quality, and the better your bandwidth, the better your experience will be.

Where unlimited bandwidth is available, Teams can provide up to 1080p video resolution. In fact, HD quality video can be delivered in under 1.2 Mbps, which shows that Teams only uses what it needs in order to deliver the best possible experience. Overall, though, the better your bandwidth, the better your experience is going to be.

Microsoft has provided the following guidance on minimum bandwidth requirements in relation to **Microsoft Teams**:

- For peer-to-peer audio calls, a minimum of 30 Kbps is recommended.

- For peer-to-peer audio calls and screen sharing, a minimum of 130 Kbps is recommended.

- For peer-to-peer 360p video calls at 30 fps, a minimum of 500 Kbps is recommended.

- For peer-to-peer 720p HD video calls at 30 fps, a minimum of 1.2 Mbps is recommended.

- For peer-to-peer 1080p HD video calls at 30 fps, a minimum of 1.5 Mbps is recommended.

- For group video calls, 500 Kbps/1 Mbps is suggested.

- For HD group video calls of 540p on a 1080p screen, 1 Mbps/2 Mbps is suggested.

Understanding the preceding requirements will help you to successfully plan your organization's Teams deployment.

Now that we have set the scene in terms of what is required, let's look at how you can interrogate your network to assess and determine your readiness and establish your network requirements.

Using the Teams Network Planner and Network Testing Companion to assess readiness and determine your network requirements

When setting out to identify your organization's network requirements for Microsoft Teams, there are two tools that are available to you. These are **Network Planner** and **Network Testing Companion**. In this section, we will introduce you to both tools and show you how to use them to help plan for your Teams deployment.

Using Network Planner

Network Planner is a tool that can be found in the **Teams admin center** and is used to calculate and plan your organization's network requirements for connecting to Microsoft Teams. By inputting details relating to your network, and your anticipated usage of Teams, the Network Planner tool will provide calculations for network requirements for you to successfully deploy Teams to your business locations.

The tool works by using personas, which you may create, or you can use some built-in personas that are recommended by Microsoft. These personas are then used to assess some typical usage scenarios. Running these persona exercises then enables you to extract reports that will guide you on your network requirements.

So how does this work? Let's look at running the Network Planner by completing the following steps:

1. From your internet browser, log in to the **Teams admin center** by navigating to `https://admin.teams.microsoft.com` and signing in with your Microsoft 365 credentials:

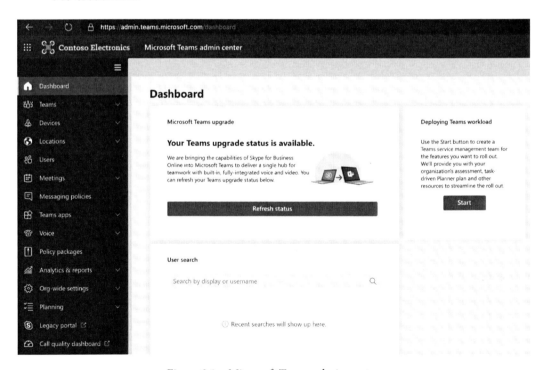

Figure 2.1 – Microsoft Teams admin center

2. From the admin center, choose **Planning | Network planner** as shown in *Figure 2.2*:

Planning
Teams advisor
Network planner

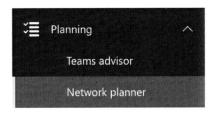

Figure 2.2 – Network planner

You will now see **Network planner** options as shown in *Figure 2.3*:

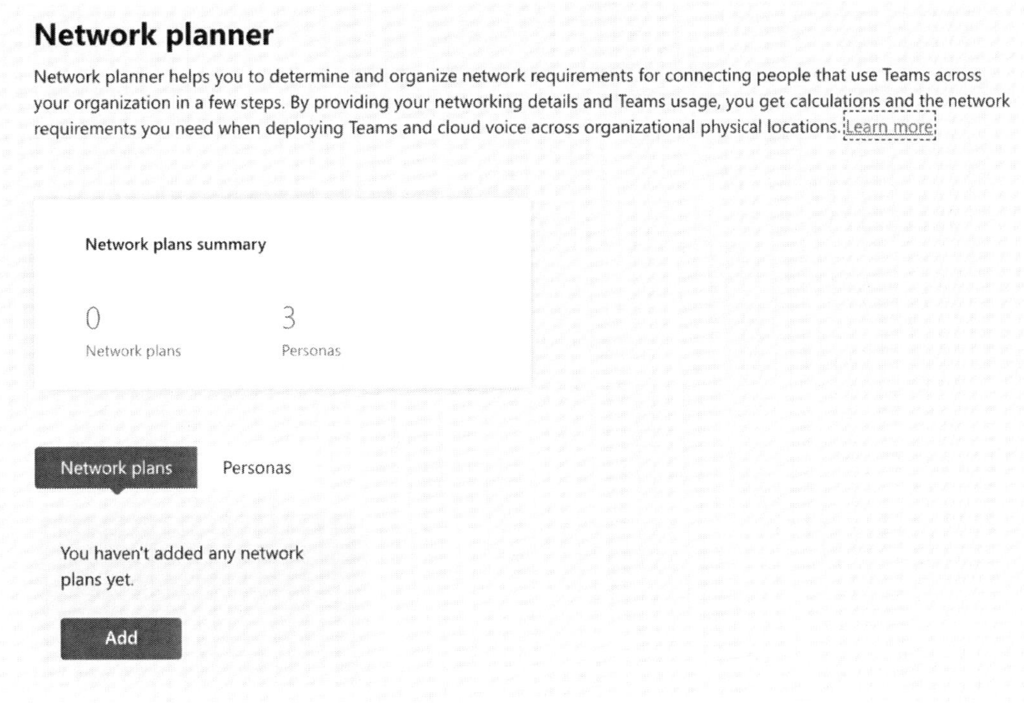
Network planner
Network planner helps you to determine and organize network requirements for connecting people that use Teams across your organization in a few steps. By providing your networking details and Teams usage, you get calculations and the network requirements you need when deploying Teams and cloud voice across organizational physical locations. Learn more
Network plans summary
0
Network plans
3
Personas
Network plans
Personas
You haven't added any network plans yet.
Add

Figure 2.3 – Network planner

3. The first step we need to carry out is to use a built-in persona, or we can create a custom persona. To do this, click on **Personas**. This will show you the three built-in Microsoft personas, which are **Teams Room system**, **Remote worker**, and **Office worker**, as illustrated in *Figure 2.4*:

Figure 2.4 – Built-in personas

4. You may examine the settings of these built-in personas by clicking on each one. However, you are unable to edit these personas. This is shown in *Figure 2.5*:

Figure 2.5 – Built-in personas

5. In most situations, the built-in personas will suffice. However, you may also click **+ Add** to create your own custom personas. This allows you to be more selective in the persona settings you choose as shown in *Figure 2.6*:

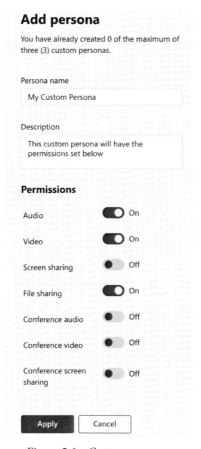

Figure 2.6 – Custom persona

6. Click **Apply** to finish creating your custom persona. You will see your new custom persona displayed as shown in *Figure 2.7*:

Figure 2.7 – New custom persona

7. Now that we have examined our available personas, we need to build a network plan. To do this, we need to click on **Network plans**, and select **Add**:

Figure 2.8 – Add a network plan

8. Enter a name and description for your plan, then click **Apply**:

Figure 2.9 – Create a network plan

Your newly created network plan will now show in the list of **Network plans**, as
shown in *Figure 2.10*:

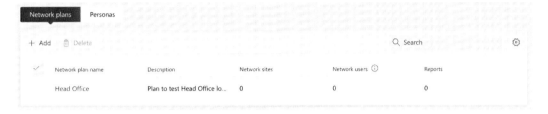

Figure 2.10 – Network plans

9. Next, click on your new plan to view it:

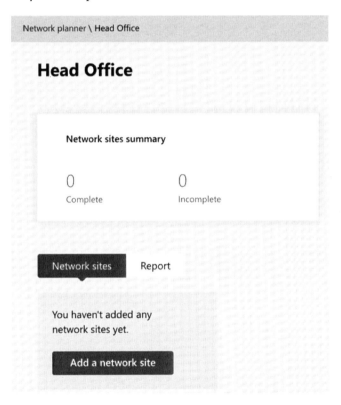

Figure 2.11 – Add a network site

10. Click on **Add a network site** and add the details for your site as per the example in *Figure 2.12*. A site may represent a location or a building complex. It is best practice to first create local sites, prior to creating sites that connect remotely through the internet or **Public Switched Telephone Networks** (**PSTNs**):

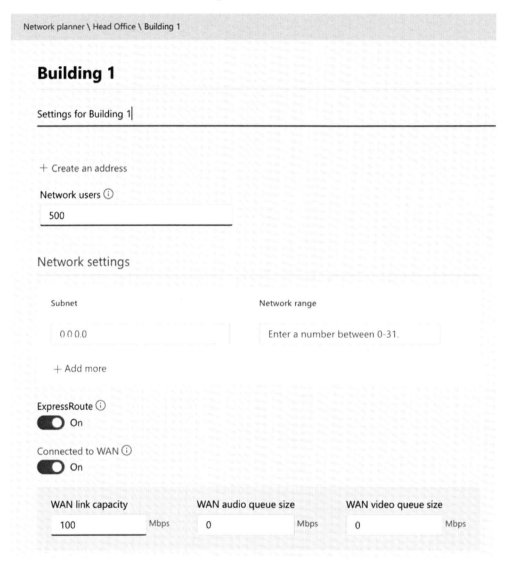

Figure 2.12 – Adding a network site

11. Scroll down and set the values for the settings shown in *Figure 2.13* and click **Save**:

Figure 2.13 – Saving your network site

Your new network site will now be shown in the list of sites:

Figure 2.14 – New network site

12. Now that you have your network sites ready, we can use these sites to create reports. To do this, select **Report**, then click on **Start a report**:

Figure 2.15 – Start a report

13. By default, the Microsoft default personas will be selected here, and the network user amounts will be automatically calculated. You may add further personas if required and distribute the user numbers manually. Once you have made your choices, click on **Generate report**:

Figure 2.16 – Generate report

The projected impact of the settings that you chose will now be shown as illustrated in *Figure 2.17*:

Figure 2.17 – Projected impact

14. You may run the report again later if you wish and use the options at the top right of *Figure 2.17* to switch between views and export your report to a PDF.

So, you can see how the Network Planner can help you to prepare to introduce Teams to your business locations. Another tool that can be used to assess our Teams deployment requirements is the Network Testing Companion.

Using the Network Testing Companion

The **Network Testing Companion** tool can be used to run quality and connectivity tests on your network. In order to run this tool, we need to complete the following steps:

1. Run PowerShell as an administrator and run the following command:

    ```
    Install-Module -Name NetworkTestingCompanion
    ```

    The results of running this command are shown in *Figure 2.18*:

```
PS C:\Users\RisingP> Install-Module -Name NetworkTestingCompanion

Untrusted repository
You are installing the modules from an untrusted repository. If you trust this repository, change its
InstallationPolicy value by running the Set-PSRepository cmdlet. Are you sure you want to install the modules from
'PSGallery'?
[Y] Yes  [A] Yes to All  [N] No  [L] No to All  [S] Suspend  [?] Help (default is "N"): y
PS C:\Users\RisingP>
```

Figure 2.18 – Installing the Network Testing Companion tool

2. Next, run the following command:

    ```
    Invoke-ToolCreateShortcuts
    ```

    This command is shown in *Figure 2.19*:

```
PS C:\windows\system32> Invoke-ToolCreateShortcuts
Successfully created Desktop shortcut.
Successfully created Start Menu shortcut.
PS C:\windows\system32>
```

Figure 2.19 – Creating a desktop shortcut

A shortcut for the Network Testing Companion launcher will now be created on your desktop:

Figure 2.20 – Shortcut creation

3. Double-click the shortcut and the application will start to launch:

Figure 2.21 – Launching the application

4. The application will open as shown in *Figure 2.22*. Click on the green **Install** button:

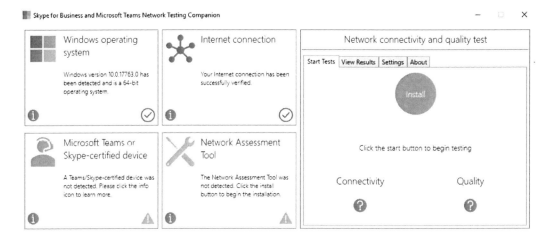

Figure 2.22 – Installing the tool

5. Once completed, you will see the message **Successfully installed the tool!**. Click **Start** to run a connectivity and quality test:

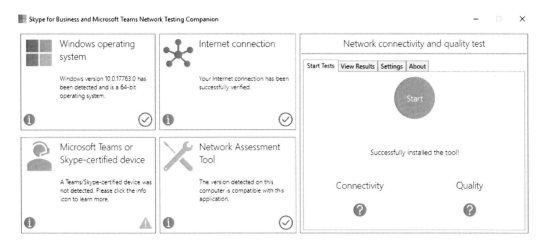

Figure 2.23 – Installation complete

6.   The test begins as shown in *Figure 2.24*:

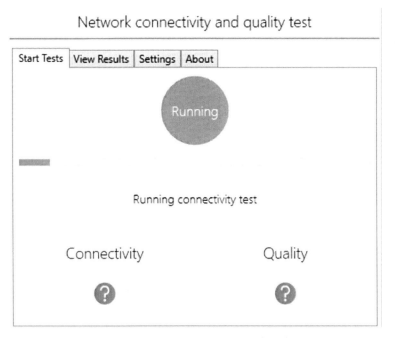

Figure 2.24 – Running connectivity and quality tests

7. At this point, you may be prompted to allow the application access via Windows Defender Firewall. Click on **Allow access**:

Figure 2.25 – Allow access through Windows Defender Firewall

8. The tests will complete and can be inspected in the **View Results** tab. In *Figure 2.26*, we can see that in this example, the network connectivity tests failed, but the network quality tests succeeded:

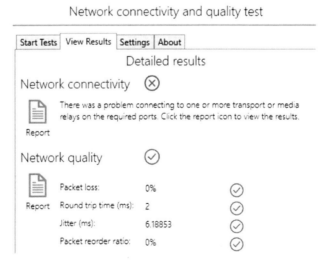

Figure 2.26 – Viewing the test results

9. Click on the **Report** icon to the left of each of the test results to view the results and troubleshoot any issues before running the tests again. *Figure 2.27* shows the results of the unsuccessful connectivity test:

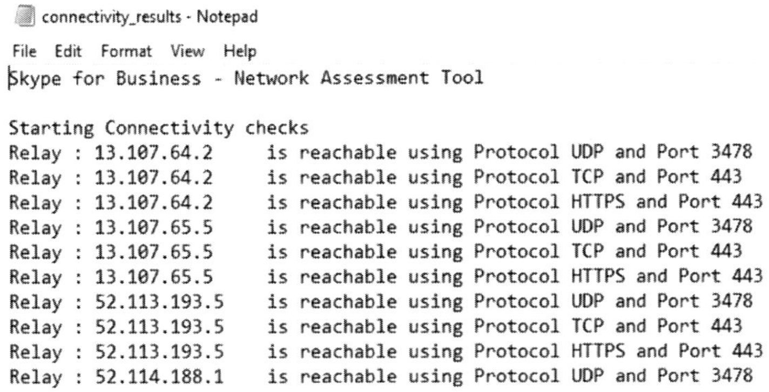


```
Skype for Business - Network Assessment Tool

Starting Connectivity checks
Relay : 13.107.64.2     is reachable using Protocol UDP and Port 3478
Relay : 13.107.64.2     is reachable using Protocol TCP and Port 443
Relay : 13.107.64.2     is reachable using Protocol HTTPS and Port 443
Relay : 13.107.65.5     is reachable using Protocol UDP and Port 3478
Relay : 13.107.65.5     is reachable using Protocol TCP and Port 443
Relay : 13.107.65.5     is reachable using Protocol HTTPS and Port 443
Relay : 52.113.193.5    is reachable using Protocol UDP and Port 3478
Relay : 52.113.193.5    is reachable using Protocol TCP and Port 443
Relay : 52.113.193.5    is reachable using Protocol HTTPS and Port 443
Relay : 52.114.188.1    is reachable using Protocol UDP and Port 3478
```

Figure 2.27 – Connectivity test results report

In this section, we have shown you how to use the Network Planner, and Network Testing Companion to assess your network's and locations' readiness for a Microsoft Teams deployment.

Next, we will show you the network ports and protocols that the Teams client application uses.

Configuring network ports and protocols to be used by the Teams client application

We've understood the bandwidth requirements and how to use planning tools for our Microsoft Teams deployment. Next, we need to familiarize ourselves with a number of network ports and protocols that will need to be opened up on your organization's firewalls in order to ensure that Teams works correctly.

Opening media ports

The following ports must be opened at all your business locations for Teams media requirements:

- UDP ports `3478` through `3481` for IP addresses `13.107.64.0/18`, `52.112.0.0/14`, and `52.120.0.0/14`

Now, let's learn how to create DNS for Skype for Business.

Creating DNS required to federate with Skype for Business

Should you require your Teams deployment to federate with **Skype for Business**, you will need to add the following **CNAME** DNS record values to your domain hosting control panel for all your domains using Teams.

The first of these records is as follows:

- Hostname – `sip`
- TTL – `3600`
- Value – `sipdir.online.lync.com`

The second of these records is as follows:

- Hostname – `lyncdiscover`
- TTL – `3600`
- Value – `webdir.online.lync.com`

In addition to the preceding ports and DNS records, there are several more ports and protocols that relate to both **Microsoft Teams and Skype for Business**. It is highly recommended that you review and familiarize yourself with these by reviewing the Microsoft documentation, which can be found at `https://docs.microsoft.com/en-us/microsoft-365/enterprise/urls-and-ip-address-ranges?view=o365-worldwide#skype-for-business-online-and-microsoft-teams`.

> **Important note**
> In a hybrid setup, all DNS records will need to point to *on-premises*.

Understanding the steps that you need to complete in relation to these ports and protocols is a key part of ensuring the success of your **Microsoft Teams** deployment.

Next, we will show you how to optimize your media configuration in Microsoft Teams using QoS.

Optimizing your Teams media configuration using QoS

QoS is a process that allows network traffic that may be sensitive to delay (such as Teams voice and video calls or meetings), to "*jump the queue*" ahead of less critical traffic. In Microsoft Teams, QoS can be configured via the Teams admin center, and in conjunction with **Group Policy objects** using a routing principle known as **Port-based Access Control**. This essentially allows you to dedicate part of your network bandwidth to critical Teams functions such as voice and video.

When should you implement QoS?

You should consider implementing **QoS** for Teams if you are encountering any of the following issues:

- Packet loss – packets getting dropped. You may encounter poor voice quality.

- Jitter – with Jitter, packet fluctuations may result in a break in voice fluidity during calls.

- Delayed round-trip time – packets taking too long to reach their destination, meaning delays encountered in conversations, leading to people unintentionally interrupting each other during calls.

If you are encountering any of the preceding issues, and don't wish to absorb the cost of upgrading your bandwidth and connectivity, QoS can provide you with a potentially cost-effective solution.

> **Important note**
>
> Make sure QoS is deployed consistently throughout your network locations. Any weak link in the chain can negate your QoS settings and lead to a degraded experience.

So, now that we understand what QoS does, let's examine how we configure it for Microsoft Teams.

Configuring QoS for Microsoft Teams

In order to configure QoS for Teams, we need to begin in the Teams admin center at `https://admin.teams.microsoft.com` and complete the following steps:

1. Navigate to **Meetings | Meeting settings**:

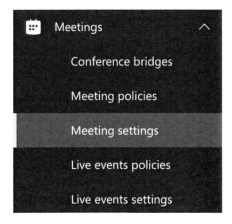

Figure 2.28 – Meeting settings

2. Scroll down to the **Network** section and move the slider next to **Insert Quality of Service (QoS) markers for real-time media traffic** to **On** as shown in *Figure 2.29*:

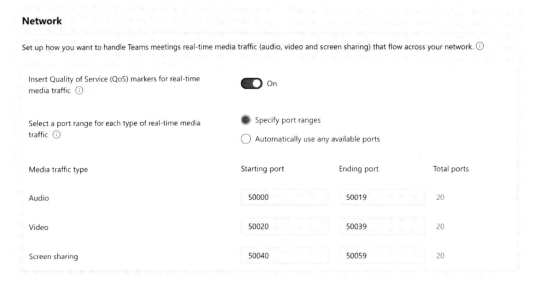

Figure 2.29 – Meeting Network settings

3. By default, **Specify port ranges** is selected here, and these will be set to Microsoft's recommended port ranges for the three media types, which are **Audio**, **Video**, and **Screen sharing**. You may also choose the option to **Automatically use any available ports**. If you choose the latter option, any available ports in the range of `1024-65535` may be used:

Select a port range for each type of real-time media traffic ⓘ

◉ Specify port ranges

○ Automatically use any available ports

Figure 2.30 – Selecting a port range

4. When you have chosen your **Network** settings, click on **Save** to complete the configuration:

Media traffic type	Starting port	Ending port	Total ports
Audio	50000	50019	20
Video	50020	50039	20
Screen sharing	50040	50059	20

Save   Discard

Figure 2.31 – Saving port ranges

Now that we have chosen and enabled the QoS settings in the Teams admin center, we need to configure a Group Policy Object for each of the three media traffic types by using the Group Policy Management Cnsole on a domain controller or server in your network.

Configuring the Group Policy objects

In order to create the Group Policy objects that are required, we need to complete the following steps:

1. From your domain controller or server, open the **Group Policy Management console** by clicking on the Windows Start button, typing in gpmc.msc, and pressing the *Enter* key.

2. Navigate to **Computer Configuration | Windows Settings | Policy-based QoS** as shown in *Figure 2.32*:

Figure 2.32 – Policy-based QoS

3. Right-click on **Policy-based QoS** and select **Create new policy**:

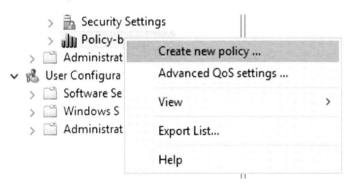

Figure 2.33 – Create new policy

4. Under **Policy name**, type in **Teams Audio policy**, and then make sure that **Specify DSCP Value** is checked and has the value set to 46. Click **Next**:

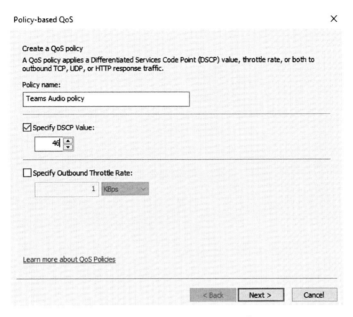

Figure 2.34 – Creating a QoS policy

5.   In the **This QoS policy applies to** section, ensure that **Only applications with this executable name** is checked, and set the value to `Teams.exe`. Click **Next**:

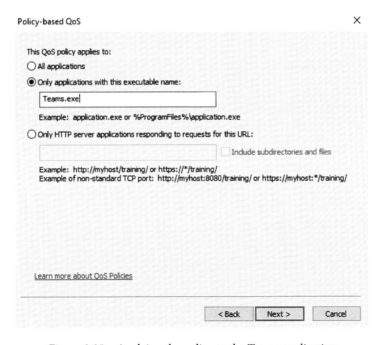

Figure 2.35 – Applying the policy to the Teams application

6. On the next screen, leave the default selections in place. Click **Next**:

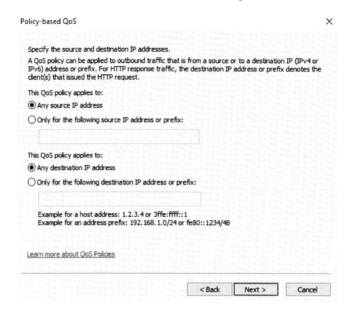

Figure 2.36 – Specify source and destination IP addresses

7. Under **Specify the protocol and port numbers**, choose **From this source port number or range**, and enter the Teams audio range of `50000:50019`. Click **Finish**:

Figure 2.37 – Specify the protocol and port numbers

Once completed, you will need to repeat this process for the Teams video and Teams screen sharing media types. The required DSCP values for these media types are 34 and 18. When you have completed the setup for all three media types, the **Policy-based QoS** section of **Computer Configuration** will appear as shown in *Figure 2.38*:

Policy Name	Application Name ...	Protocol	Source Port	Destination ...	Source IP / ...	Destination ...	DSCP Value	Throttle Rate
Teams Audio policy	Teams.exe	TCP and UDP	50000:50019	*	*	*	46	-1
Teams Video policy	Teams.exe	TCP and UDP	50020:50039	*	*	*	34	-1
Teams Sharing policy	Teams.exe	TCP and UDP	50040:50059	*	*	*	18	-1

Figure 2.38 – Teams media policies

Once you have deployed these group policy settings, they can be confirmed on each target device by inspecting the Windows registry at the following path:

```
Computer\HKEY_LOCAL_MACHINE\SOFTWARE\Policies\Microsoft\
Windows\QoS\
```

> **Important note**
> Should QoS not be effective in improving your Teams media performance, it is recommended that you investigate improving your network capacity and bandwidth to improve your users experience in Microsoft Teams.

In this section, we have introduced you to the principles of QoS for Microsoft Teams. We showed you the scenarios in which you need to consider deploying QoS, how to set it up in the *Meeting settings* section of the Teams admin center, and how to deploy it to your users by setting up Group Policy objects.

Summary

In this chapter, we explained the steps for assessing your network readiness for a Microsoft Teams deployment. You learned what the network and bandwidth requirements are, and how to interrogate your network for readiness with tools such as the Network Planner and Network Testing Companion. We also explained that there are a number of ports and protocols that need to be configured on your network to allow Microsoft Teams to work, and finally, we showed you how QoS can be used to prioritize network bandwidth to ensure that your users get the best experience with Teams media types such as audio, video, and screen sharing.

In the next chapter, we will explain the governance and lifecycle settings within Microsoft Teams. You will learn how templates can be used to set up Teams, how to use policies for setting up Microsoft 365 groups, and how to apply classification settings, expiration policies, and naming policies to the Microsoft 365 groups that are associated with your Teams.

Questions

As we conclude, here is a list of questions for you to test your knowledge regarding this chapter's material. You will find the answers in the *Assessments* section of the *Appendix*:

1. Which of the following PowerShell commands must be used to install the Network Testing Companion tool?

    a. `Add-Module -Module NetworkTestingCompanion`

    b. `Add-Module -Name NetworkTestingCompanion`

    c. `Install-Module -Module NetworkTestingCompanion`

    d. `Install-Module -Name NetworkTestingCompanion`

2. Which of the following is not one of the specified port ranges for Teams media types?

    a. `50000:50019`

    b. `50020:50039`

    c. `50040:50059`

    d. `50060:50079`

3. True or false: QoS in Microsoft Teams is designed to improve media performance during Teams meetings.

    a. True

    b. False

4. Which of the following is not one of the available options in the Network Planner tool?

    a. Report

    b. Personas

    c. Network plans

d. Network organization chart

e. Network sites

5. True or false: When configuring QoS in the Teams admin center, selecting the option to automatically set the media ports will result in the ports from range `1024-65535` being used.

a. True

b. False

6. Which of the following is not one of the media services within Teams that can be improved by using QoS?

a. Teams audio

c. Teams video

d. Teams chat

e. Teams screen share

7. Where in the Teams admin center would you configure the network settings for QoS?

a. **Meetings | Live events policies**

b. **Meetings | Meeting policies**

c. **Meetings | Meeting settings**

d. **Meetings | Live events settings**

8. True or false: To configure the Network Testing Companion, you need to use Windows PowerShell.

a. True

b. False

9. Which of the following is not one of the built-in Microsoft personas that can be used with the Network Planner tool?

a. Teams Room system

b. Office worker

c. Firstline worker

d. Remote worker

10. True or false: Using the Teams Network Planner, it is not possible to create custom personas.

a. True

b. False

Further reading

Here are links to more information on some of the topics that we have covered in this chapter:

- Prepare your organization's network for Microsoft Teams: `https://docs.microsoft.com/en-us/microsoftteams/prepare-network`

- Use the Network Planner for Microsoft Teams: `https://docs.microsoft.com/en-us/microsoftteams/network-planner`

- Using Network Planner – example scenario: `https://docs.microsoft.com/en-US/microsoftteams/tutorial-network-planner-example`

- Review Teams networking requirements: `https://docs.microsoft.com/en-gb/learn/modules/m365-teams-collab-prepare-deployment/review-networking-requirements`

- Network ports and protocols for Microsoft Teams: `https://docs.microsoft.com/en-us/microsoft-365/enterprise/urls-and-ip-address-ranges?view=o365-worldwide#skype-for-business-online-and-microsoft-teams`

- Implement QoS in Microsoft Teams: `https://docs.microsoft.com/en-US/microsoftteams/qos-in-teams`

3

Planning and Implementing Governance and Life Cycle Settings in Microsoft Teams

In this chapter, we will introduce you to the governance and life cycle settings that are available to you as a **Microsoft Teams** administrator. You will learn how to use templates for setting up Teams and how to create policies for the setup of Microsoft 365 groups. We will also show you how to apply classification settings, expiration policies, and naming policies to Microsoft 365 groups for Microsoft Teams.

In this chapter, we're going to cover the following main topics:

- Using templates to create teams
- Setting up policies to manage the creation of Microsoft 365 groups
- Configuring classifications, expiration policies, and naming policies for Microsoft 365 groups and Microsoft Teams
- Archiving, restoring, and deleting a team

Technical requirements

In this chapter, you will need to have access to the **Microsoft Teams admin center**, which you can reach at `https://admin.teams.microsoft.com`. You will need to be either a **global administrator** or a **Teams service administrator** in order to carry out the steps covered in this chapter.

You will also need to be able to access Windows PowerShell in order to configure settings for who in your organization can create Microsoft 365 groups.

Using templates to create teams

Creating a team is quick and easy and can be done by users from within Microsoft Teams itself, or by administrators from the **Teams admin center**. When you create a team, however, it provides you with some very basic team settings and the single **General** channel, and you will have some work to do to customize the team for your needs.

This is where Teams templates come in. If you have a set of channels, apps, and settings that you would like to be immediately available when you create a new team, templates can provide this. A **template** for a team can include all the structure definitions relating to your business requirements. In this section, we will show you how to use the pre-built templates included in Teams, and how to create your own templates.

Teams pre-built templates

There are several pre-built Teams templates now available in Microsoft Teams. You can create a new team from one of these templates by completing the following steps:

1. Open the Microsoft Teams app on your computer, or from your browser, and navigate to `https://teams.microsoft.com`. The Teams experience is consistent across devices and browsers as shown in *Figure 3.1*:

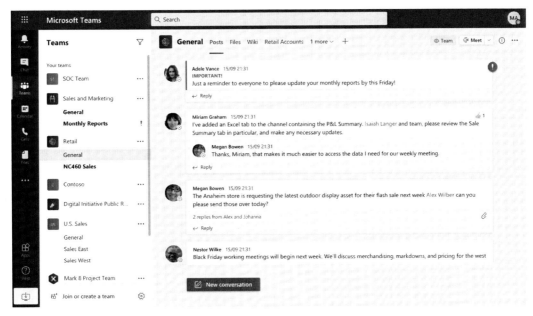

Figure 3.1 – Teams client experience

2. Click on **Join or create a team**:

Figure 3.2 – Join or create a team

3. Click on **Create team**:

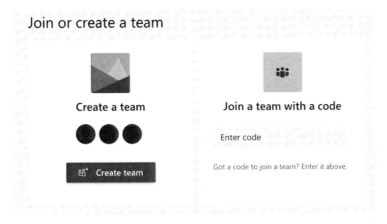

Figure 3.3 – Create team

4. In the **Select from a template** section, you will see several templates that you can choose from to build your team, as shown in *Figure 3.4*:

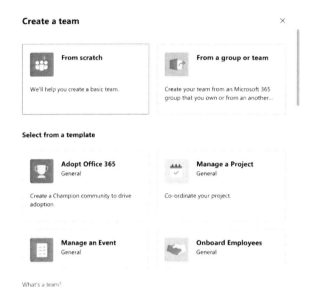

Figure 3.4 – Select from a template

5. For this example, we will choose the **Adopt Office 365** template:

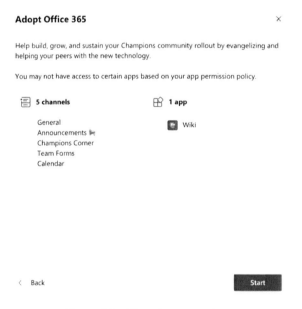

Figure 3.5 – Choosing a template

6. Next, we have the option to choose between a **Private** or **Public** team. Here, we will choose **Public**:

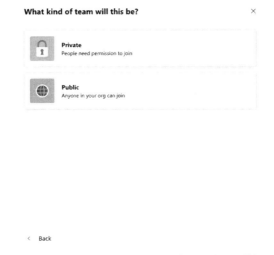

Figure 3.6 – Choose what kind of team this will be

7. Next, we need to give the team a name and description. We will call this team **Digital transformation**:

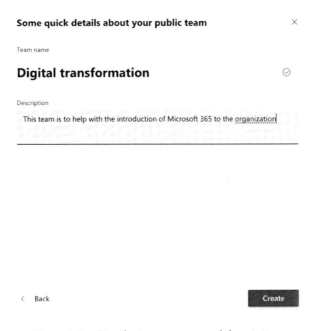

Figure 3.7 – Give the team a name and description

8. Click **Create** and the team will be provisioned as shown in *Figure 3.8*. This step can take some time to complete and you can click **Close** and skip to the next step if you prefer:

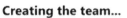

Figure 3.8 – Creating the team

9. Next, you may add some members to your new team. In this example, we will choose to **Skip** this step:

Figure 3.9 – Adding members to the team

10. The team is created, and as you can see in *Figure 3.10*, it is provisioned with four extra channels to the standard **General** channel:

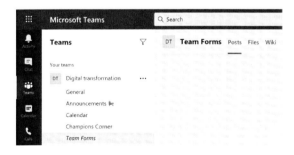

Figure 3.10 – New team created from a template with pre-built channels

Administrators may view the available Teams templates from the Teams admin center at `https://admin.teams.microsoft.com` and by navigating to **Teams | Team templates**:

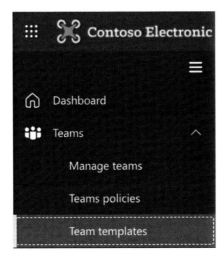

Figure 3.11 – View Teams templates in the Teams admin center

The pre-built templates are shown in *Figure 3.12*:

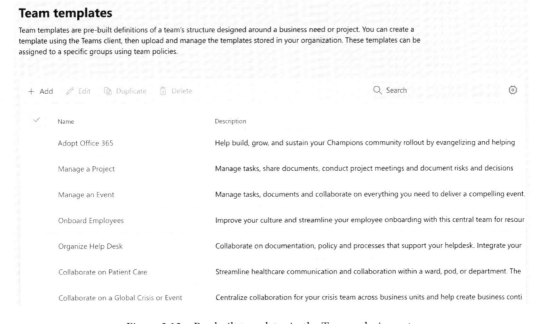

Figure 3.12 – Pre-built templates in the Teams admin center

> **Important note**
> The pre-built templates may not be edited. However, you can use the **Duplicate** option to copy the template settings to your own custom template.

Next, let's look at how to create your own custom templates.

Creating a custom template for a team

In addition to using the pre-built templates, it is also possible to create custom templates. This can be done from the Teams admin center and comprises the following steps:

1. Go to the **Teams admin center** and navigate to **Teams | Team templates**:

Figure 3.13 – Add a team template

2. Click on **+ Add** and you will see the options for creating a new template as shown in *Figure 3.14*. You may choose to **Create a brand new template**, **Use an existing team as a template**, or **Start with an existing template**:

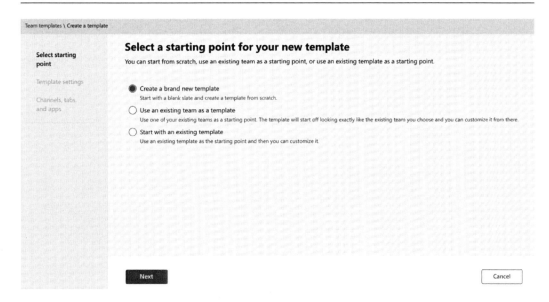

Figure 3.14 – Select a starting point for your new template

3. For this example, we will select **Create a brand new template**. Click **Next**. In the next step, we need to enter our template name, a long and a short description, and a locale (such as **English (United States)**). This is shown in *Figure 3.15*. Click **Next**:

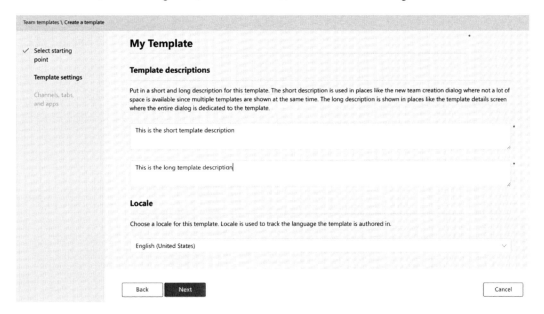

Figure 3.15 – Enter the name, descriptions, and locale for your template

4. Next, we need to add our required **Channels** and **Apps** for our new template. Under **Channels**, click **+ Add**:

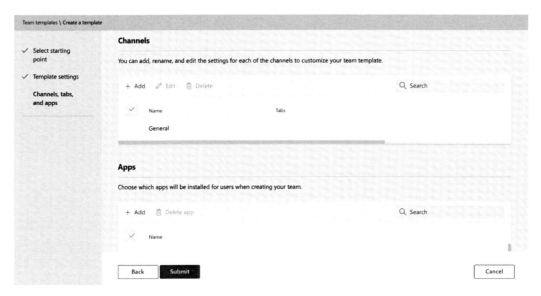

Figure 3.16 – Configure Channels and Apps

5. Enter a name and description for your channel. You may also choose whether you want the channel to be **Shown by default**, or whether it is a hidden channel. From this section, you may also optionally choose to include a tab to **Add an app for this template**. In *Figure 3.17*, we have added the **Evernote** app:

Figure 3.17 – Add a channel to the template

6.   Click on **Apply**:

Figure 3.18 – Configuring channel and tab settings

7. *Figure 3.19* shows our new channel added to the template. In addition, the tab we added for **Evernote** is shown under the **Apps** section. This app could also have been explicitly added to the template by adding it from the **Apps** section. Click on **Submit** to create your template:

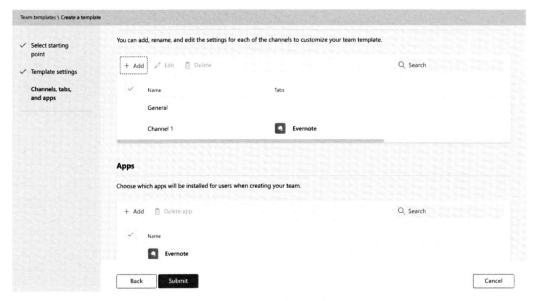

Figure 3.19 – New channel ready for creation

8. The new template is shown in *Figure 3.20* in the list of templates:

Figure 3.20 – New template shown in the list of Teams templates

Now let's look at some of the current Teams template capabilities.

Teams template capabilities

Microsoft has advised that more features will be added to templates over time, but at the time of writing, the following features and settings are available and may be configured with Teams templates:

- Name
- Description
- Adding apps
- Adding tabs

The following features are currently not available:

- Setting team membership
- Setting the team picture
- Configuring the channel settings
- Setting up connectors

> **Important note**
> Teams templates are currently limited to 15 channels per template, 20 tabs per channel in a template, and 50 apps per template.

Next, we will show you how to manage the creation of Microsoft 365 groups using policies.

Setting up policies to manage the creation of Microsoft 365 groups

One of the challenges faced by Microsoft Teams administrators is the fact that all users have the ability by default to create Microsoft 365 groups. **Microsoft 365 groups** are used and associated with many things within Microsoft 365, and among these is the fact that when a Team is created from scratch, a Microsoft 365 group is also created.

This can lead to challenges such as teams being created without expiration policies and then forgotten and discarded. As a result, administrators have the challenge of cleaning up surplus or orphaned teams and Microsoft 365 groups.

One way to address this challenge is to limit who in your organization can create Microsoft 365 groups. This is achieved by using **Windows PowerShell** and by completing the following steps.

> **Important note**
>
> In order to implement the following process, the administrator who configures the group creation settings, and any members of the security group that we will be creating, must be assigned an Azure AD Premium license.

The first step is to create a security group that contains any users that you wish to have permission to create Microsoft 365 groups:

1. Go to the Azure portal at `https://portal.azure.com` and navigate to **Azure Active Directory | Groups**:

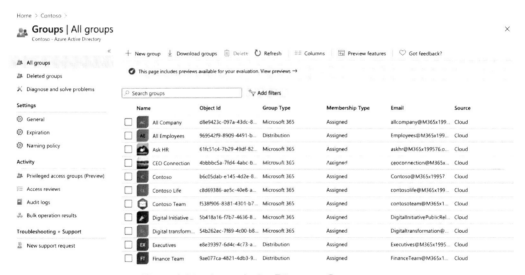

Figure 3.21 – Azure Active Directory Groups page

2. Click on + **New group**. Complete the new group settings to add the required members who will be able to create Microsoft 365 groups. Click **Create** to finish setting up the new group:

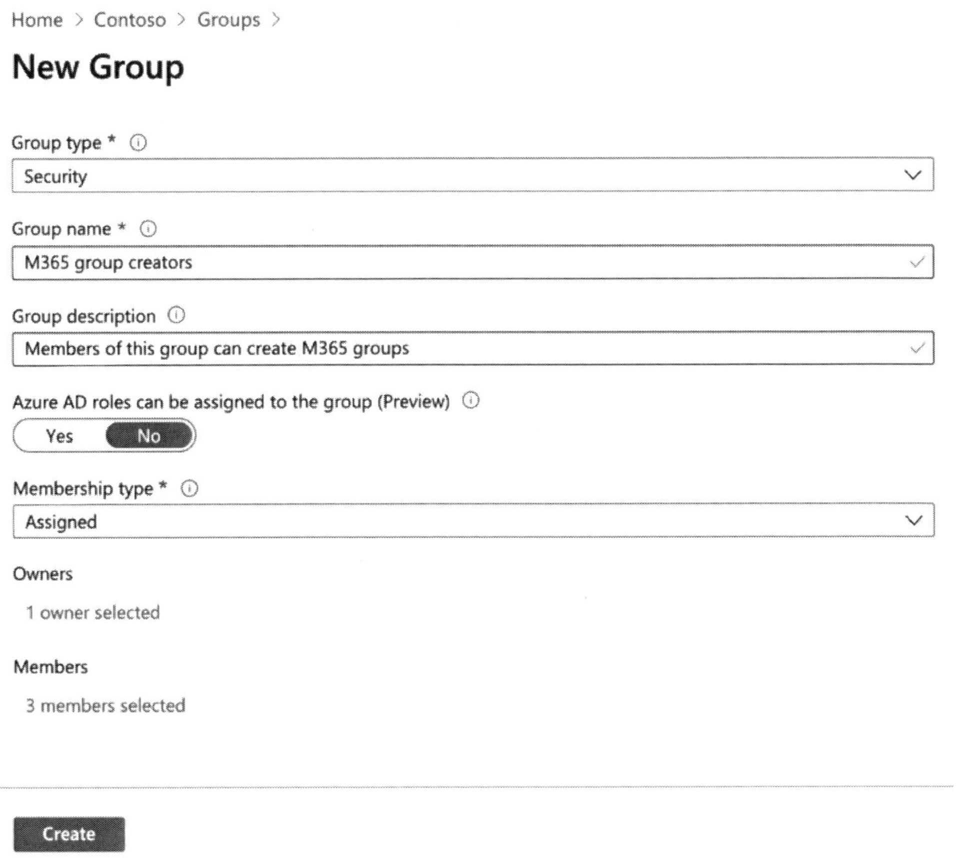

Home > Contoso > Groups >

New Group

Group type * ⓘ

| Security | ⌄ |

Group name * ⓘ

| M365 group creators | ✓ |

Group description ⓘ

| Members of this group can create M365 groups | ✓ |

Azure AD roles can be assigned to the group (Preview) ⓘ

Yes   No

Membership type * ⓘ

| Assigned | ⌄ |

Owners

1 owner selected

Members

3 members selected

Create

Figure 3.22 – New security group

3.   Next, connect to PowerShell as an administrator, run the following command, and type *Y* for yes:

```
Install-module azureadpreview
```

Below is the output of the preceding command:

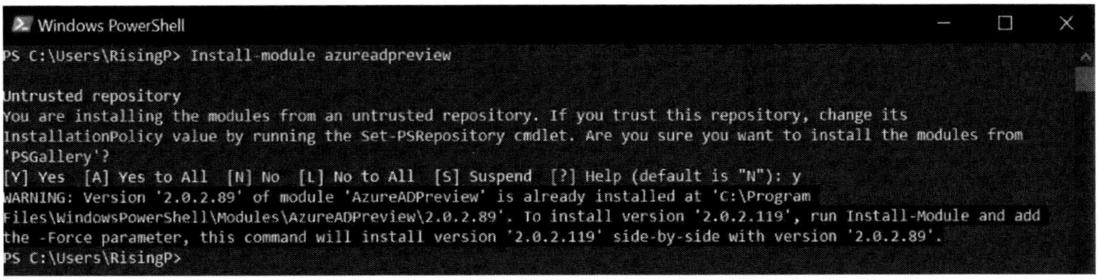

```
Windows PowerShell                                                    —    □    ×
PS C:\Users\RisingP> Install-module azureadpreview

Untrusted repository
You are installing the modules from an untrusted repository. If you trust this repository, change its
InstallationPolicy value by running the Set-PSRepository cmdlet. Are you sure you want to install the modules from
'PSGallery'?
[Y] Yes  [A] Yes to All  [N] No  [L] No to All  [S] Suspend  [?] Help (default is "N"): y
WARNING: Version '2.0.2.89' of module 'AzureADPreview' is already installed at 'C:\Program
Files\WindowsPowerShell\Modules\AzureADPreview\2.0.2.89'. To install version '2.0.2.119', run Install-Module and add
the -Force parameter, this command will install version '2.0.2.119' side-by-side with version '2.0.2.89'.
PS C:\Users\RisingP>
```

Figure 3.23 – Installing the AzureADPreview PowerShell module

4. Next, enter the following command to connect to Azure AD:

```
$AzureADCred = Get-Credential
```

5. Enter your Microsoft 365 administrator login name and password, and once connected, run the following command to connect the PowerShell session to Azure AD:

```
Connect-AzureAD -Credential $AzureAdcred
```

The results of the preceding commands are shown in *Figure 3.24*:

Figure 3.24 – Connecting to Azure AD PowerShell

6. Next, we need to run the following script to restrict M365 group creation:

```
$GroupName = "M365 group creators"
$AllowGroupCreation = "False"


Connect-AzureAD


$settingsObjectID = (Get-AzureADDirectorySetting | Where-
object -Property Displayname -Value "Group.Unified" -EQ).
id
if(!$settingsObjectID)
{
            $template =
Get-AzureADDirectorySettingTemplate | Where-object {$_.
displayname -eq "group.unified"}
```

```
    $settingsCopy = $template.CreateDirectorySetting()
    New-AzureADDirectorySetting -DirectorySetting
$settingsCopy
    $settingsObjectID = (Get-AzureADDirectorySetting |
Where-object -Property Displayname -Value "Group.Unified"
-EQ).id
}


$settingsCopy = Get-AzureADDirectorySetting -Id
$settingsObjectID

$settingsCopy["EnableGroupCreation"] =
$AllowGroupCreation


if($GroupName)
{
            $settingsCopy["GroupCreationAllowedGroupId"]
= (Get-AzureADGroup -SearchString $GroupName).objectid
}else {
$settingsCopy["GroupCreationAllowedGroupId"] = $GroupName
}
Set-AzureADDirectorySetting -Id $settingsObjectID
-DirectorySetting $settingsCopy


(Get-AzureADDirectorySetting -Id $settingsObjectID).
Values
```

The preceding script sets the target security group name and then ensures that only members of this group may create Microsoft 365 groups.

Important note

Note that the $GroupName parameter at the start of the preceding PowerShell command must match the name of the security group shown in *Figure 3.24* – which is M365 group creators in this example.

The output of the preceding script is shown in *Figure 3.25*, which illustrates the **M365 group creators** security group being set as the only group that has permissions to create Microsoft 365 groups:

Figure 3.25 – PowerShell script to set the security group

7. Note that the final line of the PowerShell output shown in *Figure 3.25* shows **EnableGroupCreation** set to **False**. This means that only members of the security group we have created will be able to create Microsoft 365 groups.

8. *Figure 3.26* shows a user logged into Teams who is not a member of the **M365 group creators** security group. You will note that the option to **Create team** is not visible:

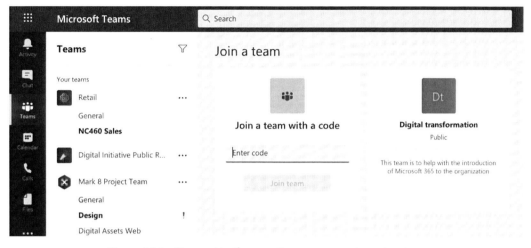

Figure 3.26 – User not in the security group cannot create a team

> **Important note**
> The preceding steps will not prevent users who have privileged roles such as
> global administrator from creating Microsoft 365 groups.

Next, we will show you the process of setting up classifications, expiration policies, and
naming policies using Microsoft 365 groups.

Configuring classifications, expiration policies, and naming policies for Microsoft 365 groups and Microsoft Teams

In this section, you will learn about the classification feature, expiration policies, and
naming policies, and how these three features may be configured using Microsoft
365 groups that are associated with Microsoft Teams. We will start with the group
classification feature.

Configuring group classification

The **group classification** feature enables users who can create Microsoft 365 groups to
create visual descriptions (much like labels) that can provide descriptive information
about the group.

> **Important note**
>
> Microsoft now recommends using sensitivity labels in conjunction with Microsoft 365 groups in preference over group classification. However, as the exam outline has not been changed to reflect this at the time of writing, we will focus on the classification feature in this section. Links to sensitivity labeling in relation to Microsoft 365 will be included in the *Further reading* section at the end of the chapter.

Group classifications can be created using **Windows PowerShell**. Examples of classification settings are the following:

- **Normal**
- **Confidential**
- **Highly Confidential**

An example of how this could work is shown as follows with the creation of a classification list. You will need to be connected to Azure AD in PowerShell as shown previously in the chapter:

```
$setting["ClassificationList"] = "Normal, Confidential, Highly
Confidential"
```

Now that we have our classification list created, we need to apply some descriptions to those list items. This is achieved as follows:

```
$setting["ClassificationDescriptions"] = "Normal: General,
Confidential: Internal only, Highly Confidential: Executive
access only"
```

Now that you have your list of classifications and their associated descriptions, you may set a classification to a chosen new or existing Microsoft 365 group as shown in the following examples:

```
Set-UnifiedGroup groupname@domainname.com -Classification
Normal
```

Or use the following:

```
New-UnifiedGroup groupname@domainname.com -Classification
Confidential -AccessType Private
```

Next, we will examine expiration policies.

Configuring expiration policies

Expiration policies are a means of managing the life cycle of your Microsoft 365 groups
to ensure that they are deleted when they are no longer used or required. To configure an
expiration policy, we need to complete the following steps:

1. Go to the Azure portal at `https://portal.azure.com` and navigate to **Azure
    Active Directory | Groups**:

Figure 3.27 – Azure AD Groups in the Azure portal

2. Under **Settings**, select **Expiration**, as shown in *Figure 3.27*.

Figure 3.28 – Groups Expiration settings

3.   Complete the settings shown in *Figure 3.28* for **Group lifetime** (this can be set to 180 days, 365 days, or a custom setting of 30 days or more), **Email contact for groups with no owners**, and **Enable expiration for these Microsoft 365 groups** (can be set to **All**, **Selected**, or **None**). Click **Save** to confirm your settings.

When expiration settings have been applied to a Microsoft 365 group, the following conditions will apply:

- If a group is still active when the expiration date approaches, the group will be automatically renewed.

- When a group is not auto-renewed, the group owners are alerted via email to renew the group.

- All groups that are not renewed will be deleted.

- When a Microsoft 365 group is deleted, it can be recovered within 30 days of its deletion.

You should consider configuring an expiration policy for your Microsoft 365 groups as it will help to prevent stale or orphaned groups within Azure AD.

Now, let's look at naming policies for Microsoft 365 groups.

Configuring a naming policy

A **group naming policy** is a means of applying a naming convention for Microsoft 365 groups when they are created. This can be highly useful for administrators to identify the function of a group and provides the ability to create and manage a blocked word list for group names or aliases.

To create a group naming policy, we need to complete the following steps:

1.   Go to the Azure portal at `https://portal.azure.com` and navigate to **Azure Active Directory** | **Groups**:

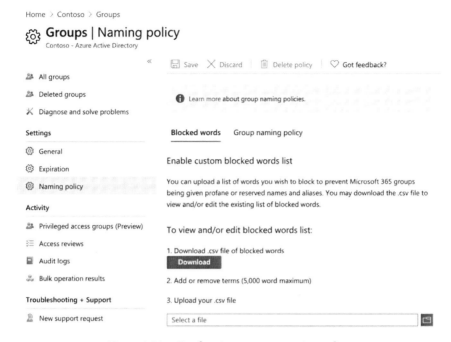

Figure 3.29 – Configuring a group naming policy

2.   Under **Settings**, select **Naming policy** as shown in *Figure 3.29.*

3.   Choose the **Group naming policy** tab as shown in *Figure 3.30.* We have two options
     here to set a prefix or a suffix to our group names. Or, we can add both:

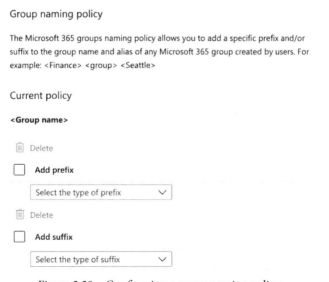

Figure 3.30 – Configuring a group naming policy

4. Using the example of a prefix, you will see that you may choose either an **Attribute** or **String** value:

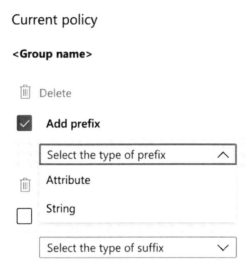

Figure 3.31 – Set up a prefix using an attribute or string value

5. *Figure 3.32* uses the example of a suffix and shows a **String** value of **Contoso**, which is the name of the organization. We have also chosen an **Attribute** value of **Office**:

Figure 3.32 – String and Attribute values applied to a suffix

6. *Figure 3.33* shows the available **Attribute** values that may be chosen:

Figure 3.33 – Available attribute values

7. The effect of the suffix settings that we have chosen is that when a user goes to create
    a team, the suffix values will be appended to the end of the team name. *Figure 3.34*
    shows a user named **Adele Vance** created a team called **Operations**. The string
    suffix value of **Contoso** is appended to the team name, followed by the attribute
    value, which is acquired from the **Office** field within the user's account:

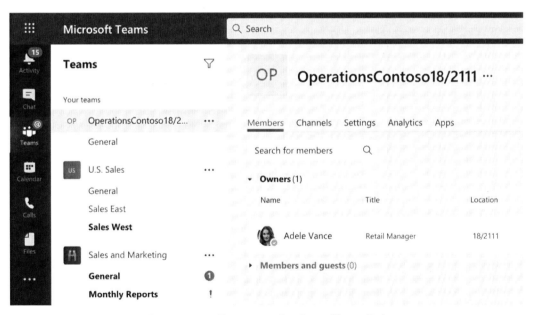

Figure 3.34 – Team created with a suffix applied

8. *Figure 3.35* shows the **Office** field setting within the contact information settings for the user **Adele Vance**.

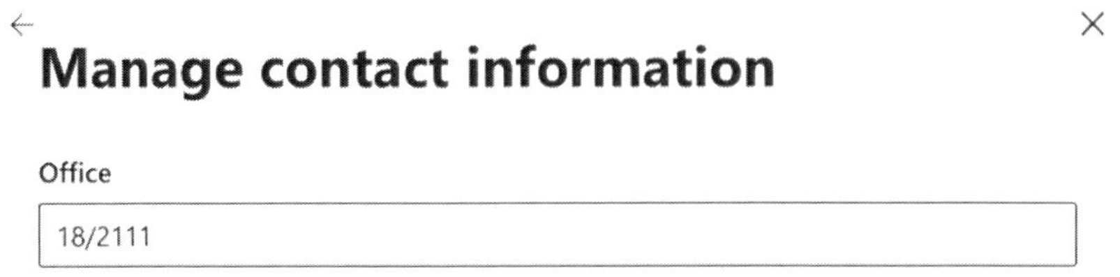

$\leftarrow$ $\times$

Manage contact information

Office

18/2111

Figure 3.35 – Office field setting

> **Important note**
> If Microsoft teams or groups are set up by users who have privileged roles such as a global administrator, the group naming policy will not be applied.

In this section, we described how to use Microsoft 365 groups to configure classification features, expiration policies, and naming policies.

Next, we will go through the process of archiving, restoring, or deleting a team.

Archiving, restoring, and deleting a team

The teams that you have in your Microsoft 365 environment may not be needed indefinitely. In this situation, there are several things you can do to ensure that stale or unused teams are removed and that only currently used teams remain active.

In this section, we will show you the options that you have to archive, restore, or fully delete teams.

Archiving a team

If there are any teams in your Microsoft 365 environment that are no longer in active use, but there may be a future requirement to access them, then you have the option to archive that team. Once you archive a team, any files and conversations within it are changed to read-only.

To archive a team, we need to complete the following steps:

1. Open **Microsoft Teams** and choose **Teams** from the left menu:

Figure 3.36 – Open the Teams app

2. At the bottom of the list of teams, next to **Join or create a team**, click on the cogwheel symbol:

Figure 3.37 – Select the cogwheel

3. A list of all teams is presented, as shown in *Figure 3.38*:

Figure 3.38 – Manage teams

4. Choose the team that you wish to archive and click the ellipsis. Then choose **Archive team**. You must be a Teams service administrator or higher in order to archive a team:

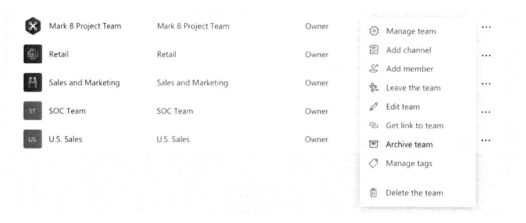

Figure 3.39 – Archive a team

5. When prompted, check the **Make the SharePoint site read-only for team members** box and click on **Archive**:

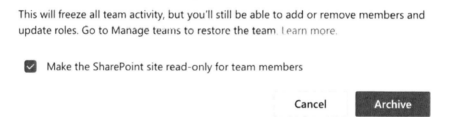

Figure 3.40 – Archive a team

6. The team is moved from the **Active** section to the **Archived** section. When the team is archived, you may open it from here to view conversations but you will not be able to start any new conversations:

Figure 3.41 – The team is successfully archived

Next, we will show you how to restore an archived team.

Restoring a team

The steps to restore an archived team are equally simple:

1. From the **Archived** section of the **Manage teams** area, click the ellipsis next to the team you wish to restore, and click on **Restore team**:

Figure 3.42 – Restoring a team

2. The team will be moved from the **Archived** section back to the **Active** section.

Archiving is a simple way of moving unused teams out of the active teams list and then restoring them should they become needed again.

> **Important note**
> It is also possible to archive teams from the **Microsoft Teams admin center**, in the **Teams | Manage Teams** section.

Next, we will show you how to delete a team.

Deleting a team

While archiving a team is easily reversed, deleting a team is a more permanent action. When a team is deleted, the mailbox and calendar for the team are removed from Exchange and the associated SharePoint site will be deleted, as will any OneNote notebooks, Planner plans, Power BI, or Stream content.

When a team is deleted, administrators or team owners can recover it within a 30-day period.

To delete a team, take the following steps:

1. From the same **Manage teams** section of the Teams app, under **Active** teams, click the ellipsis next to the team you wish to fully delete, and select **Delete the team**:

Figure 3.43 – Deleting a team

2. Check the box next to **I understand that everything will be deleted** and click on **Delete team**:

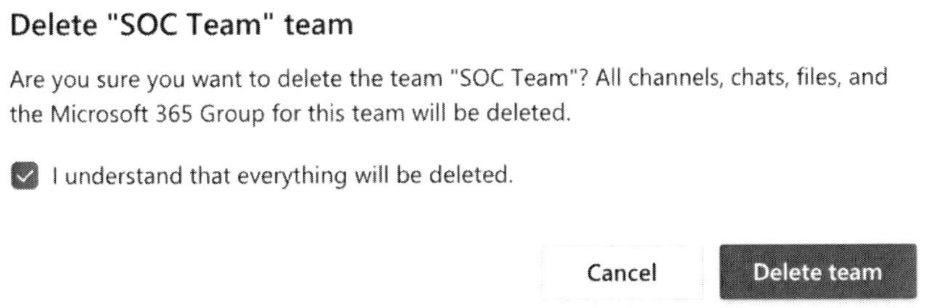

Delete "SOC Team" team

Are you sure you want to delete the team "SOC Team"? All channels, chats, files, and the Microsoft 365 Group for this team will be deleted.

☑ I understand that everything will be deleted.

Cancel   Delete team

Figure 3.44 – Deleting a team

The team will now be completely deleted.

Summary

In this chapter, we introduced you to the principles of creating teams using the built-in Teams templates that are available. We also showed you how to create your own Teams templates from the Teams admin center. You also learned how to set up a policy to control who in your organization can create Microsoft 365 groups.

In addition, we showed you how Microsoft 365 groups can be used to set classification features, expiration policies, and naming policies, and finally, you learned how to archive, restore, and completely delete teams from within the Teams app.

In the next chapter, we will examine the options for configuring guest access for users outside of your organization in Microsoft Teams. You will learn how to access the Teams admin center to control and set the permissions for guest users, and how to configure the meeting, messaging, and calling experience for those guest users. Then, we will show you how to remove guests from Microsoft Teams, and how access reviews can be used to review the existing guest access to the teams in your environment. Finally, we will demonstrate how guest access settings may be controlled from the Azure AD portal.

Practice questions

As we conclude, here is a list of questions for you to test your knowledge regarding this chapter's material. You will find the answers in the *Assessments* section of the *Appendix*:

1. Which of the following are possible prefix and suffix settings for a group naming policy (choose two)?

   a. Attribute

   b. Vector

   c. String

   d. Vertices

2. True or false – when a team is archived, it cannot be restored.

   a. True

   b. False

3. Which of the following is not a setting option for a group expiration policy?

   a. 365 days

   b. 730 days

   c. 180 days

   e. Custom

4. True or false – global administrators are not bound by the Teams naming policy.

   a. True

   b. False

5. Where in the Azure portal would you go to configure an expiration policy?

   a. **Azure Active Directory | Properties**

   b. **Azure Active Directory | Users**

   c. **Azure Active Directory | Groups**

   d. **Azure Active Directory | User settings**

6. When a Team is deleted, how long does an administrator or team owner have to restore it before it cannot be recovered?

    a. 14 days

    b. 25 days

    c. 30 days

    d. 50 days

7. True or false – to control who in your organization can create Microsoft 365 groups, you do not need to create a security group.

    a. True

    b. False

8. Which of the following statements about pre-built Teams templates is incorrect?

    a. Pre-built Teams templates may not be edited.

    b. Pre-built Teams templates may be duplicated.

    c. Pre-built Teams templates may be edited.

    d. Pre-built Teams templates can include channels and apps.

9. True or false – when a team is created from scratch, a Microsoft 365 group is always created.

    a. True

    b. False

10. True or false – Teams templates may be created from the **Teams admin center**.

    a. True

    b. False

Further reading

Here are links to more information on some of the topics that we have covered in this chapter:

- Get started with Teams templates in the Teams admin center: `https://docs.microsoft.com/en-us/microsoftteams/get-started-with-teams-templates-in-the-admin-console`

- Get started with Teams templates using Microsoft Graph: `https://docs.microsoft.com/en-us/microsoftteams/get-started-with-teams-templates`

- Manage who can create Microsoft 365 groups: `https://docs.microsoft.com/en-us/microsoft-365/solutions/manage-creation-of-groups?view=o365-worldwide`

- Configure the expiration policy for Microsoft 365 groups: `https://docs.microsoft.com/en-us/azure/active-directory/enterprise-users/groups-life cycle`

- Configure classifications for Microsoft 365 groups `https://docs.microsoft.com/en-us/microsoft-365/enterprise/manage-microsoft-365-groups-with-powershell?view=o365-worldwide#create-classifications-for-microsoft-365-groups-in-your-organization`

- Configure sensitivity labeling for Microsoft 365 groups, SharePoint sites, and Teams: `https://docs.microsoft.com/en-us/microsoft-365/compliance/sensitivity-labels-teams-groups-sites?view=o365-worldwide`

- Microsoft 365 groups naming policy: `https://docs.microsoft.com/en-us/microsoft-365/solutions/groups-naming-policy?view=o365-worldwide`

- Microsoft 365 groups expiration policy: `https://docs.microsoft.com/en-us/microsoft-365/solutions/microsoft-365-groups-expiration-policy?view=o365-worldwide`

- Archive or restore a team: `https://support.microsoft.com/en-us/office/archive-or-restore-a-team-dc161cfd-b328-440f-974b-5da5bd98b5a7?ui=en-us&rs=en-us&ad=us`

- Delete a team: `https://support.microsoft.com/en-us/office/delete-a-team-c386f91b-f7e6-400b-aac7-8025f74f8b41?ui=en-us&rs=en-us&ad=us`

4
Configuring Guest Access in Microsoft Teams

In this chapter, we will examine the options for configuring guest access for users outside of your organization in **Microsoft Teams**. You will learn how to access the **Microsoft Teams admin center** to control and set the permissions for guest users and how to configure the meeting, messaging, and calling experience for these guest users.

Then, we will show you how to remove guests from Microsoft Teams, and how access reviews can be used to review existing guest access to the teams in your environment.

Finally, we will demonstrate how guest access settings may be controlled from the Azure **Active Directory (AD)** portal.

In this chapter, we're going to cover the following main topics:

- Configuring guest users and permissions for Microsoft Teams
- Configuring meeting, messaging, and calling options for guests in Microsoft Teams
- Removing guests from teams, and reviewing guest access to teams with Azure AD access reviews
- Configuring guest access from the Azure AD portal

Technical requirements

In this chapter, you will need to have access to the **Microsoft Teams admin center**, which you can reach at `https://admin.teams.microsoft.com`. You will also require access to the **Microsoft 365 admin center** at `https://admin.microsoft.com` and the **SharePoint admin center**, which can be reached via the Microsoft 365 admin center.

You will need to be a **global administrator** to complete some of the tasks in this chapter, but a **Teams service administrator** role will suffice for some of the other tasks that are included.

In order to carry out **Azure AD access reviews**, you will also require an **Azure AD Premium P2** subscription.

Configuring guest users and permissions for Microsoft Teams

With Microsoft Teams, your core users are the people within your organization who have a licensed Microsoft 365 account. However, it is also possible to grant access to people who are not members of your organization, and who do not have access to your Microsoft 365 tenant from a school or work account. Typical examples of this would be partner organizations, suppliers, vendors, and customers.

To grant such access to Teams, we need to set up guest user access. An invited guest user can be provided with access to your Microsoft Teams environment in order to participate in chats, access documents in channels, and even use the applications that you have made available within Teams. Although this feature is not automatically enabled at the time of writing, Microsoft have announced that they plan to enable guest access for all Microsoft 365 tenants in the near future.

In order for a guest to be granted access, they must meet the following criteria:

- Have an Azure AD account on their own Microsoft 365 tenant

- Have a consumer email account, such as an **Outlook** or **Gmail** account

The level of access granted to guest users and the features they are able to consume are determined by the settings configured by the Teams administrators.

> **Important note**
> Guest user access to Teams does have some limitations compared to the full user experience. A full list of the capabilities of guest users may be found in the *Further reading* section at the end of this chapter.

Let's look at how we can set up guest access for Microsoft Teams.

Setting up guest access

To fully set up guest access for Microsoft Teams, there are a number of settings within Microsoft 365 that you are going to need to configure. These include configurations for Azure AD, Microsoft 365 Groups, SharePoint Online, and the Teams admin center. We will now go through each of these, starting with Azure AD.

Azure AD

Azure AD is the highest level of governance for sharing within Microsoft 365. You will need to check and configure the following settings to enable guest access:

1. Log in to the Azure portal at `https://portal.azure.com` and navigate to **Azure AD**. Then click on **External Identities**, as shown in *Figure 4.1*:

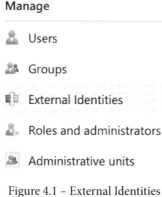

Figure 4.1 – External Identities

2. Next, click on **External collaboration settings**, as shown in *Figure 4.2*:

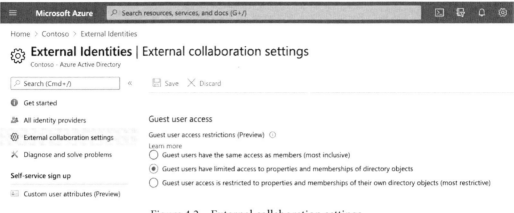

Figure 4.2 – External collaboration settings

3. From the right navigation pane, scroll down to **Guest invite settings** and ensure that both the **Admins and users in the guest inviter role can invite** and **Members can invite** options are set to **Yes**. If this requires you to change the present configuration, click **Save**. This is shown in *Figure 4.3*:

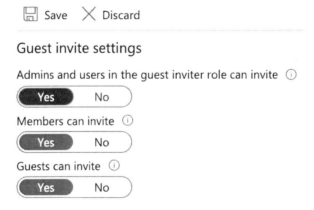

Figure 4.3 – Guest invite settings in the Azure portal

4. Scroll down further and check the **Collaboration restrictions** to ensure that any domains you wish to allow guest access from are not being blocked:

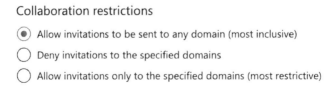

Figure 4.4 – Collaboration restrictions settings

Now that you understand how to check the Azure AD settings for guest access, let's look at Microsoft 365 groups.

Microsoft 365 groups

Teams are connected to **Microsoft 365 group** memberships. The guest settings for Microsoft 365 groups must also be enabled in order for team guest access to be available. This can be configured by going through the following steps:

1. Go to the **Microsoft 365 admin center** at `https://admin.microsoft.com`, navigate to **Settings | Org settings | Services**, and select **Microsoft 365 Groups**. This is shown in *Figure 4.5*:

Figure 4.5 – Microsoft 365 group settings in the admin center

2. Ensure that the **Let group owners add people outside your organization to Microsoft 365 Groups as guests** option is selected, as shown in *Figure 4.6*:

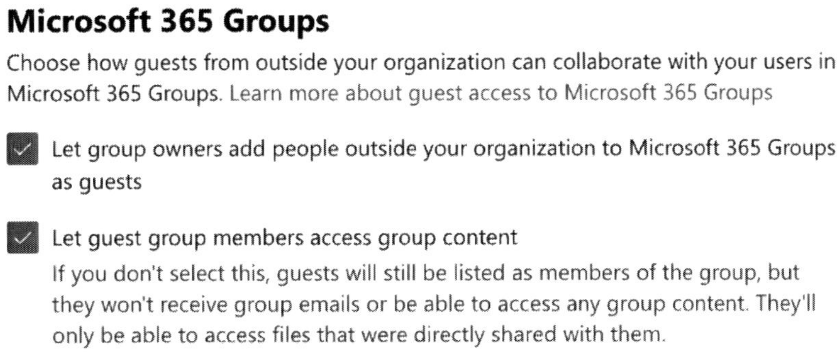

Microsoft 365 Groups

Choose how guests from outside your organization can collaborate with your users in Microsoft 365 Groups. Learn more about guest access to Microsoft 365 Groups

☑ Let group owners add people outside your organization to Microsoft 365 Groups as guests

☑ Let guest group members access group content
If you don't select this, guests will still be listed as members of the group, but they won't receive group emails or be able to access any group content. They'll only be able to access files that were directly shared with them.

Figure 4.6 – Microsoft 365 group settings

Next, we will need to check the SharePoint Online settings.

SharePoint Online

Files and folders in Teams are actually stored within SharePoint Online. Therefore, in order for any guests that you invite to your organization to access files and folders within Teams, you will need to enable the SharePoint organization-level sharing settings. This can be done by going through the following steps:

1. Go to the **Microsoft 365 admin center** at `https://admin.microsoft.com` and navigate to **Admin centers | SharePoint**:

Figure 4.7 – Navigating to the SharePoint admin center

2. Under **Policies | Sharing**, check whether **External sharing** is set to one of the more permissive settings, such as **Anyone**, **New and existing guests**, or **Existing guests**. This is shown in *Figure 4.8*:

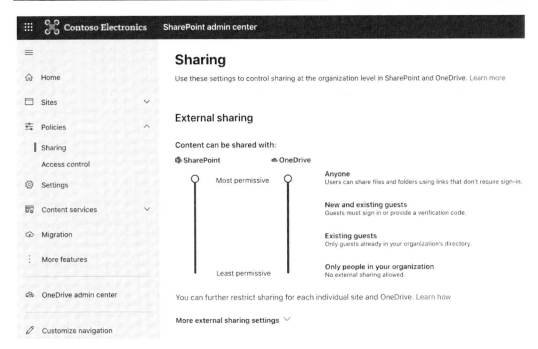

Figure 4.8 – SharePoint External sharing controls

3. By scrolling further down the **Sharing** page, you will see some options related to
    File and folder links, as shown in *Figure 4.9*:

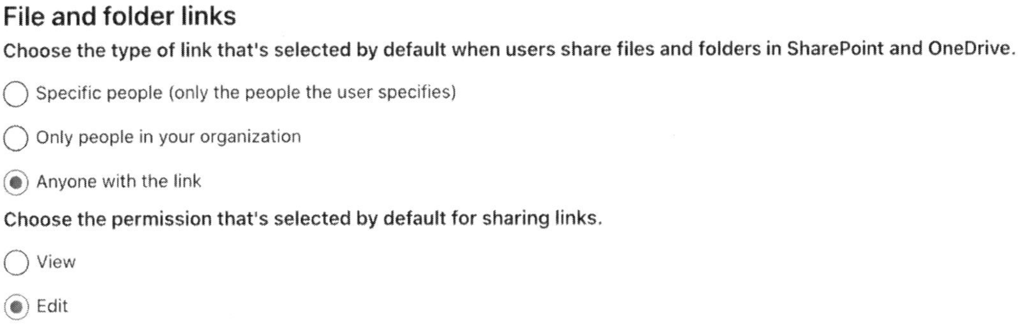

File and folder links

Choose the type of link that's selected by default when users share files and folders in SharePoint and OneDrive.

◯ Specific people (only the people the user specifies)

◯ Only people in your organization

◉ Anyone with the link

Choose the permission that's selected by default for sharing links.

◯ View

◉ Edit

Figure 4.9 – SharePoint file and folder links settings

The **Specific people** option is most appropriate if you anticipate the need to share files and
folders on a regular basis.

> **Important note**
> The sharing settings described here are set for SharePoint at organization level. Sharing settings may also be set at site level, and it is important to check these settings for the SharePoint sites that contain any files and folders for the teams you have created.

Finally, we need to look at the actual Teams guest access settings.

Teams

Guest access must also be configured within the **Teams admin center**. By default, guest access is turned off and therefore must be explicitly enabled should you wish to invite guest users into Teams. However, as mentioned earlier in the chapter, Microsoft are planning to change this so that guest access is enabled by default. You can configure this by going through the following steps:

1. Log in to the **Teams admin center** at `https://admin.teams.microsoft.com` and navigate to **Org-wide settings | Guest access**. This is shown in *Figure 4.10*:

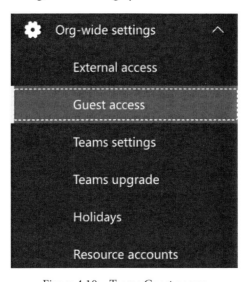

Figure 4.10 – Teams Guest access

2. Move the slider next to the **Allow guest access in Teams** option to the **On** position, as shown in *Figure 4.11*:

Guest access

Guest access in Teams lets people outside your organization access teams and channels. When you turn on Guest Access, you can turn on or off features guest users can or can't use. Make sure to follow the steps in this checklist to set up the prerequisites and so Team owners can add guest users to their teams. Learn more

Allow guest access in Teams  On

Figure 4.11 – Allow guest access in Teams

3. Enabling guest access will show you some further options that you can configure for the **Calling**, **Meeting**, and **Messaging** settings for guest users. We will discuss these in further detail in the *Configuring meeting, messaging, and calling options for guests in Microsoft Teams* section of this chapter. To finish enabling guest access in Teams, click **Save**:

Figure 4.12 – Save the guest user settings

So, now that we have guest access configured, how are guests invited to a team, and how do they gain access? Let's take a look.

Adding a guest to a team

Guests may be added to teams either by the team owner or a Microsoft 365 administrator. This is achieved by going through the following steps:

1. Open **Microsoft Teams** and select the team that you wish to invite a guest user to. In the following example, we will add an external guest to the **Retail** team, as shown in *Figure 4.13*:

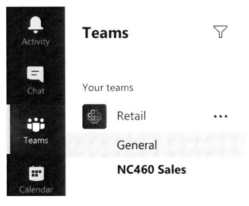

Figure 4.13 – Retail team shown in Teams

2.   Click the ellipsis next to the team name and then select **Add member**:

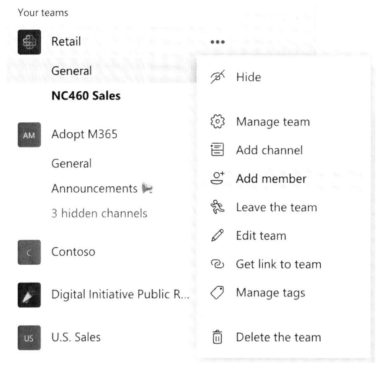

Figure 4.14 – Add member

3.   In this example, we will add a Gmail account, as shown in *Figure 4.15*:

Figure 4.15 – Add a guest to a team

4. Once added, click **Close**:

Figure 4.16 – Add a guest to a team

5. The invitation will be received by the invited guest, as shown in *Figure 4.17*:

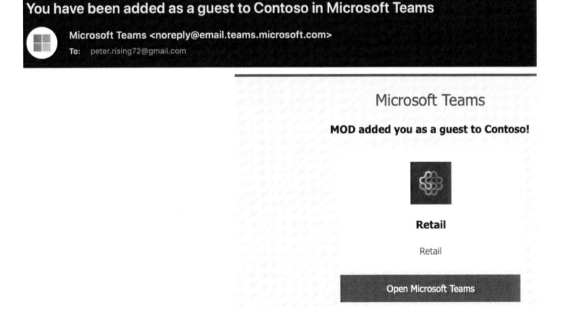

Figure 4.17 – Invitation received by the guest

6. If the guest user's account is not already set up as a Microsoft school or work account when they click on **Open Microsoft Teams** in the email invitation, then they will be guided through the necessary steps to automatically create one; otherwise, they will be prompted to log in, as shown in *Figure 4.18*:

Figure 4.18 – Logging in to Teams as a guest

7. After entering their credentials and clicking **Next**, the guest user will be prompted to review and accept permissions, as shown in *Figure 4.19*:

Figure 4.19 – Review and accept the guest permissions

8. Upon clicking **Accept**, the guest user will be shown the message **You're joining Teams as a guest**, as shown in *Figure 4.20*:

You're joining Teams as a guest
Welcome! As a guest, you can work and chat with others and navigate across topics, files and more through channels.

Figure 4.20 – Joining teams as a guest

9. Clicking **Next** to complete the invitation will take the guest user into Teams and grant them immediate access to the team they were invited to:

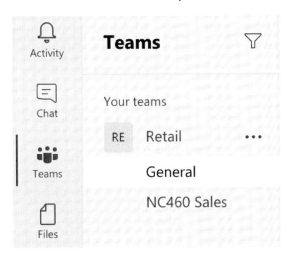

Figure 4.21 – The guest user can now access the team

10. When the team owner checks the members and guests within the team, the guest user will now be shown as a guest, as shown in *Figure 4.22*:

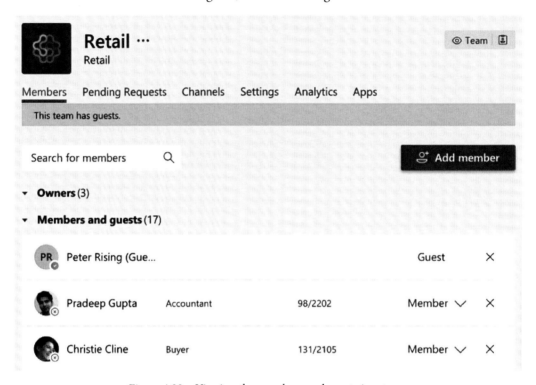

Figure 4.22 – Viewing the members and guests in a team

In this section, we have shown you the four key areas within Microsoft 365 where you can enable and configure guest user access so that people from outside of your organization can be invited into your Microsoft Teams environment. You also learned how guest users are invited to the team, and the steps they need to go through to accept the invitation and gain access to the team.

Next, we will look at how to configure the meeting, messaging, and calling options for the guest users that we have set up in Microsoft Teams.

Configuring the meeting, messaging, and calling options for guests in Microsoft Teams

In the previous section, we showed you how to enable guest access within the Microsoft Teams admin center. Once guest access has been enabled, it provides some settings that can be configured for guest users in relation to the calling, meeting, and messaging settings. These settings may be configured by going through the following steps:

1. Log in to the Teams admin center and navigate to **Org-wide settings | Guest access**. This is shown in *Figure 4.23*:

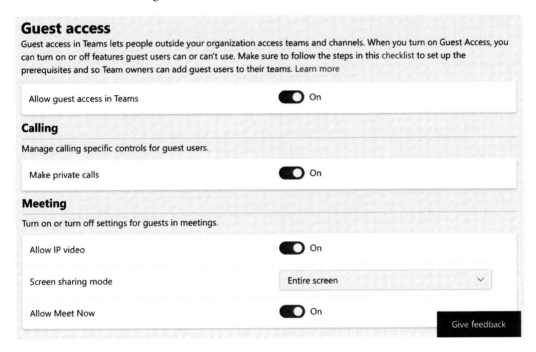

Figure 4.23 – Guest access settings in the Teams admin center

2. The first section you will see here is the **Calling** options. This contains one setting that enables or disables the guest users' ability to make private calls:

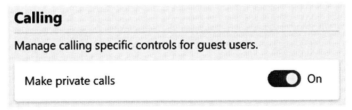

Figure 4.24 – Guest calling options

3. The next section contains the guest **Meeting** options. Here, you can set the guest users' abilities to access meeting features within Teams, such as IP video and screen-sharing settings, as shown in *Figure 4.25*:

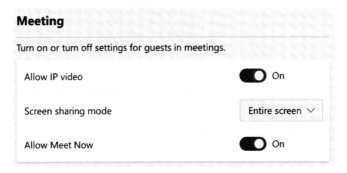

Figure 4.25 – Guest meeting options

4. The final section contains the guest **Messaging** options. Here, you can set the guest users' abilities to use settings within chats or channel conversations. These include settings such as being able to edit or delete sent messages or use chat. These options are shown in *Figure 4.26*:

Figure 4.26 – Guest messaging options

5. Should you wish to make any changes to these organization-wide guest access settings, you must click on **Save** to apply these changes.

It is also possible to configure guest user permissions at the individual team level. This can be done by going through the following steps:

1. Select the team whose guest permissions you wish to set, click the ellipsis, and then select **Manage team**, as shown in *Figure 4.27*:

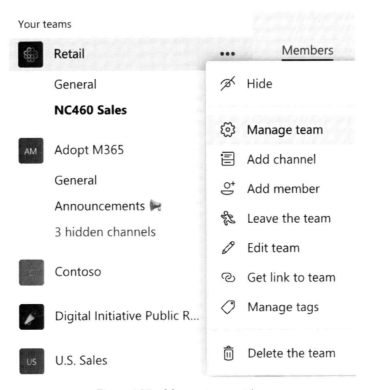

Figure 4.27 – Manage team settings

2. Click on the **Settings** menu and then expand **Guest permissions**, as shown in *Figure 4.28*:

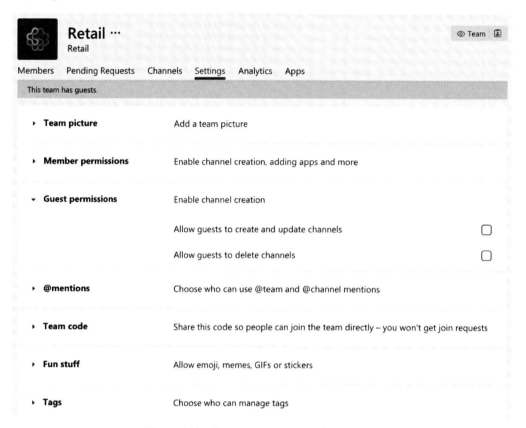

Figure 4.28 – Guest permissions within a team

The permissions that can be set here relate to the guests' ability to create, update, and delete channels within the team.

So, to recap what we have learned in this chapter so far, we have showed you how to enable guest user access for Microsoft Teams and how to configure guest permissions at both the organization and the individual team level. Next, we will demonstrate how to remove guests from Teams, and how Azure AD access reviews can be used to review existing guest access.

Removing guests from Teams and reviewing guest access to Teams with Azure AD access reviews

When you allow guest users to access your Azure AD organization and Microsoft Teams, it is important to regularly review who has access and assess and determine whether that access can or should be removed or whether it will be allowed to continue.

This can be achieved either by manually removing a guest user or by using Azure AD access reviews. In this section, we will examine both methods.

Removing a guest from a team

When you wish to remove a guest user from a team, you will need to complete the following steps:

1. From **Microsoft Teams**, a team owner can select the team, click the ellipsis, select **Manage Team**, and then select the **Members** tab:

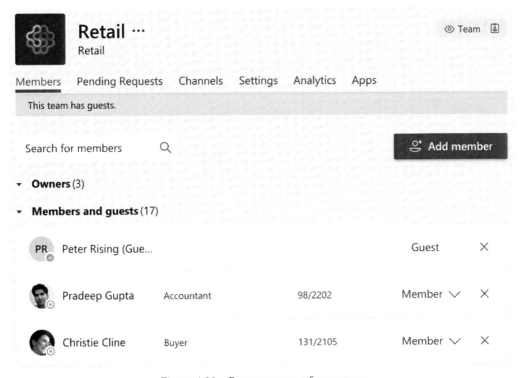

Figure 4.29 – Remove a guest from a team

2. Find the guest member in the **Members and Guests** section and click on the **X** next to the guest user. This will immediately remove the guest user from the team—there is no confirmation button.

> **Important note**
>
> When you remove a guest user from a team, this does not remove the guest user entirely from Azure AD. This must be done from the Azure portal by going through the following steps:

3. Log in to the Azure portal at `https://portal.azure.com`.

4. Navigate to **Azure AD | Users**.

5. Select the guest from the list, select the **Delete User** option, and click **OK**.

Now let's look at access reviews in Azure AD.

Using Azure AD access reviews to review guest access to Azure AD and Microsoft Teams

Azure AD access reviews provide Microsoft 365 administrators with the ability to ensure that users and guest users have the appropriate level of access. In this section, we will show you how to start an access review to assess and manage guest user access.

> **Important note**
>
> To use access reviews, you must have an Azure AD Premium P2 subscription.

In order to create an access review, you will need to go through the following steps:

1. Log in to the Azure portal at `https://portal.azure.com` and navigate to **Azure AD | Identity Governance** or **Azure AD | External Identities**:

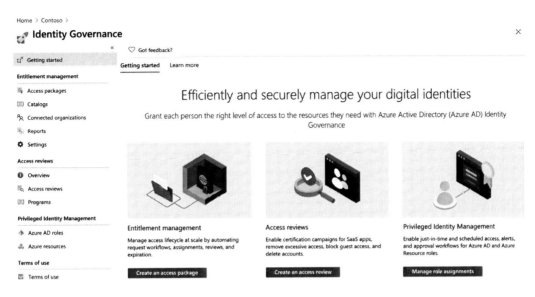

Figure 4.30 – Identity Governance in the Azure portal

2. Under the **Access reviews** section, click on **Access reviews**. You will see the options shown in *Figure 4.31*:

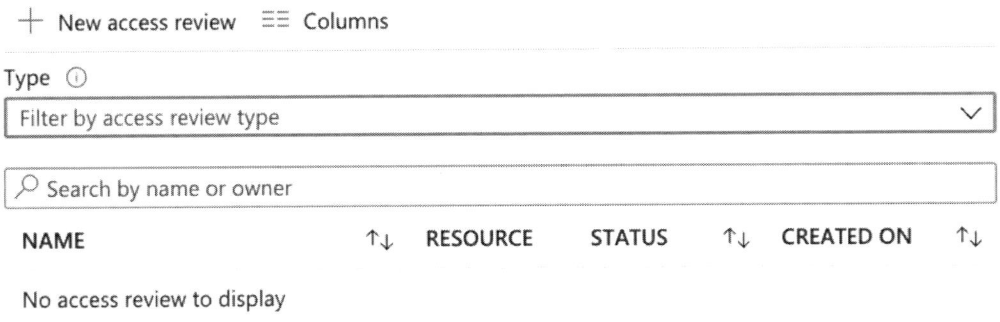

+ New access review   ▤ Columns

Type ⓘ

Filter by access review type   ⌄

🔍 Search by name or owner

NAME	⇅	RESOURCE	STATUS	⇅	CREATED ON	⇅

No access review to display

Figure 4.31 – Access reviews settings

3. Click on **+ New access review**. This will show the **Create an access review** options. The first section of these options is shown in *Figure 4.32*. In this example, we have provided a name and description for the access review. We have also set the frequency to run **One time** (other options available from the drop-down menu range from weekly to annually). Under **Users to review**, we will select the **Members of a group** option. It is also possible to select the **Assigned to an Application** option. Finally, under the **Scope** options, we will select **Guest users only**:

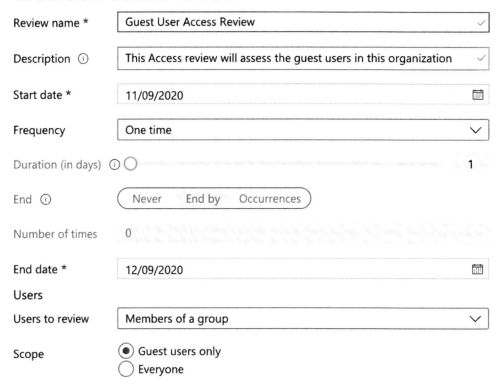

Figure 4.32 – Access review options

4. Scrolling down, we have some further options to select for our access review. We need to select the group. In this example, we will select the Microsoft 365 group called **Retail**. This group contains the members and guest members of the retail team shown earlier in this chapter. Under **Reviewers**, we may also choose who is going to carry out this access review. We can choose between **Group owners**, **Selected users**, or **Members (self)**:

Figure 4.33 – Access review options

5. For this example, we will choose the **Members (self)** option. The effect of this will be that each guest that accepted an invitation will receive an email from Azure AD that contains a link to the access review so that they may complete it themselves. Finally, you may choose some options that will take effect when the access review is completed, along with some advanced options. These are shown in *Figure 4.34*:

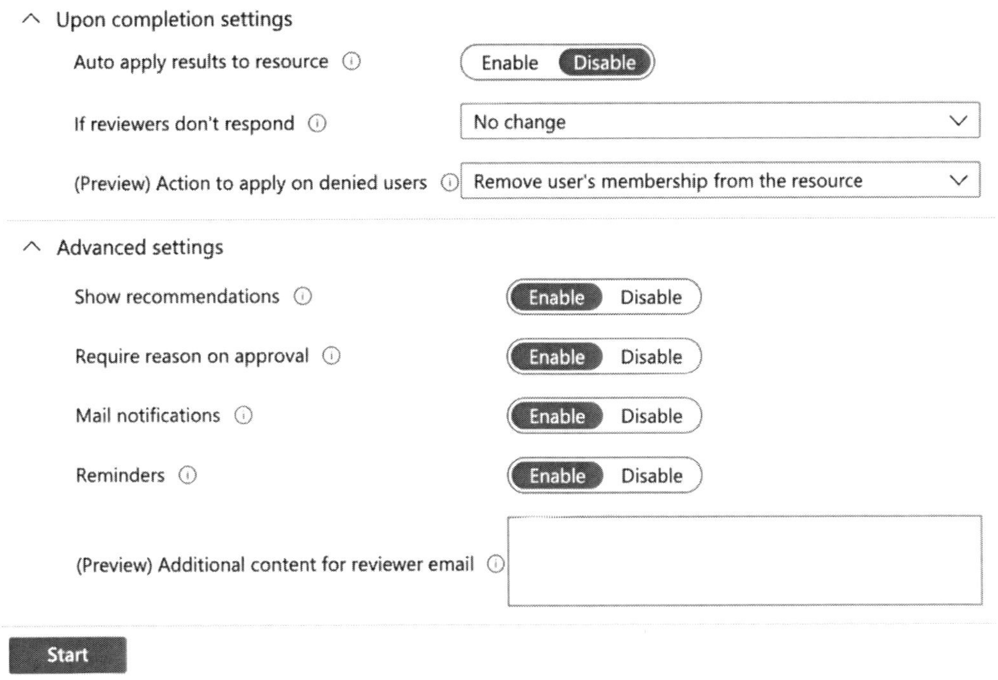

Figure 4.34 – Completion and advanced settings

6. Click on **Start** to begin the access review. The access review will now appear in the list and will have an **Initializing** status, as shown in *Figure 4.35*:

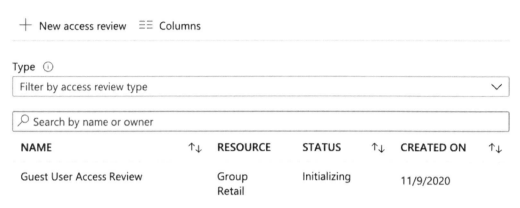

Figure 4.35 – New access review created

7. Now, any guest users within the retail group will receive an email asking them to **review access**, as shown in *Figure 4.36*:

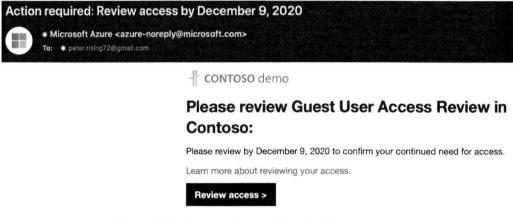

Figure 4.36 – Access review email received by guest user

8. Upon opening the review, the guest user is then asked if they still need access to the retail group, as shown in *Figure 4.37*:

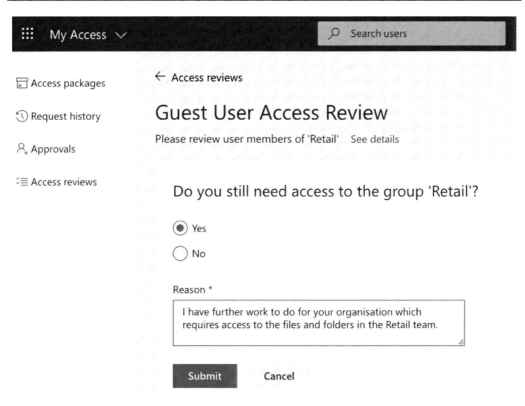

Figure 4.37 – Guest user completes the access review

9.   Upon clicking **Submit**, the access review progress is shown in *Figure 4.38*:

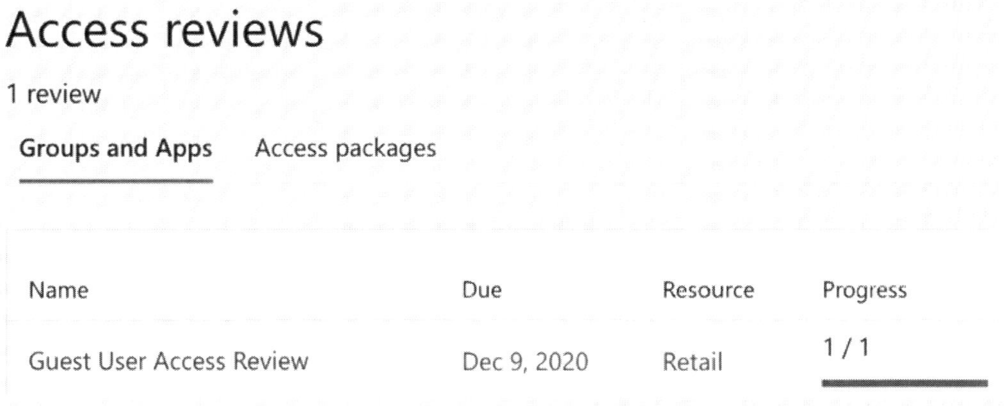

Access reviews

1 review

Groups and Apps   Access packages

Name	Due	Resource	Progress
Guest User Access Review	Dec 9, 2020	Retail	1 / 1

Figure 4.38 – Access review completed by guest user

10. Once completed, the Azure AD administrator who set up the access review can check the results in the **Identity Governance** section of the Azure portal, as shown in *Figure 4.39*:

Figure 4.39 – Completed access review checked by the Azure AD administrator

In this section, you learned how to remove guest users from a team. We also demonstrated how Azure AD **access reviews** can be used to assess the guest users in your organization and determine whether they need to retain access to Microsoft 365 groups. Once the reviews have been completed, recommended actions may be applied.

Next, we will look at how to configure guest access from the Azure AD portal.

Configuring guest access from the Azure AD portal

Earlier in this chapter, we showed you how to configure the external-collaboration settings for guest user access from within the **Azure portal**. We also showed you how to invite a guest user directly from Microsoft Teams. Creating a guest user from Teams will also create a guest user object directly within Azure AD. However, it is also possible to invite users directly from the Azure portal. This provides tenant-, directory-, and application-level control of the guest experience as opposed to just at the Microsoft Teams level. In this section, we will show you how to invite guest users from the Azure portal by going through the following steps:

1. Log in to the Azure portal at `https://portal.azure.com` and navigate to **Azure AD | Manage | Users**. You will see the list of Azure AD users, as shown in *Figure 4.40*:

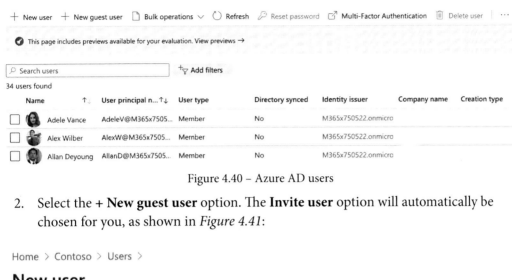

Figure 4.40 – Azure AD users

2. Select the **+ New guest user** option. The **Invite user** option will automatically be chosen for you, as shown in *Figure 4.41*:

Home > Contoso > Users >

New user

Contoso

♡ Got feedback?

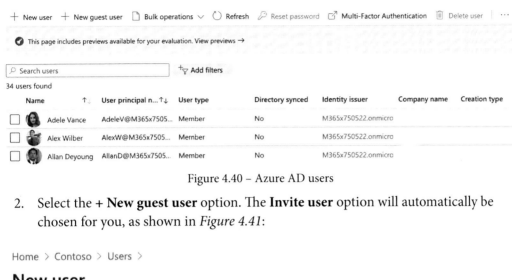

Figure 4.41 – Invite user

3. Scroll down and fill in the details of the guest user that you would like to invite. You can choose to include a personal message with the invitation:

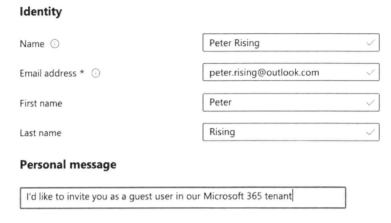

Figure 4.42 – Guest user invitation with personal message

4. Scroll down again and select the groups that you would like to invite the guest user to join. In this example, we will invite the guest user to join the same retail group that we used earlier in this chapter, which will provide the new guest with access to the retail team within **Microsoft Teams**. In this section, we can also set some sign-in options and a usage location, and optionally include some job information:

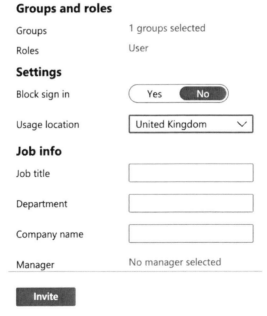

Figure 4.43 – Completing the guest user invitation

5. When clicking on **Invite**, the invitation is immediately emailed to the user, as shown in *Figure 4.44*:

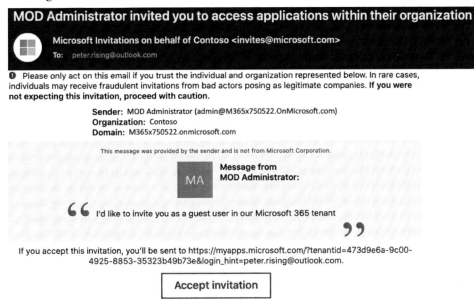

Figure 4.44 – Guest access invitation received by the user

6. When the invited user clicks on **Accept invitation**, they are prompted to review and accept permissions, as shown in *Figure 4.45*:

Figure 4.45 – Accepting the guest user invitation

7.   The user will then be taken to the **My Apps** page, as shown in *Figure 4.46*:

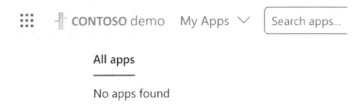

Figure 4.46 – New guest user logged in to the My Apps page

8.   If the new guest user logs in to the Teams app or opens Teams in a browser via `https//teams.microsoft.com`, they will also be able to connect to the organization and access the retail team. First, they will need to choose the organization that invited them, as shown in *Figure 4.47*:

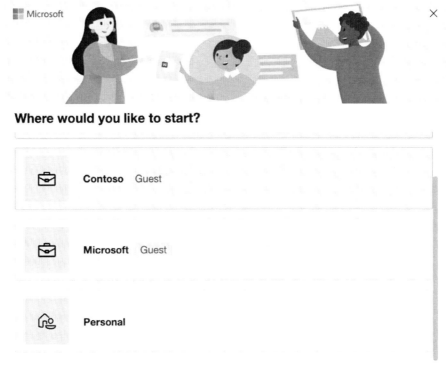

Figure 4.47 – Choosing which Teams organization to connect to

9.   Then, once they are logged into Teams, the retail team will be available, as shown in *Figure 4.48*:

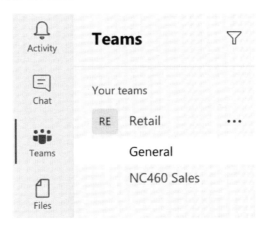

Figure 4.48 – Guest user signed in to Teams

As you can see, this process is very similar to how we invited a guest user via Teams earlier in the chapter.

In this section, we showed you how to invite a guest user into your Microsoft 365 organization using the Azure portal. We demonstrated how to send the invitation, which included group settings, and then how to accept the invitation as the invited user and access Microsoft 365 services, including Microsoft Teams.

Summary

In this chapter, we introduced you to the principles of configuring guest user access within Microsoft Teams. You learned that there are a number of different areas within **Microsoft 365** that you need to configure guest user access for in when providing guest user access to **Microsoft Teams**. These included the **Azure AD portal**, **Microsoft 365 group settings**, the **SharePoint admin center**, and the **Microsoft Teams admin center**.

In addition, we showed you how to configure the permissions for guest users in Teams from both an organizational level and from a Teams level. We also looked at how to remove guest users from Microsoft Teams and how to use Azure AD access reviews to assess the access requirements of your guest users.

Finally, we demonstrated how to invite users into your **Microsoft 365** organization directly from the Azure portal, add them to a **Microsoft 365** group with a team attached to it, and then accept the invitation and gain access to the team.

In the next chapter, we will examine the principles of security and compliance within Microsoft Teams. You will learn about the different Teams admin roles that are available and what they do. You will also gain an understanding of the compliance features for Teams, such as retention and sensitivity policies, and we will also show you how to set up security- and compliance-related alerting for Microsoft Teams. Additionally, we will introduce you to information barrier policies, which can be used to separate groups of Teams users so that they cannot communicate directly. Lastly, we will examine some of the available security reporting features for Microsoft Teams.

Questions

As we conclude this chapter, here is a list of questions for you to test your knowledge regarding this chapter's material. You will find the answers in the *Assessments* section of the *Appendix*:

1. Which of the following cannot be used to set guest user access relating to Microsoft teams?

    a. Microsoft 365 group settings

    b. Security group settings

    c. The Teams admin center

    d. The Azure portal

2. When configuring SharePoint external-sharing policies, which of the following is not one of the available options?

    a. Specific people

    b. Specific guests

    c. Only people in your organization

    d. Anyone with the link

3. True or false: Guest users who you invite into your organization must use an existing Microsoft 365 account or a personal email account, such as an Outlook or Gmail account—which can be enabled as a Microsoft organizational account—or a **one-time passcode** (**OTP**) for guest access.

    a. True

    b. False

4. Which of following would you use to access existing guest user access permissions?

    a. Azure AD identity protection

    b. Azure AD access reviews

    c. Azure AD privileged identity management

    e. Azure AD conditional access

5. True or false: To use Azure AD access reviews, you must have an Azure AD Premium P1 license.

    a. True

    b. False

6. Where in the Teams admin center would you go to configure guest access settings?

    a. **Org-wide settings | Guest permissions**

    b. **Org-wide settings | Guest user access**

    c. **Org-wide settings | Guest access**

    d. **Org-wide settings | External access**

7. Which of the following is not one of the available options for configuring guest access from the Teams admin center?

    a. Meeting

    b. Calling

    c. Collaboration

    d. Messaging

8. True or false: When a guest is removed from a team, their guest account is also removed from Azure AD.

    a. True

    b. False

9. Where in the Azure portal could you go to configure access reviews (choose two options)?

    a. **External Identities | Access reviews**

    b. **Administrative Units | Access reviews**

    c. **Identity Governance | Access reviews**

    d. **User Settings | Access reviews**

10. True or false: Access reviews can be completed by members of the group that is being reviewed.

   a. True

   b. False

Further reading

Here are some links to more information on some of the topics that we have covered in this chapter:

- Guest access in Microsoft Teams: `https://docs.microsoft.com/en-us/microsoftteams/guest-access`

- Comparison of team member and guest capabilities: `https://docs.microsoft.com/en-us/microsoftteams/guest-experience#comparison-of-team-member-and-guest-capabilities`

- Collaborate with guests in a team: `https://docs.microsoft.com/en-us/microsoft-365/solutions/collaborate-as-team?view=o365-worldwide`

- Turning guest access to Microsoft Teams on or off: `https://docs.microsoft.com/en-us/microsoftteams/set-up-guests`

- Remove someone from a team: `https://support.microsoft.com/en-us/office/remove-someone-from-a-team-91610d8b-c182-4cab-8f31-1ed8d3d316ee?ui=en-us&rs=en-us&ad=us`

- Manage guest access with Azure AD access reviews: `https://docs.microsoft.com/en-us/azure/active-directory/governance/manage-guest-access-with-access-reviews`

- Add guest users to your directory in the Azure portal: `https://docs.microsoft.com/en-us/azure/active-directory/external-identities/b2b-quickstart-add-guest-users-portal`

- Add a guest user with PowerShell: `https://docs.microsoft.com/en-us/azure/active-directory/external-identities/b2b-quickstart-invite-powershell`

5
Managing the Security and Compliance Settings in Microsoft Teams

In this chapter, we will examine the principles of security and compliance within Microsoft Teams. You will learn about the different Teams admin roles that are available and what they do, gain an understanding of compliance features for Teams, such as retention policies and sensitivity policies, and we will also show you how to set up security- and compliance-related alerting for Microsoft Teams. Additionally, we will introduce you to information barrier policies, which can be used to separate groups of Teams users so that they may not communicate directly, and finally examine some of the security reporting features available for Microsoft Teams. Learning about these principles will help you to manage Microsoft Teams on a day-to-day basis and also help you to pass the MS-700 exam.

In this chapter, we're going to cover the following main topics:

- Understanding and assigning the Teams admin roles

- Managing retention and sensitivity policies for Microsoft Teams

- Setting up alerts for security and compliance in Microsoft Teams

- Understanding and implementing information barrier policies for Microsoft Teams

- Understanding the security reports available within Microsoft Teams

Technical requirements

In this chapter, you will need to have access to the **Microsoft Teams admin center**, which you can reach at `https://admin.teams.microsoft.com`. You will need to be a **Global Administrator** in order to carry out most of the steps covered in this chapter. However, the **Compliance Administrator** role will be enough for many of the activities described.

You will also need to be able to access **Windows PowerShell** to configure **Information Barrier** segments and policies.

Understanding and assigning the Teams admin roles

When configuring Microsoft Teams for your organization, it is necessary to understand and assign the appropriate administrator roles so that only authorized staff may configure user settings and features for Teams. It is important to only grant the access that is needed and no more.

To facilitate only the required level of administrative access, Microsoft Teams comes with five administrator roles, which can be assigned to the appropriate people in your organization who need to manage Teams workloads. These roles range from having full permissions, and subsets of permissions, to the features and settings that may be configured from the Microsoft Teams admin center and Windows PowerShell.

In this section, we will examine each of these roles and explain the tools and features that are available to those assigned to these roles.

The roles available are as follows:

Role	Role Description	Access Level
Teams Service Administrator	Teams service, and Microsoft 365 group management	This role has access to all features within the Teams admin center.
Teams Communications Administrator	To manage calling and meeting features	This role can be used to configure meeting policies and settings, calling policies and phone number allocation, view user profile pages, and troubleshoot call quality from the Call Quality Dashboard.
Teams Communications Support Engineer	To troubleshoot communications problems with an advanced toolset	This role can be used to view user profile pages and troubleshoot call quality using advanced tools from the Call Quality Dashboard.
Teams Communications Support Specialist	To troubleshoot communications problems with a basic toolset	This role can be used to search a specific user's profile and view information to troubleshoot call quality using basic tools from the Call Quality Dashboard.
Teams Device Administrator	To manage devices configured to use Teams	This role can manage device settings and updates, apply profiles to devices, restart devices, and monitor the health of devices.

> **Important note**
> The **Global Administrator** role within Microsoft 365 has all the same permissions and capabilities that are assigned to the Teams Service Administrator role.

So, now that you are aware of these available admin roles for Teams, let's look at how you can assign these roles to users in your organization.

Assigning Teams admin roles to users

To assign a Teams admin role to your users, you will need to connect to the Azure portal as a **Global Administrator**. In the following example, we will assign the **Teams Communications Support Engineer** role to a user named **Adele Vance**. This is achieved by completing the following steps:

1. From the Azure portal at `https://portal.azure.com`, navigate to **Azure Active Directory** and then, under the **Manage** section, choose **Users**, as shown in *Figure 5.1*:

Figure 5.1 – Accessing users from the Azure portal

2. Next, under **Users | All users (Preview)**, we need to choose the user, and click to open it to assign the role to, which in this case is **Adele Vance**, as shown in *Figure 5.2*:

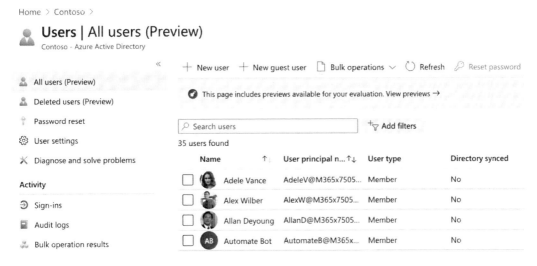

Figure 5.2 – Selecting the user to assign the role to

3. Once you have clicked to open the user object, click on **Assigned roles**, as shown in *Figure 5.3*:

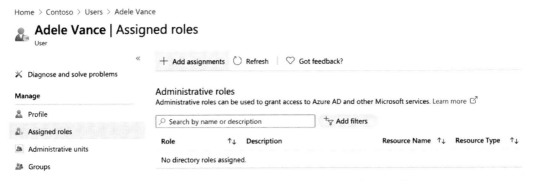

Figure 5.3 – Choosing Assigned roles from within the user object

4. Click on + **Add assignments** and, in the **Directory roles** search box, type in "*Teams*" and hit *Enter* (you can also scroll through the full list of roles). The list of Teams admin roles is now as shown in *Figure 5.4*:

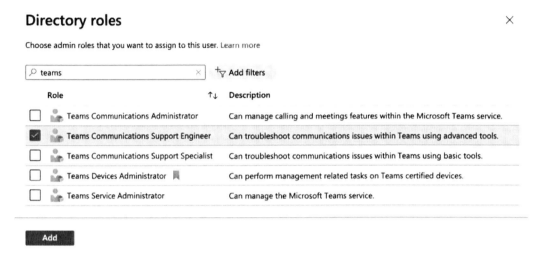

Figure 5.4 – Searching for directory roles

5. Select the **Teams Communications Support Engineer** role and click on **Add**. The role will now be added to the user as shown in *Figure 5.5*:

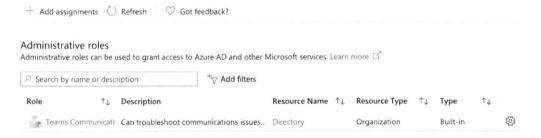

Figure 5.5 – The Teams Communications Support Engineer role added to the user

It is also possible to add a Teams admin role by using **Windows PowerShell**. This can be achieved by completing the following steps:

1. Open PowerShell and run the following command to connect to Azure **Active Directory** (**AD**):

```
Connect-AzureAD
```

2. Enter your **Global Administrator** credentials when prompted and you will be connected to Azure AD. In the following example, we will assign a user named **Alex Wilber** to the **Teams Service Administrator** role by running the following PowerShell commands:

```
$userName="alexw@m365x750522.onmicrosoft.com"
$roleName="Teams Service Administrator"
$role = Get-AzureADDirectoryRole | Where {$_.displayName -eq $roleName}
if ($role -eq $null) {
$roleTemplate = Get-AzureADDirectoryRoleTemplate | Where {$_.displayName -eq $roleName}
Enable-AzureADDirectoryRole -RoleTemplateId $roleTemplate.ObjectId
$role = Get-AzureADDirectoryRole | Where {$_.displayName -eq $roleName}
}
Add-AzureADDirectoryRoleMember -ObjectId $role.ObjectId -RefObjectId (Get-AzureADUser | Where {$_.UserPrincipalName -eq $userName}).ObjectID
```

3. When executed, this is shown as displayed in *Figure 5.6*:

Figure 5.6 – Adding a Teams admin role to a user with Windows PowerShell

4. Now, if we check **Alex Wilber** in the Azure portal, we can see the role assignment successfully applied as shown in *Figure 5.7*:

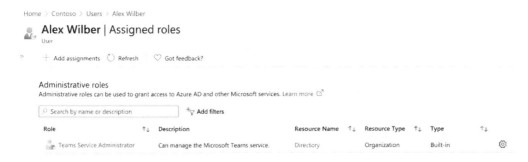

Figure 5.7 – Teams admin role successfully assigned to a user via PowerShell

So, to recap what you have learned in this section, we have introduced you to the five Teams admin roles that are available within Azure AD. We showed you how you can assign these roles to your users via the Azure portal, and by using Windows PowerShell.

Next, we will look at configuring retention and sensitivity policies for Microsoft Teams.

Managing retention and sensitivity policies for Microsoft Teams

In this section, we will show you how to configure retention policies and sensitivity labels for use with your Microsoft Teams deployment. **Retention policies** ensure that the information stored in your Microsoft 365 locations are appropriately retained or deleted based on industry regulations or internal policies. **Sensitivity labels** allow you to control access to your company data stored in Microsoft Teams to ensure that only authorized personnel can access this content. We will look at retention policies first.

Retention policies for Microsoft Teams

When you use retention policies with Microsoft Teams, the most important consideration is to determine your industry obligations and any internal policies that your organization has in place. This is to ensure that data is retained as long as required, but also not retained longer than it should be.

Teams retention policies enable you to do the following:

- Retain Teams chats and channel messages for a defined time period, and then take no action.

- Retain Teams chats and channel messages for a defined time period, and then delete the content.

- Delete Teams chats and channel messages following a defined time period.

Teams private chat messages are stored in an Azure-powered chat service and ingested to the user's Exchange mailbox for compliance, while Teams group chats are stored in the group mailbox.

When a user makes changes or deletes content within Teams chats or channels that is subject to a retention policy, a copy of the original content is saved to a hidden folder named **Substrateholds**, while the retention policy remains in effect.

While the retention policy remains in effect, the content may be searched for by compliance admins by using **eDiscovery**. Once the retention period passes, however, and the content is permanently deleted, it cannot be searched for.

Before you configure retention policies for Teams, it is important to be aware of the following limitations:

- Teams retention policies may not be configured together with other Microsoft 365 workload, such as Exchange Online, OneDrive, or SharePoint. They must be configured separately.

- Teams retention policies only work with standard Teams channels. Private channels are not supported.

- Advanced retention settings, such as keywords, are not supported.

- If one or more retention policies have conflicting settings, then retention will always win out over deletion.

To create a retention policy for Microsoft Teams, you will need to complete the following steps:

1. Log in to the Microsoft Compliance center as a **Global Administrator**, a **Compliance Administrator** at `https://compliance.microsoft.com`, and navigate to **Solutions | Catlog**, as shown in *Figure 5.8*:

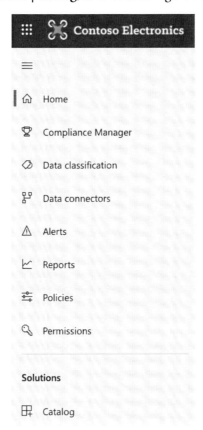

Figure 5.8 – Microsoft 365 Compliance center

2. Under **Information governance**, click **View**:

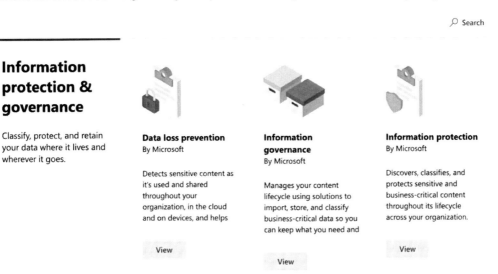

Figure 5.9 – Information governance in the compliance center

3. Next, click on **Open solution**:

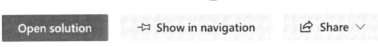

Figure 5.10 – Opening the information governance solution

4. From the **Information governance** screen, select the **Retention** tab shown in *Figure 5.11*:

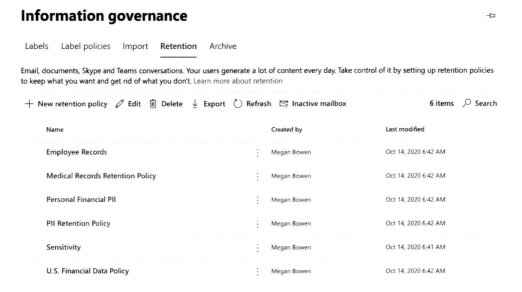

Figure 5.11 – Opening the retention tab

5. Click on **+ New retention policy**. Add a name and description for your retention policy. In this example, we will name the policy **Teams retention policy**, as shown in *Figure 5.12*:

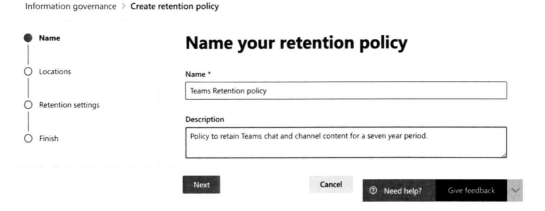

Figure 5.12 – Name your retention policy

6. Click **Next**, and you will be taken to the choices for the Microsoft 365 service locations that you may include in your retention policy. You will note that when you select either or both of the Teams retention policies, all other locations are automatically toggled to **Off**. This is due to the fact that Teams retention policies may not coexist with other Microsoft 365 workloads in the same policy as we described earlier in this chapter.

For this example, we will select both **Teams channel messages** and **Teams chats**. These could be selected in separate policies if required. It is also possible to filter the Teams that will be targeted by the policy. However, in this example, we will leave **All Teams** selected for the policy, as illustrated in *Figure 5.13*:

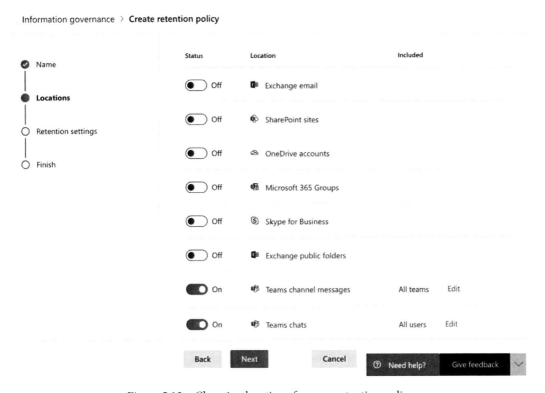

Figure 5.13 – Choosing locations for your retention policy

7.   Click **Next**. Now we can choose our retention settings. In this example, we will set the policy to retain items for a 7-year period and then delete the content automatically. This is shown in *Figure 5.14*:

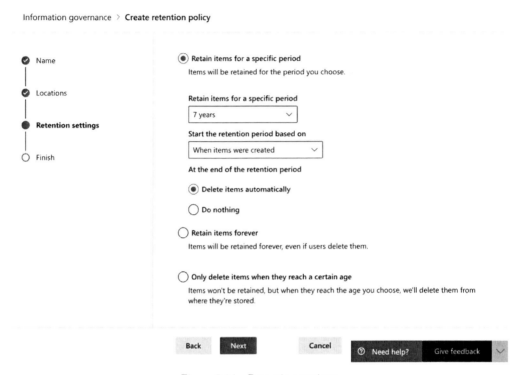

Figure 5.14 – Retention settings

8. Click **Next**. Now we can review the settings. *Figure 5.15* shows the settings we have configured, along with a warning that content will be automatically deleted after the retention period:

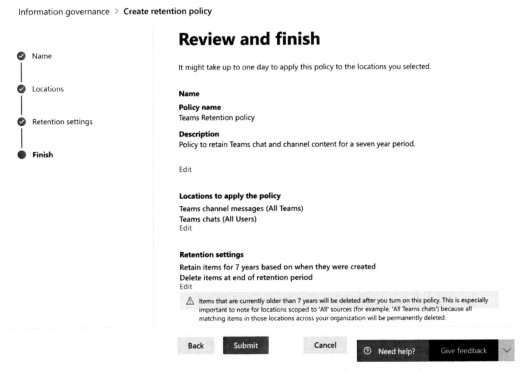

Figure 5.15 – Reviewing and finishing configuring the retention policy

9.   Click **Submit**. Then, click **Done**, as shown in *Figure 5.16*:

Figure 5.16 – The policy has been created

So, our policy has now been successfully created, and will retain items within Teams chat and channel messages for 7 years, based on when the items were created. At the end of the retention period, the content will be automatically deleted.

> **Important note**
>
> Any files that are shared in private chats will be stored in OneDrive for the user who shared the file. In addition, if users upload any files to a channel chat, these will be stored in the SharePoint site for that team. To retain such content, you must also create retention policies for OneDrive and SharePoint Online.

Next, we will look at sensitivity labels.

Sensitivity labels

When **sensitivity labels** are applied to a team, the collaborative content within the team is regulated to ensure that only authorized users may gain access. Sensitivity labels are created from the **Microsoft 365 Compliance center**. In the following example, we will create and publish a label that will apply to all users in the organization and select the group and site settings so that the label may be applied to a team.

> **Important note**
> The following steps include instructions relating to groups and sites in relation to sensitivity labels. Sensitivity labeling for sites and groups is not enabled by default. This must be explicitly enabled in Microsoft 365 tenants. More details on this can be found at the end of this chapter in the *Further reading* section.

To do this, we need to complete the following steps:

1. Log in to the compliance center at `https://compliance.microsoft.com` as a **Global Administrator**, a **Compliance Administrator**, a **Compliance Data Administrator**, or as a **Security Administrator**. From **Solution catalog**, which we accessed earlier to create our retention policy, this time choose the **Information protection** section and then click **View**:

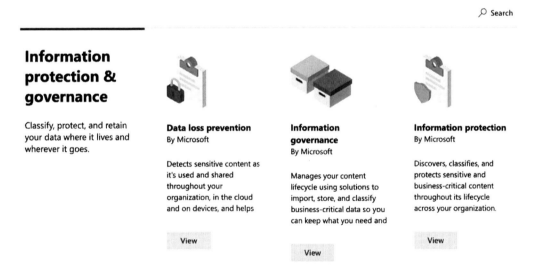

Figure 5.17 – Selecting information protection from the compliance center

2. Click on **Open solution**, as shown in *Figure 5.18*:

Figure 5.18 – Opening the Information protection solution from the compliance center

3. This will take you to the **Labels** section, as shown in *Figure 5.19*. We can see that in the demo tenant we are using in this example, there are some labels already configured. If you are working in a production tenant, you will need to create some labels. In this example, we will modify the **Public** label to configure it for use with **Groups & Sites** so that it may be used with Microsoft Teams:

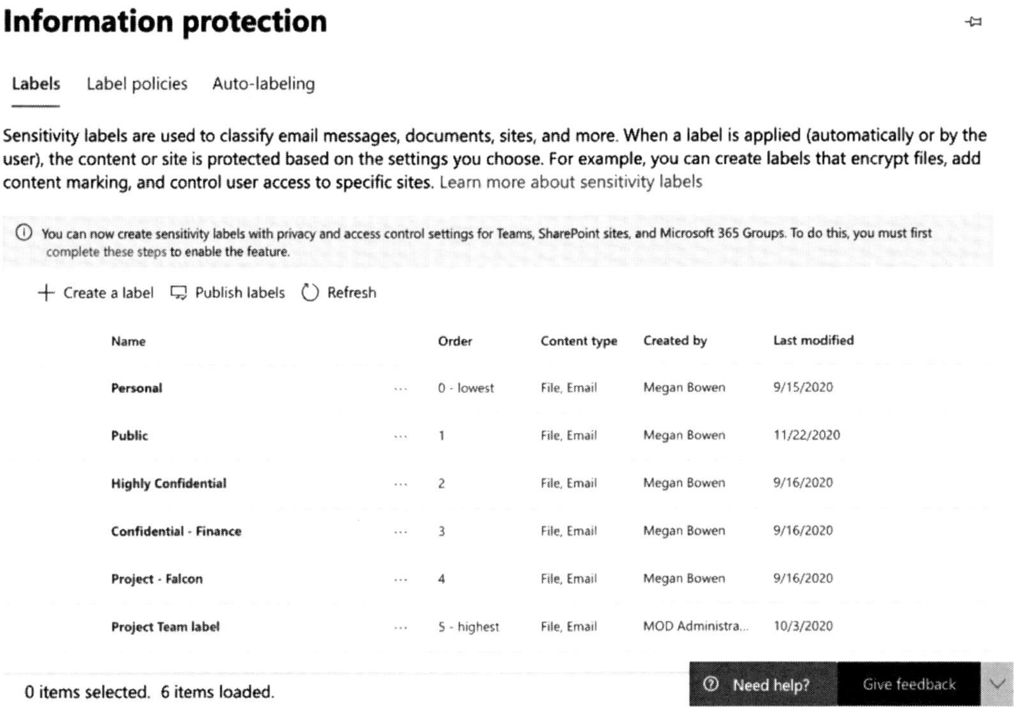

Figure 5.19 – Labels in the compliance center

4. Click on the **Public** label and then keep clicking **Next** until you reach the
    Scope | Groups & sites section where you will see **Define the scope for this label**:

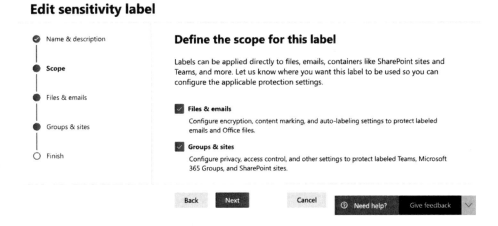

Figure 5.20 – Defining the scope for this label

5. Click **Next** and then select the checkboxes next to the privacy and device access
    settings as shown in *Figure 5.21*:

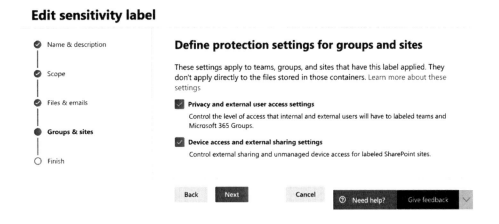

Figure 5.21 – Selecting the privacy and device access checkboxes

6. Click **Next**, and here we will set the privacy level for the label to be **Public**:

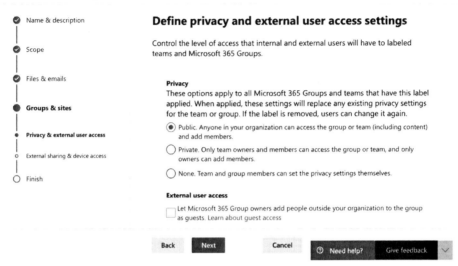

Figure 5.22 – Setting the privacy level for the label

7. Under **Define external sharing and device access settings**, we will choose the **Allow full access from desktop apps, mobile apps, and the web** option:

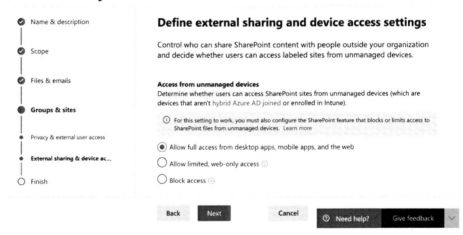

Figure 5.23 – Setting external sharing and device access settings

8. Click **Next** and complete the label wizard to save your changes.

Now that we have amended our label, the next step is to apply it to a team. You can do this by creating a new team or editing an existing team. In this example, we will set up a new team by completing the following steps:

1. Log in to **Microsoft Teams** and select **Join or create a team | Create a Team | From Scratch**. For this example, we will choose the option of a **Public** team. We also have the option to set a sensitivity label for our team. In *Figure 5.24*, the sensitivity label has been set to **Public** by selecting it from the drop-down option:

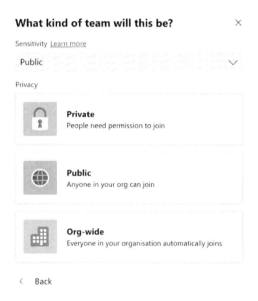

Figure 5.24 – Choosing a sensitivity label and privacy option for the team

2. Once the team has been created, you will note that the label assigned to the team is shown in the top-right corner next to the **Meet** button:

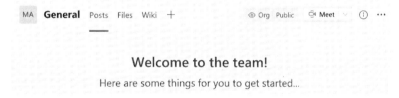

Figure 5.25 – Sensitivity label for the team shown in the General channel

In this section, we examined the principles of applying retention policies and sensitivity labels in Microsoft Teams. We created a retention policy and a sensitivity label.

Next, we will look at how you can set up alerts for security and compliance within Microsoft Teams.

Setting up alerts for security and compliance in Microsoft Teams

As a Microsoft Teams administrator, you will need to regularly monitor your environment to ensure that user activities are in line with the policies and settings that you have put in place. To do this, you can create alert policies from the Microsoft 365 **Security & Compliance Center**. You can monitor for activities, such as when teams were created or deleted, or when the settings of a team have been modified.

> **Important note**
> In the following steps, we will use the security and compliance center. However, the audit log search may now also be carried out from the compliance center at `https://compliance.microsoft.com`.

This can be achieved by completing the following steps:

1. Log in to the security and compliance center at `https://protection.office.com` and navigate to **Search | Audit log search**:

Figure 5.26 – Audit log search in the security and compliance center

2. Under the search option, type in the word *"Team"* and by clicking to show the results for all activities, you will see all the alert options available to you for **Microsoft Teams**, as shown in *Figure 5.27*. We will choose the **Created team** option in this example:

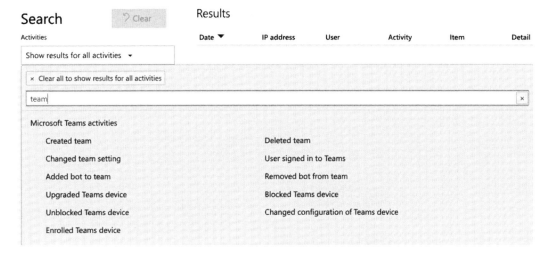

Figure 5.27 – Microsoft Teams activities in the audit log search

3. Once you have selected **Created team**, and clicked to get out of the search area, select **+ New alert policy**, as shown in *Figure 5.28*:

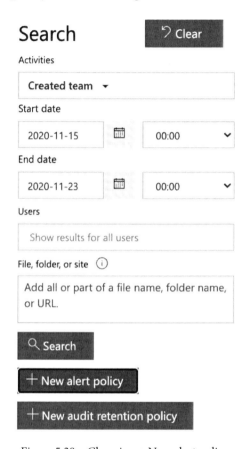

Figure 5.28 – Choosing + New alert policy

4. Next, we need to provide a name and description for our alert policy, setting it to **Send this alert when…** and the activity to **Created team**. For this example, we will leave the **Users** field set to **Show results for all users**:

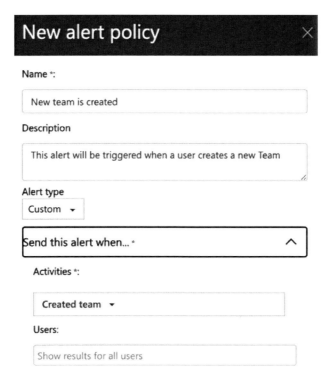

Figure 5.29 – Settings for a new alert policy

5. Scroll down further, and you can set the recipients for the alert policy as shown in *Figure 5.30*:

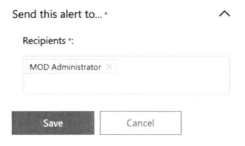

Figure 5.30 – Settings for a new alert policy

6. Click **Save**. The saved alert policy can be viewed by clicking on **Activity alerts**, as shown in *Figure 5.31*:

Activity alerts

! We are working on a better experience for you to manage and view security and compliance alerts. Go to Alert policies

+ New alert policy

Name	Recipients	Status	Date modified
New team is created	admin@M365x750522.OnMicrosoft.com	On	2020-11-22 10:57:26

Figure 5.31 – New alert policy shown in the Activity alerts section

The result of this is that when a new team is created by any user in the organization, an alert will be sent to the recipients chosen in the alert policy.

In this section, we have shown you how to set up alert policies for activities related to Microsoft Teams. Next, we will talk about implementing information barrier policies.

Understanding and implementing information barrier policies for Microsoft Teams

Information barriers may be configured in Microsoft 365 if you have departments or individuals who must be prevented from communicating with one another, or even prevented from finding each other in lookups. To configure information barrier policies, we need to use PowerShell commands from the Microsoft 365 compliance center, and you must have one of the following admin roles assigned to you:

- Global administrator
- Compliance administrator
- IB compliance management

In the following example, we will create two information barrier segments called *Retail* and *Marketing*. These segments will refer to the department field for all user objects to determine which users will be affected. We will then create an information barrier policy to prevent users in the retail department from communicating with users in the marketing department.

In order to configure information barriers for Microsoft Teams, we need to complete the following steps:

1. Log in to the **Teams admin center** and navigate to **Org-wide settings | Teams settings**. Scroll down to **Search by name** and set the **Scope directory search using an Exchange address book policy** option to **On**. Then, click **Save**:

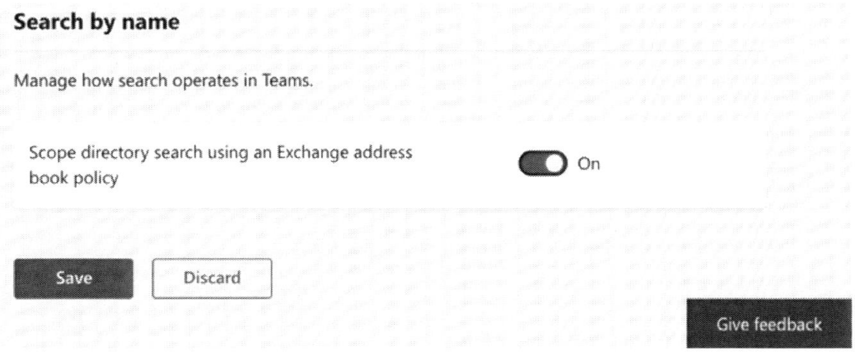

Figure 5.32 – Setting up a scoped directory search in the Teams admin center

2. Next, we have to create two information barrier segments for the departments we wish to keep separate. This is achieved by running the following PowerShell commands to connect to Security and Compliance PowerShell:

```
$UserCredential = Get-Credential
$Session = New-PSSession -ConfigurationName Microsoft.
Exchange -ConnectionUri https://ps.compliance.
protection.outlook.com/powershell-liveid/ -Credential
$UserCredential -Authentication Basic -AllowRedirection
Import-PSSession $Session -DisableNameChecking
```

3. Now that we are connected to Security and Compliance PowerShell, we need to create our information barrier segments as follows:

```
New-OrganizationSegment -Name "Retail" -UserGroupFilter
"Department -eq 'Retail'"
```

The preceding command sets up an information barrier segment called `Retail`. We now have to repeat this process and create another segment called `Marketing`.

The results of these PowerShell inputs are shown in *Figure 5.33*:

Figure 5.33 – Configuring information barrier segments

4. Now that we have our two segments configured, we can create our information barrier policy to prevent these two departments from communicating with each other:

```
New-InformationBarrierPolicy -Name "Retail-Marketing"
-AssignedSegment "Retail" -SegmentsBlocked "Marketing"
-State Inactive
```

The execution of the preceding command is shown in *Figure 5.34*:

```
PS C:\Users\RisingP> New-InformationBarrierPolicy -Name "Retail-Marketing" -AssignedSegment "Retail" -SegmentsBlocked "M
arketing" -State Inactive

Note: Information barrier policy will restrict communication, collaboration and people search between users.

For Teams  - including Teams Channel (Microsoft 365 Groups), Teams Meeting & Teams Communication (Chat, Call)
 * Access to communication/content access/people search/SharePoint site
   connected to the Teams will be restricted based on Information Barrier
   policy assigned to user's segments.

For OneDrive
 * Access and sharing of OneDrive content will be restricted based on the
   information barrier policy assigned to the OneDrive owner.

For SharePoint- including Microsoft 365 Groups connected and non-connected sites
 * Segments are associated to a SharePoint site (communication sites,
   classic sites, modern sites) based on the site creator's segment or by
   adding segments explicitly to a site.
 * Access and sharing of a SharePoint site will be restricted to the
   segments associated to the site.
   More Details - https://aka.ms/SPOInfobarriers.

Are You Sure You Want To Proceed?
[Y] Yes  [N] No  [?] Help (default is "Y"): y
```

Figure 5.34 – Setting up a new information barrier policy

5.   Press **Y** to confirm that you wish to proceed:

```
RunspaceId               : e30cb06d-2cf4-45f8-9155-f3d6f2b4e137
Type                     : InformationBarrier
AssignedSegment          : Retail
SegmentsAllowed          : {}
ExoPolicyId              : a1e1cb37-47e0-4903-b5b1-1183313b8da0
SegmentsBlocked          : {Marketing}
SegmentAllowedFilter     :
BlockVisibility          : True
BlockCommunication       : True
State                    : Inactive
ObjectVersion            : 8f2a3075-a335-4897-e257-08d88ee78f63
CreatedBy                : MOD Administrator
LastModifiedBy           : MOD Administrator
Comment                  :
ModificationTimeUtc      : 22/11/2020 13:07:26
CreationTimeUtc          : 22/11/2020 13:07:26
Identity                 : FFO.extest.microsoft.com/Microsoft Exchange Hosted
                           Organizations/M365x750522.onmicrosoft.com/Configuration/Retail-Marketing
Id                       : FFO.extest.microsoft.com/Microsoft Exchange Hosted
                           Organizations/M365x750522.onmicrosoft.com/Configuration/Retail-Marketing
ExchangeVersion          : 0.20 (15.0.0.0)
Name                     : Retail-Marketing
DistinguishedName        : CN=Retail-Marketing,CN=Configuration,CN=M365x750522.onmicrosoft.com,OU=Microsoft Exchange
                           Hosted Organizations,DC=FFO,DC=extest,DC=microsoft,DC=com
ObjectCategory           :
ObjectClass              : {msExchUnifiedPolicy}
WhenChanged              : 22/11/2020 13:07:26
WhenCreated              : 22/11/2020 13:07:26
WhenChangedUTC           : 22/11/2020 13:07:26
WhenCreatedUTC           : 22/11/2020 13:07:26
ExchangeObjectId         : bd43f86c-1d30-43fb-bcc0-46a4a8438571
OrganizationId           : FFO.extest.microsoft.com/Microsoft Exchange Hosted Organizations/M365x750522.onmicrosoft.com -
                           FFO.extest.microsoft.com/Microsoft Exchange Hosted
                           Organizations/M365x750522.onmicrosoft.com/Configuration
Guid                     : bd43f86c-1d30-43fb-bcc0-46a4a8438571
OriginatingServer        :
IsValid                  : True
ObjectState              : New

WARNING: Your changes will take into affect after you run Start-InformationBarrierPoliciesApplication cmdlet.
Start-InformationBarrierPoliciesApplication cmdlet only applies Active state policies.
```

Figure 5.35 – New information barrier policy created

6. Finally, run the following command to apply the information barrier policy settings:

```
Start-InformationBarrierPoliciesApplication
```

The execution of this command is shown in *Figure 5.36*:

```
PS C:\Users\RisingP> Start-InformationBarrierPoliciesApplication
WARNING: It may take several hours for the application to finish. Please check the status using
Get-InformationBarrierPoliciesApplicationStatus cmdlet. Execution of New/Set cmdlets will be prevented until start/stop
is finished.


RunspaceId                 : e30cb06d-2cf4-45f8-9155-f3d6f2b4e137
Identity                   : 7c357f8e-65d2-4a78-8d47-fec169cf673a
CreatedBy                  : MOD Administrator
CancelledBy                :
Type                       : ExoApplyIBPolicyJob
ApplicationCreationTime    : 11/22/2020 13:10:54
ApplicationEndTime         :
ApplicationStartTime       : 11/22/2020 13:10:54
TotalBatches               : 0
ProcessedBatches           : 0
PercentProgress            : 0
TotalRecipients            : 0
SuccessfulRecipients       : 0
FailedRecipients           : 0
FailureCategory            : None
Status                     : NotStarted
IsValid                    : True
ObjectState                : Unchanged


PS C:\Users\RisingP>
```

Figure 5.36 – Starting the information barrier policies application

7. Once you have completed the aforementioned steps, it will be several hours before the settings applied take effect. Once successfully applied, users with department attributes that match the information barrier segments will not be able to search for each other in Teams, as shown in *Figure 5.37*:

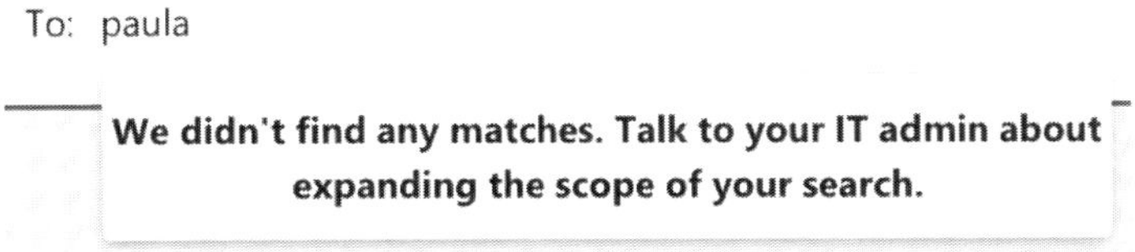

To: paula

> **We didn't find any matches. Talk to your IT admin about expanding the scope of your search.**

Figure 5.37 – A user cannot be found in Teams due to an information barrier being applied

It is also possible to apply multiple segments to an information barrier policy, as well as explicitly allowing just one segment to be able to communicate with another segment.

In this section, we introduced you to the principles of information barriers in Microsoft Teams. We showed you how to create segments based on Azure AD attributes and then create policies that define which segments can communicate with each other.

In the final section of this chapter, we will examine the security reports available within Microsoft Teams.

Understanding the security reports available within Microsoft Teams

The **Teams admin center** includes many reports that you can access from the **Analytics & reports** menu. In this section, we will show you how to access these reports and explain their functions.

In order to access these reports, you must have one of the following admin roles assigned to you:

- Global administrator
- Teams service administrator
- Skype for Business administrator

We can access these reports by completing the following steps:

1. Log in to the **Teams admin center** and navigate to **Analytics & reports | Usage reports**, as shown in *Figure 5.38*:

Figure 5.38 – Analytics & reports in the Teams admin center

2. You will now see the options shown in *Figure 5.39*:

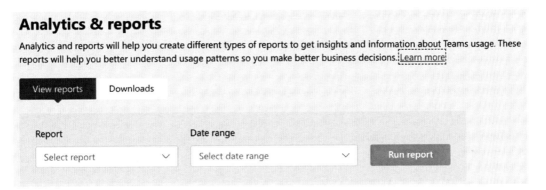

Figure 5.39 – Viewing the available reports

3. Click on the dropdown under **Report** and choose the report you wish to run:

Figure 5.40 – Available reports

4. In this example, we will choose the **Teams user activity** report, and select a date range of **90 days**. There are two other date range options you can select. These are **7 days** and **30 days** (however, other available reports have different date range options). With these settings selected, we then need to click on **Run report**:

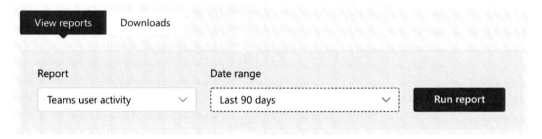

Figure 5.41 – Running a report

5. The report is run and displayed immediately in graph format, as shown in *Figure 5.42*:

Figure 5.42 – Viewing the report results

6. At the top right of the report, you have three options. These are **Export to Excel**, **Full Screen**, and **Edit Columns**:

Figure 5.43 – Report view options

7. Selecting the **Export to Excel** option will make the report available to you in the **Downloads** tab, as shown in *Figure 5.44*:

Figure 5.44 – Report download completed

Important note

The Live event usage report is not one that can be exported.

The reports available within the **Analytics & reports** section are described as follows:

Report	Report output
Apps usage	App name
	Active users
	App type
	Active teams
	Publisher
	Version
PSTN blocked users	Display name
	Phone
	Blocked reason
	Blocked action
	Blocked time
PSTN minute and SMS pools	Country or region
	Capability description
	Total minutes or SMS units
	Minutes or SMS units used
	Minutes or SMS units available
	Capability
PSTN and SMS usage	Start time
	Display name
	Username
	Phone number
	Caller ID
	Call / SMS type
Teams device usage	Reports on usage of users who use:
	Windows devices
	Apple macOS devices
	Apple iOS devices
	Android phones
Teams live event usage	Number of views of the live event
	Start time
	Event status
	Organizer
	Presenters
	Producers
	Recording setting
	Production type

Report	Report output
Teams usage	Active users
	Active channels
	Active users in teams and channels
	Messages
	Teams privacy settings
	Guests in a team
Teams user activity	1:1 calls which a user joined
	Team chat messages post by user
	Private chat messages posted by user
	Users last activity date

The preceding reports will provide invaluable information to Teams administrators about usage and activity within their environment.

In this section, we showed you how to access the available reports for Teams within the **Teams admin center**. You learned how to access these reports from the **Analytics & reports** section, and we showed you a description of what each report does.

Summary

In this chapter, we have introduced you to the principles of managing the security and compliance settings for Microsoft Teams. You learned that there are several admin roles for Teams that can be assigned to users in your organization depending on their roles. We showed you how to view and assign these roles from the **Teams admin center**.

You also learned about retention policies and sensitivity labels and how to use the **compliance center** to configure these for Teams workloads.

In addition, we demonstrated how to configure **alert policies** for Microsoft Teams activities, and how **information barriers** can be used to set up segments based on Azure AD attributes to ensure that departments in your organization that should not be allowed to communicate would not be able to search for each other within Teams.

Finally, we explained the available security reports within **Microsoft Teams** and how to access and run these reports from the **Analytics & reports** section of the Teams admin center.

In the next chapter, we will show you how to manage devices to use Microsoft Teams. This will include deploying the Teams client to devices such as Windows, virtual desktops, macOS, and mobile devices. You will also learn how to manage the settings, which are deployed to these devices by setting up configuration profiles. Finally, we will examine the subject of Teams Rooms and show how to configure Teams Rooms devices and Collaboration bars.

Questions

As we conclude, here is a list of questions for you to test your knowledge regarding this chapter's material. You will find the answers in the *Assessments* section of the *Appendix*:

1. Which of the following is not a Teams admin role?

    a. Teams service administrator

    b. Teams device administrator

    c. Teams communications administrator

    d. Teams device support engineer

2. True or false: The Teams service administrator has access to all features and settings within the Teams admin center.

    a. True

    b. False

3. Where would you go to configure alert policies for Microsoft Teams?

    a. The security center

    b. The compliance center

    c. The security and compliance center

    d. The Microsoft 365 admin center

4. True or false: Sensitivity labels cannot be configured for use with Microsoft Teams.

    a. True

    b. False

5. Which of the following best describes information barriers?

    a. They prevent users from communicating with external users.

    b. They prevent users from communicating with other users by configuring information barrier segments.

c. They prevent users from using information protection features.

d. They prevent users from using information governance features.

6. Which of the following is not a possible action of a retention policy?

a. Retain, then delete.

b. Retain, then do nothing.

c. Delete after a dynamically determined time period.

d. Delete after a defined time period.

7. True or false: Retention policies for Teams can be set up in the same policy as other Microsoft 365 workloads.

a. True

b. False

8. Which of the following is a possible action after running a report from the Teams admin center?

a. Download the report and export to Power BI.

b. Download the report and export to Excel.

c. Download the report and export to PDF.

d. Download the report and export to a TXT file.

9. True or false: Retention policies can be applied to private channels in Teams.

a. True

b. False

10. What is the least privileged Teams admin role that can be used to configure meeting policies and meeting settings?

a. Teams service administrator

b. Teams communications administrator

c. Teams communications support engineer

d. Teams communications support specialist

Further reading

- Using Microsoft Teams administrator roles to manage Teams: `https://docs.microsoft.com/en-us/MicrosoftTeams/using-admin-roles`

- Retention policies in Microsoft Teams: `https://docs.microsoft.com/en-us/microsoftteams/retention-policies`

- Sensitivity labels for Microsoft Teams: `https://docs.microsoft.com/en-us/microsoftteams/sensitivity-labels`

- Configuring sensitivity labels for Groups, Teams, and SharePoint sites: `https://docs.microsoft.com/en-us/microsoft-365/compliance/sensitivity-labels-teams-groups-sites?view=o365-worldwide`

- Alert policies in the security and compliance center: `https://docs.microsoft.com/en-us/microsoft-365/compliance/alert-policies?view=o365-worldwide`

- Information barriers in Teams: `https://docs.microsoft.com/en-us/microsoftteams/information-barriers-in-teams`

- Defining information barrier policies: `https://docs.microsoft.com/en-us/microsoft-365/compliance/information-barriers-policies?view=o365-worldwide`

- Teams analytics and reports: `https://docs.microsoft.com/en-us/microsoftteams/teams-analytics-and-reports/teams-usage-report`

- Microsoft Teams activity reports: `https://docs.microsoft.com/en-us/microsoftteams/teams-activity-reports`

- Microsoft Teams analytics and reporting: `https://docs.microsoft.com/en-us/microsoftteams/teams-analytics-and-reports/teams-reporting-reference`

6
Managing Endpoint Devices in Microsoft Teams

In this chapter, we will show you how to manage devices to use Microsoft Teams. This will include deploying the Teams client to devices such as Windows, virtual desktops, macOS, and mobile devices. You will also learn how to manage the settings that are deployed to these devices by setting up configuration profiles. Finally, we will examine the subject of Teams Rooms and explain the principles of configuring Teams Rooms devices and collaboration bars.

After reading this chapter, you will understand the different endpoint devices that can be configured with Microsoft Teams and the settings and controls that can be applied to them.

In this chapter, we're going to cover the following main topics:

- Deploying Teams clients to devices
- Managing device settings
- Managing configuration profiles
- Setting up Microsoft Teams Rooms

Technical requirements

In this chapter, you will need to have access to the **Microsoft Teams admin center**, which you can reach at `https://admin.teams.microsoft.com`. You will need to be either a *Global Administrator*, a *Teams Service Administrator*, or a *Teams Communications Administrator* in order to carry out the steps covered in this chapter.

Deploying Teams clients to devices

In this section, we will examine how Microsoft Teams may be installed or deployed across many devices and platforms, including Windows, virtual desktops, macOS, and mobile devices.

> **Important note**
> The technologies that we will be discussing in this section, such as **Microsoft Endpoint Configuration Manager**, **Group Policy**, and **Virtualized Desktop Infrastructure**, are beyond the scope of this book. These technologies will be described only at a very high level to provide you with a basic awareness of how these technologies relate to **Microsoft Teams**.

First, we will look at the methods available to install or deploy **Microsoft Teams** to Windows devices.

Windows

Microsoft Teams may be deployed to your Windows devices using several methods. The simplest method is to use **self-service**. Microsoft Teams has been included in Microsoft 365 apps for some time now, so when a user installs Microsoft 365 to their Windows computer, Microsoft Teams will be part of that installation.

To install Microsoft Teams for Windows, please note the following minimum requirements:

- .NET Framework 4.5 or above
- Windows 8.1 or above
- Windows Server 2012 R2 or above
- Recommended minimum of 3 GB of disk space available for each user profile

To install Microsoft Teams as part of the Microsoft 365 apps installation, your users will need to have a valid license for Microsoft 365, which includes Microsoft Teams. The user may carry out the installation by completing the following steps:

1. Log in to the *Microsoft 365* portal at `https://portal.office.com/account` and choose **My account**. Then select **Office apps & devices | Install Office** as shown in *Figure 6.1*:

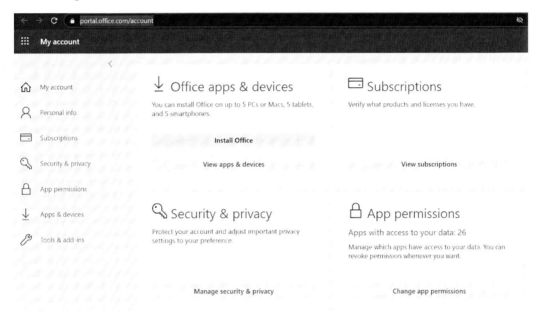

Figure 6.1 – A user installs Microsoft 365 apps including Microsoft Teams

2. You will be prompted to open the setup file and complete the installation of **Office** as shown in *Figure 6.2*:

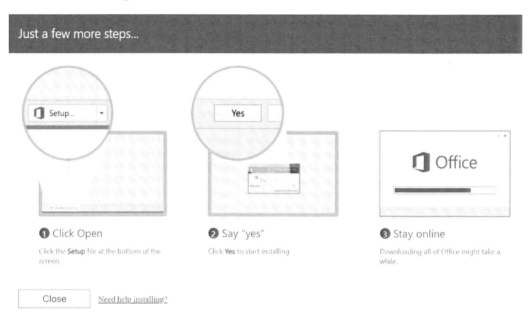

Figure 6.2 – Installing Office

However, for many organizations, it is often more effective to deploy Microsoft Teams by using a method such as **Microsoft Endpoint Configuration Manager** or **Group Policy**. To facilitate this, Microsoft has provided some MSI files, which can be used for bulk deployment scenarios. In this situation, users will not be required to install Microsoft Teams themselves.

The *MSI files* are available in either **32-bit**, **64-bit**, or **ARM64**, and there are versions for Commercial, Federal Government – GCC, Federal Government – GCC High, and Federal Government – DoD.

When you identify which MSI file you need, the steps required to deploy Microsoft Teams are as follows:

1. Download your preferred MSI package.

2. Use the prepopulated MSI defaults if possible.

3. Deploy using your chosen method, such as **Microsoft Endpoint Configuration Manager** or **Group Policy**.

Once executed, the MSI package will copy an installation package to the `Program Files` folder of the Windows device. When the user logs into their computer, the installer will be triggered, and the Microsoft Teams application will be installed on that device. The application is installed in the `AppData` folder for the user. Should Teams already be detected in this folder, the installation process will be skipped as it is not necessary.

You can also deploy Microsoft Teams to Windows devices in your environment by using the **Office Deployment Tool**. This tool allows you to include or exclude Microsoft Teams from an Office installation package that you download and configure. The following example shows Microsoft Teams being excluded from an Office XML installation file:

```xml
<Configuration>
    <Add OfficeClientEdition="64" Channel="Current">
        <Product ID="O365ProPlusRetail">
            <Language ID="en-us" />
            <ExcludeApp ID="Teams" />
        </Product>
        <Product ID="VisioProRetail">
            <Language ID="en-us" />
        </Product>
        <Product ID="ProjectProRetail">
            <Language ID="en-us" />
        </Product>
        <Product ID="LanguagePack">
            <Language ID="de-de" />
        </Product>
    </Add>
</Configuration>
```

> **Important note**
> Further reading on the Office Deployment Tool can be found at the end of this chapter.

It is also possible for users to download and install the Microsoft Teams app from the Microsoft Teams web client by clicking on their username at the top right of the screen and selecting **Download the desktop app.**

Next, we will look at virtual desktops.

Virtual desktops

Microsoft Teams is also supported within **Virtual Desktop Infrastructure** (**VDI**) environments, where desktop operating systems are hosted at a central source. The following VDI platforms support Microsoft Teams:

Vendor	Product
Microsoft	Windows Virtual Desktop
Citrix	Citrix Virtual Apps and Desktops
VMware	VMware Horizon

In the preceding environments, Microsoft Teams supports chat, collaboration, calling, and meetings.

It is possible to configure virtualized environments for multiple configuration modes, which include the following:

- Dedicated
- Shared
- Persistent (users' changes are saved when the user logs off)
- Non-persistent (users' changes are not saved when the user logs off)

It should be noted that some advanced features of Microsoft Teams may not work in VDI environments.

Microsoft Teams used in VDI environments will require the following components:

- A virtualization broker (such as Azure)
- A virtual desktop machine
- A thin client endpoint
- The Microsoft Teams desktop app

Microsoft recommends the following as the minimum configuration:

Specification	Workstation OS	Server OS
vCPU	2 cores	4, 6, or 8
RAM	4 GB	512 to 1,024 MB per user
Storage	8 GB	40 to 60 GB

To deploy the Microsoft Teams application to a VM, you must download the MSI package and install it on the VM by running one of the following commands:

- For a per-user installation, run the following command to install the Microsoft Teams app to the users, `AppData` folder. Note that a per-user installation will not work on a non-persistent setup:

```
msiexec /i <MSI path> /l*v <logfilename> ALLUSERS=1
```

- For a per-machine installation, run the following command to install the Microsoft Teams app to the `Program Files (x86)` folder. However, it should be noted that client updates will not occur using this method. In this instance, the client must be uninstalled and reinstalled with the newer version:

```
msiexec /i <MSI path> /l*v <logfilename> ALLUSER=1
ALLUSERS=1
```

Next, we will look at macOS.

macOS

Microsoft Teams for macOS is installed by using a PKG installation file, which can be downloaded from Microsoft. Administrative access will be required to complete the installation, which will be placed in the `/Applications` folder.

The installation of Microsoft Teams to macOS devices is machine-wide as opposed to user-wide.

The application can be installed on a per-machine basis, or by a broader deployment approach such as **Jamf Pro**.

Now, let's look at mobile devices.

Mobile devices

The Microsoft Teams app may be downloaded from the Apple iOS and Google Play for Android app stores and installed on devices by users.

The currently supported platforms are as follows:

- iOS – Limited to the two most recent versions of the iOS app
- Android – Limited to the last four major versions of the Android app

> **Important note**
> The mobile client for Microsoft Teams may also be deployed using Intune app protection policies. Further reading on this option may be found at the end of the chapter.

In this section, we have explained how the Microsoft Teams app can be downloaded and installed or deployed to devices and platforms in your organization such as Windows, VDI, macOS, and mobile devices.

Next, we will show you how to manage your device settings from the Microsoft Teams admin center.

Managing device settings

Any devices that are used with Microsoft Teams may be managed from the Microsoft Teams admin center. It is possible to carry out device-related tasks such as updating, restarting, and monitoring devices.

To carry out these tasks, you must be either a **Global Administrator**, a **Teams Service Administrator**, or a **Teams Device Administrator**.

When assigned one of these roles, you may manage the following devices:

- **IP phones** – Including desk phones and conference phones.

- **Teams Rooms** – Including consoles, microphones, and cameras.

- **Collaboration bars** – These are Android base units with the Microsoft Teams app, which can be connected to TVs and screens.

- **Teams displays** – All-in-one business communication devices designed for Microsoft Teams.

To manage devices in the **Microsoft Teams admin center**, we need to complete the following steps:

1. Log in to the **Microsoft Teams admin center** at `https://admin.teams.microsoft.com` and navigate to **Devices** on the left hand-side menu as shown in *Figure 6.3*:

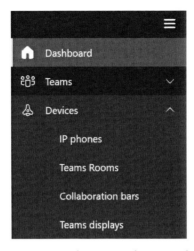

Figure 6.3 – Devices in the Microsoft Teams admin center

2. When selecting **IP phones**, you can filter phones by their categories, which include individual **User phones**, **Common area phones**, and **Conference phones**. You may edit the device settings, assign configuration, manage device tags, and add or edit **Configuration profiles** as shown in *Figure 6.4*:

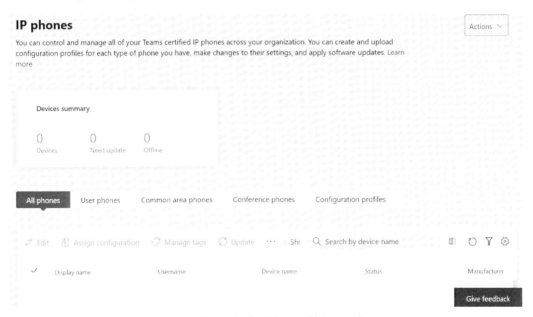

Figure 6.4 – IP phones in the Microsoft Teams admin center

3.   Similarly, the **Teams Rooms** section will show you any Rooms devices:

Figure 6.5 – Teams Rooms in the Microsoft Teams admin center

4.   Next, we can see the **Collaboration bars** section, with similar configuration options:

Figure 6.6 – Collaboration bars in the Microsoft Teams admin center

5. And finally, we can view the **Teams displays** section:

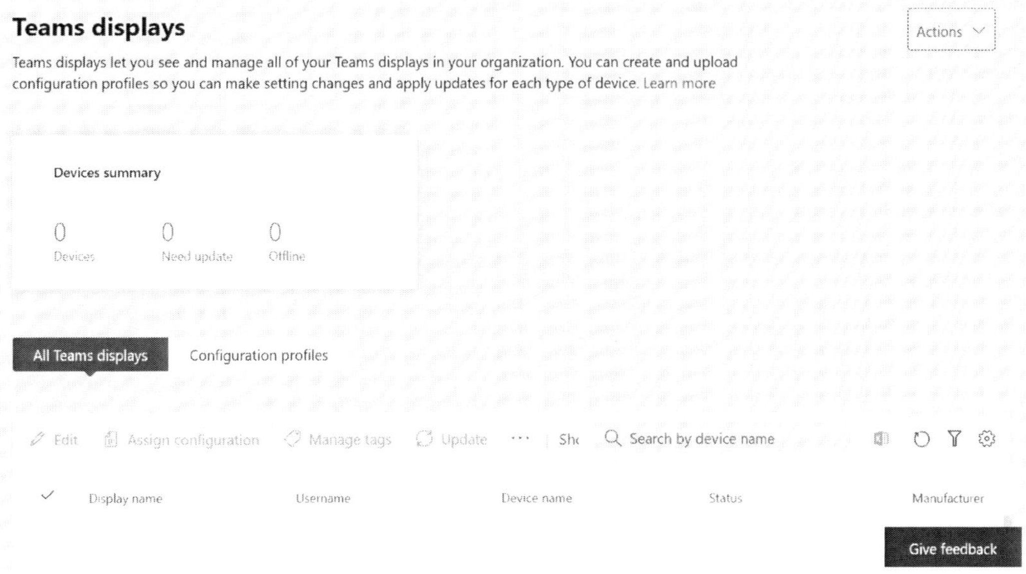

Figure 6.7 – Teams displays in the Microsoft Teams admin center

Let's take a closer look at the functions you may carry out in relation to these devices, starting with Teams Rooms devices.

Managing Teams Rooms devices

The following table lists the functions that are available to administrators in the Microsoft Teams admin center in relation to Teams Room devices:

Task	Process
Modify settings on devices	Choose the device(s), go to Edit Settings.
Restart devices	Choose the device(s), go to Restart, and you will see the option to restart immediately or to schedule a restart.
View meeting activity	Choose the device to view its details and select Activity, to see all of the meetings hosted by the device. You will be able to view the start time, the number of participants, and the meeting duration and call quality.
View meeting details	Choose the device to view its details and select Activity, then choose a meeting's details to view all participants of the meeting, how long each participant was in the call, call quality, and session types.

Next, let's examine more closely the settings available for managing phones, collaboration bars, and Teams displays.

Managing Teams phones, collaboration bars, and Teams displays

The following table lists the functions that are available to administrators in the Microsoft Teams admin center in relation to Teams phones, collaboration bars, and Teams displays:

Task	Process
Modify device information	Choose the device, go to **Edit** to modify entries such as the device name, tag, and notes.
Manage software updates	Choose the device, go to **update**, and you will see a list of software and firmware available for the device.
Upgrade a Teams phone to a Teams display	Choose the device to view its details and select Activity to see all of the meetings hosted by the device. You will be able to view the start time, the number of participants, and the meeting duration and call quality.
View meeting details	From IP phones, select a Teams phone and choose the Upgrade option.
Modify the configuration policy	Choose a device(s) and select Assign Configuration.
Modify device tags	Choose a device(s) and select Manage tags.
Restart a device	Choose a device(s) and select Restart.
Filter with device tags	Choose the Filter option and filter results by device name, manufacturer, model, display name, status, and tag.
View device history	Choose the device, select History.
View diagnostics	Choose the device, select Diagnostics.

In this section, we have shown you how you can manage Teams devices from the Microsoft Teams admin center, including IP phones, Teams Rooms, Collaboration Bars, and Teams displays.

Next, we will show you how to manage configuration profiles.

Managing configuration profiles

Configuration profiles are used to manage settings for Teams phones, collaboration bars, and Teams displays. These profiles may be configured to include settings you wish to add or remove from a device or several devices.

To create a configuration profile, we need to complete the following steps:

1. Log in to the *Microsoft Teams admin center* at `https://admin.teams.microsoft.com` and navigate to **Devices** on the left-hand-side menu as shown in *Figure 6.8*:

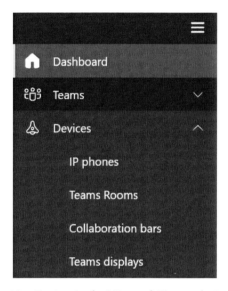

Figure 6.8 – Devices in the Microsoft Teams admin center

2. Choose either **IP phones**, **Collaboration bars**, or **Teams displays** (configuration profiles may not be applied to **Teams Rooms**). In this example, we will choose **IP phones** and select the **Configuration profiles** tab as shown in *Figure 6.9*:

Figure 6.9 – Configuration profiles tab in the IP phones section of the Microsoft Teams admin center

3.   Click **+ Add**, and then enter a name and description for your configuration profile, as shown in *Figure 6.10*:

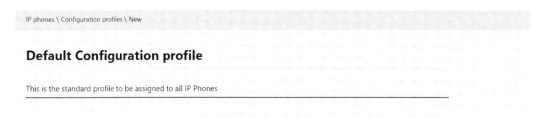

Figure 6.10 – Set the name and description for the configuration profile

4.   Scroll down to the **General** section of the new configuration profile settings and complete the required settings shown in *Figure 6.11*:

Figure 6.11 – Complete the general settings for the new configuration profile

5. Scroll to the **Device settings** section and complete the settings as required, as shown in *Figure 6.12*:

Figure 6.12 – Complete the device settings for the new configuration profile

6. Scroll down to the **Network settings** section and complete the required settings as shown in *Figure 6.13*:

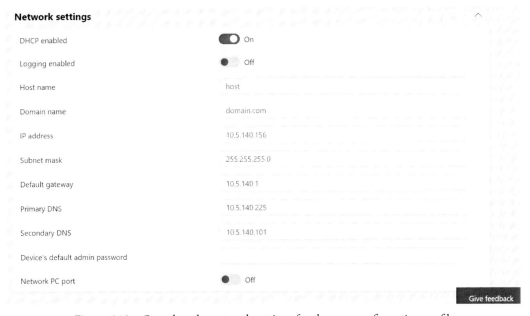

Figure 6.13 – Complete the network settings for the new configuration profile

7. When you have completed all the required settings, click on **Save**:

Figure 6.14 – Save the new configuration profile

8. The new configuration profile is now visible. Click to select the profile and choose **Assign to device** as shown in *Figure 6.15*:

Figure 6.15 – Assign the new configuration profile to a device

9. Search for the devices that you wish to apply the new configuration profile to, and then click **Apply** as shown in *Figure 6.16*:

Figure 6.16 – Apply the new configuration profile to your chosen devices

In this section, we explained how configuration profiles are groups of device settings that may be quickly and easily applied to your Teams devices from the Microsoft Teams admin center.

In the final section of this chapter, we will show you how to set up Microsoft Teams Rooms.

Setting up Microsoft Teams Rooms

With Microsoft Teams Rooms, you can use HD video and audio, and share content in meetings on supported devices in your organization's meeting and conference rooms. The **Microsoft Teams Rooms** software is run on device hardware that can be provided by a number of different vendors and that runs Windows. It is also possible to mix devices for separate functions, such as one device for the camera and another for Microsoft Teams Rooms itself.

There are many Microsoft Teams Rooms devices available for purchase, but before we talk about these devices, we need to configure accounts for Microsoft Teams Rooms to use.

The accounts that you create for Microsoft Teams Rooms will need to be set up in line with the following available deployment options:

- **Online deployment**: Where your organization is entirely based in Microsoft 365

- **On-premises deployment**: Where you have on-premises Active Directory, Exchange servers, and Skype for Business servers

- **Hybrid deployment**: Where you have a mixture of on-premises and cloud services

A device account must be set up for every Microsoft Teams Rooms device that you configure. This account is used to host the calendar for the device and to manage connectivity. The result of this is that your users can schedule a meeting on the device.

> **Important note**
>
> It is Microsoft's recommendation to create device accounts for your Microsoft Teams Rooms at least 2 to 3 weeks before you plan to install the actual device.
>
> You should also be aware of the license requirements for using Microsoft Teams Rooms and common area phones. Further reading is included at the end of the chapter.

The following table shows the minimum requirements for the configuration of a device account:

Requirement	Reason
Exchange 2013 SP1 or later mailbox or an Exchange Online mailbox	To provide the ability to send and receive meeting requests and to enable the device to display meeting information
Skype for Business enabled	To provide conference features such as video calling, screen sharing, and instant messaging.
Password enabled	The device account must be able to authenticate with Exchange or Skype for Business

The simplest method to create these accounts is by using Windows PowerShell, and Microsoft provides a script for this.

In the example that follows, we will explain the process of deploying a Microsoft Teams room with Microsoft 365. To do this, you will need to be aware of the following requirements:

- Skype for Business Online (Plan 2) or a higher plan that allows dial-in conferencing.

- An audio conferencing and phone system license if dial-in features are required.

- An audio conferencing license if dial-out features are required.

- Tenant users will require Exchange mailboxes.

To add a device account, we need to complete the following steps:

1. Connect to Exchange Online PowerShell as an administrator by completing the following commands:

   ```
   $Cred=GET-CREDENTIAL
   $s = NEW-PSSESSION -ConfigurationName Microsoft.
   Exchange -ConnectionUri https://ps.outlook.com/
   powershell -Credential $Cred -Authentication Basic
   -AllowRedirection
   $importresults=import-pssession $s
   ```

2. Now we need to create a new room mailbox and add an account to it, which will allow it to authenticate. To create a room mailbox, we need to run the following command, which will set up a new room mailbox called Conference-01:

   ```
   New-Mailbox -Name "Conference-01" -Alias
   Conference1 -Room -EnableRoomMailboxAccount $true
   ```

```
-MicrosoftOnlineServicesID conference01@domainname.com
-RoomMailboxPassword (ConvertTo-SecureString -String
'Password' -AsPlainText -Force)
```

The mailbox account is now created. Next, we will show how you can configure your Microsoft Teams Rooms console device.

Configuring a Microsoft Teams Rooms console device

Now that we have a device account ready, we can configure a **Microsoft Teams Rooms** console device. You will need to meet the hardware and software requirements that are laid out in this Microsoft guidance: `https://docs.microsoft.com/en-us/ MicrosoftTeams/rooms/requirements`.

Once you have fulfilled these requirements, you can start to configure your Microsoft Teams Rooms device by completing the following steps, which include the optional step to create USB media. Most Microsoft Teams Rooms devices now come pre-deployed with the required software:

1. Prepare the installation media. You will need to use a USB storage device with nothing else on it and with a minimum of 32 GB capacity.

2. Download the media script from `https://go.microsoft.com/ fwlink/?linkid=867842`.

3. The script is named `CreateSrsMedia.ps1` and must be run from Windows PowerShell as an administrator.

4. Running the script will download an MSI installer package for Microsoft Teams Rooms.

5. Next, you need to establish the build of Windows that will be required, download it and any required supporting elements, and place these on the installation media.

6. Plug the USB media into the Microsoft Teams Rooms device. Boot to the setup and follow the manufacturer's instructions.

7. Select and apply your desired language.

8. Windows will now install and the console will trigger its native setup upon restart.

Once you have the preceding steps completed, you can complete further steps to complete the setup of the device depending on the type of device and your environment. For example, you may need to use the **Configure Domain** option to set the settings to connect to your Skype for Business Server if applicable. You may also configure microphone and speaker settings at this point.

In this section, we have explained the principles of **Microsoft Teams Room** devices. These are certified devices that can be used to book meeting and conference rooms when an appropriate device account is set up and associated with a compatible device.

Summary

In this chapter, we explained how to install or deploy **Microsoft Teams** client apps to your devices, including **Windows**, **VDI**, **macOS**, and mobile devices. We also showed you how to configure settings for Teams devices such as **IP phones, Teams Rooms, collaboration bars**, and **Teams displays** from the **Microsoft Teams admin center**. You also learned how **configuration profiles** may be used to apply a collection of settings to the devices listed in the **Microsoft Teams admin center**. Finally, we introduced you to **Microsoft Teams Rooms** devices and explained the prerequisites and steps to configure them within your environment.

In the next chapter, we will introduce you to the principles of monitoring **Microsoft Teams**. We will show you how to view and interpret Teams-related usage reports in both the **Microsoft Teams admin center** and the **Microsoft 365 admin center**, and set up per-user call quality optimization with the call analytics feature. In addition, we will demonstrate how to access and understand the **Call Quality Dashboard**, and finally, how to use **Power BI** to detect call quality issues.

Practice questions

1. Which of the following devices may not be used with configuration profiles?

    a. Teams displays

    b. Teams Rooms

    c. Collaboration bars

    d. IP phones

2. How many recent versions of the iOS Teams app are supported?

    a. 5

    b. 6

    c. 4

    d. 2

3. True or false: It is possible to deploy the Microsoft Teams app to mobile devices via the use of Intune app protection policies?

   a. True

   b. False

4. Which of the following is not one of the minimum requirements for installing the Microsoft Teams app on Windows devices?

   a. NET Framework 4.5 or above

   b. Windows 8.1 or above

   c. Windows Server 2012 R2 or above

   d. Recommended minimum of 2 GB of disk space available for each user profile

5. How many recent versions of the Android Teams app are supported?

   a. 2

   c. 4

   d. 5

   e. 6

6. Which of the following is not one of the available setting headings for configuration profiles for an IP phone in the Microsoft Teams admin center?

   a. General

   b. Device settings

   c. More settings

   d. Network settings

7. True or false: Microsoft Teams can be deployed to VDI environments?

   a. True

   b. False

8. Which of the following is not a description in the Microsoft Teams admin center for the types of available IP phones?

   a. User phones

   b. Common area phones

   c. Shared phones

   d. Conference phones

9. True or false: Teams Rooms devices may be configured within hybrid environments?

    a. True

    b. False

10. In a VDI environment, the Teams app should be deployed in which mode?

    a. Machine

    b. User

Further reading

- Deploy Microsoft Teams with Microsoft 365 Apps: `https://docs.microsoft.com/en-us/deployoffice/teams-install`

- Microsoft Teams operations guide: `https://docs.microsoft.com/en-us/microsoftteams/upgrade-operate-my-service`

- Microsoft Teams for Virtualized Desktop Infrastructure: `https://docs.microsoft.com/en-us/microsoftteams/teams-for-vdi`

- Install Microsoft Teams using Microsoft Endpoint Configuration Manager: `https://docs.microsoft.com/en-us/microsoftteams/msi-deployment`

- Manage your devices in Microsoft Teams: `https://docs.microsoft.com/en-us/microsoftteams/devices/device-management`

- Microsoft Teams Rooms deployment overview: `https://docs.microsoft.com/en-us/MicrosoftTeams/rooms/rooms-deploy`

- Configure a Microsoft Teams Rooms console: `https://docs.microsoft.com/en-us/MicrosoftTeams/rooms/console`

- Microsoft Teams Rooms requirements: `https://docs.microsoft.com/en-us/MicrosoftTeams/rooms/requirements`

- Get clients for Microsoft Teams: `https://docs.microsoft.com/en-us/microsoftteams/get-clients`

- Configure accounts for Microsoft Teams Rooms: `https://docs.microsoft.com/en-us/MicrosoftTeams/rooms/rooms-configure-accounts`

- Configure a Microsoft Teams Rooms console: `https://docs.microsoft.com/en-us/MicrosoftTeams/rooms/console`

- Configure Microsoft Teams Rooms for Microsoft 365: `https://docs.microsoft.com/en-us/microsoftteams/rooms/with-office-365`

- Microsoft Endpoint Configuration Manager: `https://docs.microsoft.com/en-us/mem/configmgr/`

- Windows Virtual Desktop: `https://azure.microsoft.com/en-gb/services/virtual-desktop/`

- Group Policy: `https://docs.microsoft.com/en-us/troubleshoot/windows-server/group-policy/use-group-policy-to-install-software`

- Microsoft Office Deployment tool: `https://docs.microsoft.com/en-us/deployoffice/overview-office-deployment-tool`

- Deploy Teams to mobile devices using Intune app protection policies: `https://docs.microsoft.com/en-us/mem/intune/apps/manage-microsoft-teams`

- Licensing for Microsoft Teams Rooms: `https://docs.microsoft.com/en-us/microsoftteams/rooms/rooms-licensing`

- Licensing for common area phones: `https://docs.microsoft.com/en-us/microsoftteams/set-up-common-area-phones`

7
Monitoring Usage within Microsoft Teams

In this chapter, we will introduce you to the principles of monitoring **Microsoft Teams**. We will show you how to view and interpret Teams-related usage reports in both the **Microsoft Teams admin center** and the **Microsoft 365 admin center**, and set up per-user call quality optimization with the call analytics feature. In addition, we will demonstrate how to access and understand the Call Quality Dashboard, and finally, how to use Power BI to detect call quality issues.

In this chapter, we're going to cover the following main topics:

- Viewing and understanding Teams usage reports
- Viewing and understanding Microsoft 365 usage reports
- Optimizing call quality per user with call analytics
- Using the Call Quality Dashboard
- Detecting call quality issues with Power BI

Technical requirements

In this chapter, you will need to have access to the **Microsoft Teams admin center**, which you can reach at `https://admin.teams.microsoft.com`. You will need to be a *Global Administrator* or a *Teams Service Administrator* in order to carry out the steps covered in this chapter unless otherwise specified. You will also need to have access to **Power BI Desktop**.

Viewing and understanding Teams usage reports

The **Microsoft Teams admin center** provides a number of useful reports that administrators can use to gain insight into usage and activity within **Microsoft Teams**. In *Chapter 5, Managing the Security and Compliance Settings for Microsoft Teams*, we introduced you to the available reports and showed you how to access them from the **Teams admin center** by navigating to **Analytics & reports**.

In this section, we will examine these reports in a bit more detail. Firstly, as a reminder, the available reports are shown in the following table:

Report	Report output
Apps usage	App name
	Active users
	App type
	Active teams
	Publisher
	Version

Report	Report output
PSTN blocked users	Display name
	Phone
	Blocked reason
	Blocked action
	Blocked time
PSTN minute and SMS pools	Country or region
	Capability description
	Total minutes or SMS units
	Minutes or SMS units used
	Minutes or SMS units available
	Capability
PSTN and SMS usage	Start time
	Display name
	Username
	Phone number
	Caller ID
	Call / SMS type
Teams device usage	Reports on usage of users who use:
	Windows devices
	Apple macOS devices
	Apple iOS devices
	Android phones
Teams live event usage	Number of views of the live event
	Start time
	Event status
	Organizer
	Presenters
	Producers
	Recording setting
	Production type
Teams usage	Active users
	Active channels
	Active users in teams and channels
	Messages
	Teams privacy settings
	Guests in a team
Teams user activity	1:1 calls that a user joined
	Team chat messages posted by user
	Private chat messages posted by user
	User's last activity date

As there are eight available reports, we will examine two of these in detail to give you an idea of the experience. The reports we will focus on are the first two reports in the drop-down list and are the **Apps usage report** and the **PSTN blocked users report**.

Apps usage report

The **Apps usage report** shows you how the apps that you have made available to your users in **Microsoft Teams** are being used within your organization. To run the report, we need to take the following steps:

1. Log in to the **Teams admin center** and navigate to **Analytics & reports | Usage** and under the **Report** dropdown, choose **Apps usage** as shown in *Figure 7.1*:

Figure 7.1 – Apps usage report shown in the Microsoft Teams admin center

2. Choose your preferred date range for the report and click **Run report** as shown in *Figure 7.2*:

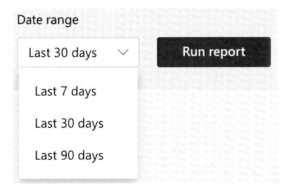

Figure 7.2 – Date range options

3. The results are displayed in the form of a graph. Hovering over a dot related to one of the dates on the graph will show you the number of active users in apps for that date. This is shown in *Figure 7.3*:

Apps usage report

Dec 13, 2020 8:32:07 AM UTC   Date range: **Nov 12, 2020** - **Dec 11, 2020**

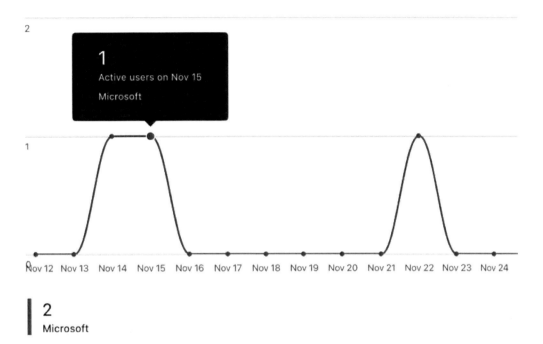

Figure 7.3 – Active users in Teams apps for a specific date

4. Scroll further down to see a searchable list of app names, as shown in *Figure 7.4*.
    Here, you can see the app name, the number of users who opened the app for the
    time period selected, the app type, the number of teams the app was used by, the
    app publisher details, and the version of the app:

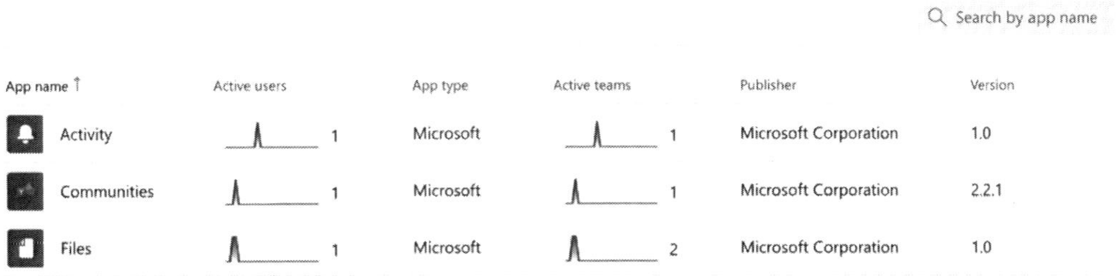

App name ↑	Active users	App type	Active teams	Publisher	Version
Activity	1	Microsoft	1	Microsoft Corporation	1.0
Communities	1	Microsoft	1	Microsoft Corporation	2.2.1
Files	1	Microsoft	2	Microsoft Corporation	1.0

Figure 7.4 – App activity in list form

5. At the top-right corner of the report results, you will see the options shown in *Figure 7.5*. These are **Export to Excel**, **Filter**, **Full screen**, and **Edit columns**:

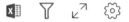

Figure 7.5 – Report options

6. **Export to Excel** will produce a downloadable report, which you can see in the **Downloads** tab. This is shown in *Figure 7.6*:

Figure 7.6 – Export to Excel

7. **Filter** allows you to sort your report results by **App name** or **App type**, and combine filters using the **+Add more** option as shown in *Figure 7.7*:

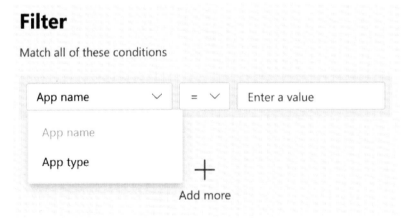

Figure 7.7 – Filter options

8. In *Step 5*, we also showed the **Full screen** and **Edit columns** icons. Using **Full Screen** will make the report easier to read in the current view and using **Edit columns** will allow you to choose the column headers that you wish to include or exclude from your report as shown in *Figure 7.8*:

Figure 7.8 – Edit the columns for your report

Next, let's take a look at the PSTN blocked users report.

PSTN blocked users

This report shows any users who are blocked from making PSTN calls in Microsoft Teams. You may view information such as the reason for the block and the assigned phone number. The report may be run as shown in the following steps:

1. Select the **PSTN blocked users** report and click **Run report**:

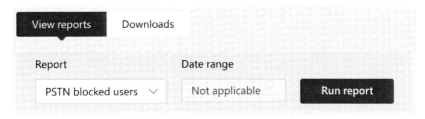

Figure 7.9 – Run the PSTN blocked users report

2. The results will be shown in the format shown in *Figure 7.10*:

PSTN blocked users

Dec 13, 2020 9:25:10 AM UTC

Display name	Phone	Blocked reason	Blocked action	Blocked time (UTC) ↓

Figure 7.10 – PSTN blocked users report results

3. This report has two options, which are **Full screen** and **Edit columns**:

Figure 7.11 – Report options

4. The **Edit columns** options for the **PSTN blocked users** report are shown in *Figure 7.12*:

Figure 7.12 – Edit the columns for the report

The remaining reports that are available in the Microsoft Teams admin center all have similar options to those shown in the two preceding examples. Date range options will sometimes vary or not be applicable.

Important note

Please take the time to familiarize yourself with all of the available reports in the Microsoft Teams admin center. Links to further reading on each report can be found at the end of this chapter.

Now that you have an understanding of the reports available from the Microsoft Teams admin center, let's look at some of the reporting options in the Microsoft 365 admin center.

Viewing and understanding Microsoft 365 usage reports

In addition to the reports that are available within the **Microsoft Teams admin center**, there are some reporting options that relate to **Microsoft Teams** that you can view in the **Microsoft 365 admin center**. To view and access these reports, you will need to be a *Global Administrator*, a *Teams Service Administrator*, or a *Teams Communications Administrator*. Additionally, the following roles also have access to these reports but are less relevant in the context of Microsoft Teams:

- Exchange Administrator
- SharePoint Administrator
- Skype for Business Administrator
- Global Reader
- Reports Reader

To access these reports, we must complete the following steps:

1. Log in to the **Microsoft 365 admin center** at `https://admin.microsoft.com` and navigate to **Reports | Usage** as shown in *Figure 7.13*:

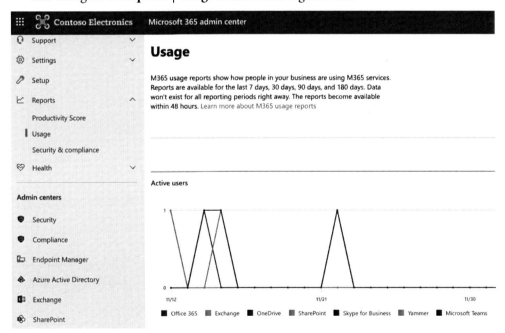

Figure 7.13 – Usage reports in the Microsoft 365 admin center

2. Scroll down to the **Microsoft Teams activity** section and click on **View more** as shown in *Figure 7.14*:

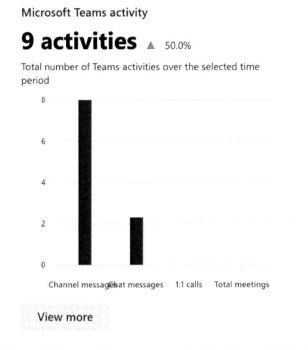

Figure 7.14 – Microsoft Teams activity usage reports in the Microsoft 365 admin center

3. This shows you the view in *Figure 7.15* where you may view **User activity** based on licensing:

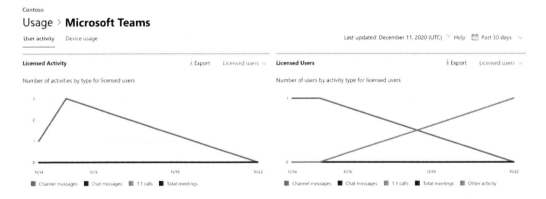

Figure 7.15 – Microsoft Teams user activity

4. You may filter the results by the date ranges shown in *Figure 7.16*:

Figure 7.16 – Filter results by date

5. Scroll down to see a list of users in the report, which may be exported to **Microsoft Excel**. You can also modify the column settings of this list by clicking on **Choose columns**:

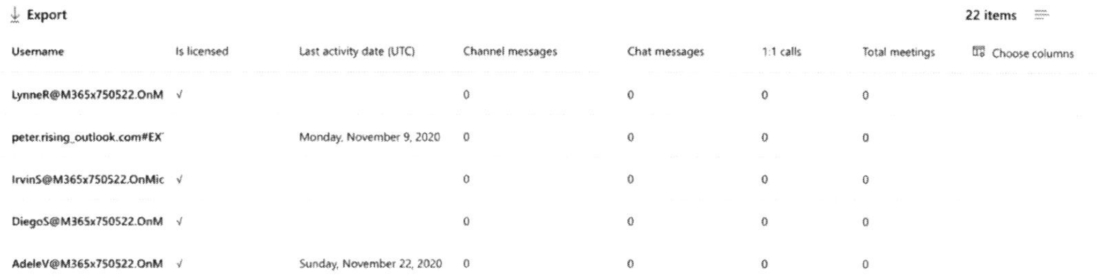

↓ Export						22 items ≡
Username	Is licensed	Last activity date (UTC)	Channel messages	Chat messages	1:1 calls	Total meetings ⊞ Choose columns
LynneR@M365x750522.OnM	√		0	0	0	0
peter.rising_outlook.com#EX		Monday, November 9, 2020	0	0	0	0
IrvinS@M365x750522.OnMic	√		0	0	0	0
DiegoS@M365x750522.OnM	√		0	0	0	0
AdeleV@M365x750522.OnM	√	Sunday, November 22, 2020	0	0	0	0

Figure 7.17 – Report results by user

6. Additionally, switch to the **Device usage** tab within the report to see statistics on licensed users by device type. This report may also be filtered by **Date range** and viewed by **Licensed users** or **All users**:

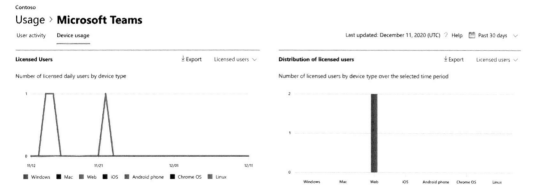

Figure 7.18 – Report results for device usage

7. Scroll down to see device-based information by username, which may also be exported to **Microsoft Excel**, and you may also choose which columns you wish to include:

Figure 7.19 – Report results by user

These reports are a useful option for **Microsoft 365** administrators who regularly examine the usage and activity within their organization for not just **Microsoft Teams** but other **Microsoft 365** workloads as well.

Next, we will look at optimizing call quality with per-user call analytics.

Optimizing call quality per user with call analytics

Call analytics allows you to view information about calls and meetings for individual users in your **Microsoft 365** environment. You can view information relating to devices, network connectivity, and call quality.

With **Call analytics**, you may view each step of a call or a meeting and use this information to troubleshoot quality issues.

To use per-user **Call analytics**, we need to complete the following steps:

1. Open the **Teams admin center** from `https://admin.teams.microsoft.com` and navigate to **Users**:

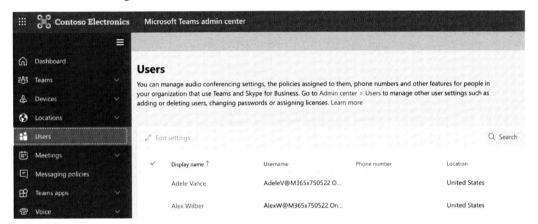

Figure 7.20 – Users in the Microsoft Teams admin center

2. Select a user from the list and click on it. Then scroll down and select **Call history** as shown in *Figure 7.21*. Here, you will see a list of calls for the user you have chosen. Click on one of the call entries in this list to view further information:

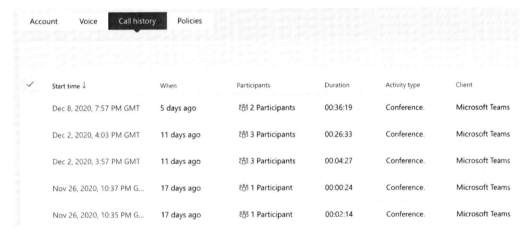

Figure 7.21 – Selecting a user

3. *Figure 7.22* shows statistics for this call. You can see the status and type of this meeting and view the participants:

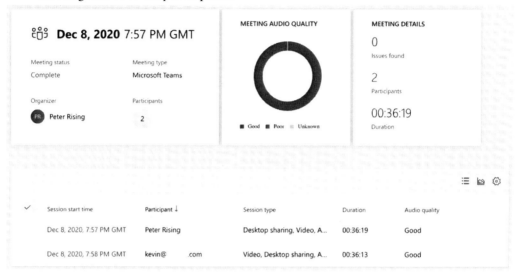

Figure 7.22 – Call details showing participants

4. Clicking on an individual participant from the call will show you an overview of that user's session with device, system, connectivity, and network statistics as shown in *Figure 7.23*:

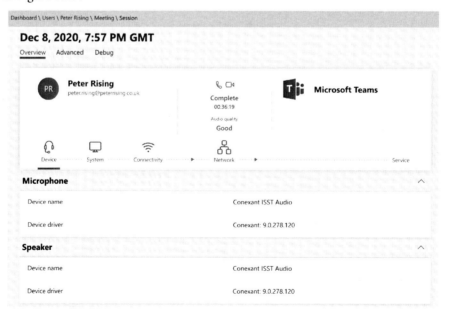

Figure 7.23 – Individual call participant statistics

5. The **Advanced** tab will show you much more detailed information and you can look for items in yellow or red, which will indicate abnormal performance or significant issues respectively. You can use this information to help you to take any required corrective measures to improve your users' experience while on calls or meetings within **Microsoft Teams**:

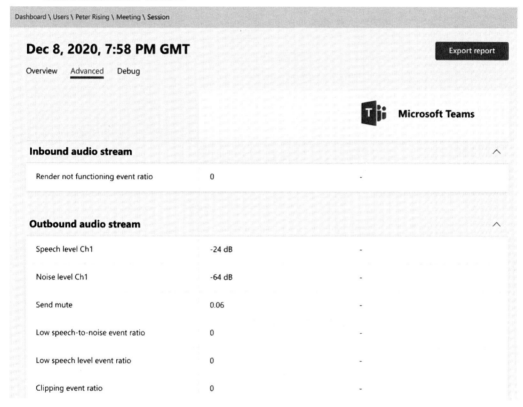

Figure 7.24 – Advanced statistics

The per-user **Call analytics** capabilities provide useful information to Microsoft Teams administrators when they are required to respond to call quality issues reported by users.

Next, we will show you how to access and use the Call Quality Dashboard.

Using the Call Quality Dashboard

The **Microsoft Teams Call Quality Dashboard** allows administrators to assess and interpret the quality of calls in **Microsoft Teams**.

To access the Call Quality Dashboard, we need to take the following steps:

1. Go to `https://cqd.teams.microsoft.com` or log in to the **Microsoft Teams admin center** and navigate to **Call Quality Dashboard** as shown in *Figure 7.25*. If this is your first time signing in to the **Call Quality Dashboard**, it will begin collecting data at this point and may take 1 or 2 hours to provide useful information in reports. The dashboard shows you graphical statistics broken down into monthly and daily trends:

Figure 7.25 – The Call Quality Dashboard

2. At the top of the **Call Quality Dashboard**, under **Summary Reports**, you may view several built-in reports, which are shown in *Figure 7.26*:

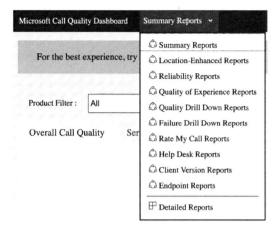

Figure 7.26 – Available summary reports

3. An example of one of the **Summary Reports** is the **Client Version Reports**, which, when accessed, will show you a **Client Version Summary** or a **Client Version by User** report as shown in *Figure 7.27*:

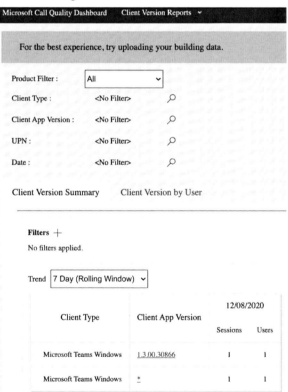

Figure 7.27 – Client Version Reports in the Call Quality Dashboard

4. Should the built-in reports not be sufficient for your needs, you can use the **Detailed Reports** option from the **Summary Reports** dropdown to create your own reports. This option is shown in *Figure 7.28*. Click **New**:

Figure 7.28 – Detailed Reports options in the Call Quality Dashboard

5. Once you have clicked **New**, the **QUERY EDITOR** will open, and you will see the options shown in *Figure 7.29*:

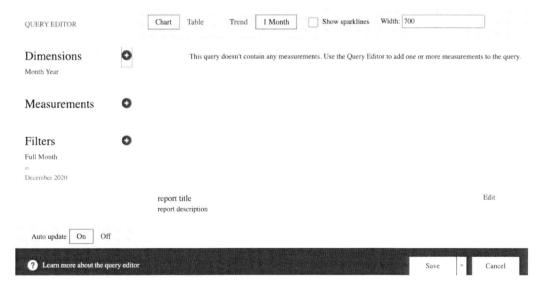

Figure 7.29 – QUERY EDITOR on the Call Quality Dashboard

6. In addition to adding your own dimensions and measurements to a new query, it is also possible to import reports into the **QUERY EDITOR** (by clicking on the **Import** option shown in *Figure 7.28*), such as the two curated Call Quality Dashboard report templates, which may be downloaded from Microsoft at `https://aka.ms/qertemplates` as a ZIP file. Once extracted, the two files may be imported. One of these templates is the **Quality of Experience Review**, which is shown after import in *Figure 7.30*:

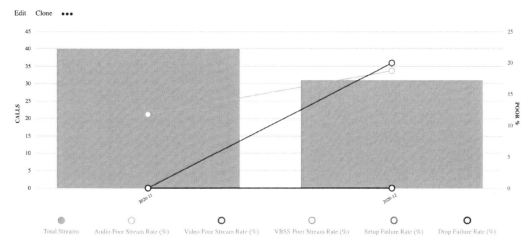

Figure 7.30 – Report template imported into the Call Quality Dashboard

Now that you know how to access the Call Quality Dashboard for Microsoft Teams, you can use it with the built-in templates, create your own, or import available templates from Microsoft.

Another way to view call quality statistics, however, is by using **Microsoft Power BI**, and we will look at this in the final section of this chapter.

Detecting call quality issues with Power BI

In Microsoft's own words, *"Power BI is a collection of software services, apps, and connectors that work together to turn your unrelated sources of data into coherent, visually immersive, and interactive insights. Your data may be an Excel spreadsheet, or a collection of cloud-based and on-premises hybrid data warehouses."*

In addition to using the Call Quality Dashboard, it is also possible to analyze call quality data using some customizable templates with **Microsoft Power BI**.

To do this, we will need to complete the following steps:

1. Download the Call Quality Dashboard Power BI query templates from Microsoft at `https://www.microsoft.com/en-us/download/details.aspx?id=102291` and unzip the files. If you already have Power BI Desktop installed, save the files to the folder called `[Documents]\Power BI Desktop\Custom Connectors`. If you do not yet have Power BI Desktop installed, it is recommended to install it at this point. The files included in the ZIP file are shown in *Figure 7.31*:

Name	Date modified	Type
CQ and AA combined Analytics 20201105.pbit	13/12/2020 15:01	Microsoft Power BI D...
CQD Helpdesk Report.pbit	13/12/2020 15:01	Microsoft Power BI D...
CQD Location Enhanced Report.pbit	13/12/2020 15:01	Microsoft Power BI D...
CQD Mobile Device Report.pbit	13/12/2020 15:01	Microsoft Power BI D...
CQD PSTN Report.pbit	13/12/2020 15:01	Microsoft Power BI D...
CQD Summary Report.pbit	13/12/2020 15:01	Microsoft Power BI D...
CQD Teams Usage Report.pbit	13/12/2020 15:01	Microsoft Power BI D...
CQD User Feedback Report (Rate My Call).pbit	13/12/2020 15:01	Microsoft Power BI D...
MicrosoftCallQuality.pqx	13/12/2020 15:01	PQX File
Power BI Connector for Microsoft Advanced CQ...	13/12/2020 15:01	Microsoft Word Doc...
Readme - Power BI query templates for Micros...	13/12/2020 15:01	Microsoft Word Doc...

Figure 7.31 – Files included in the Power BI query templates

2. If you do not already have Power BI Desktop installed on your computer, you will need to download and install it from `https://www.microsoft.com/en-in/download/details.aspx?id=58494`. Once you have completed the simple installation onto your device, open Power BI Desktop and click on **File**, select **Options and settings**, then choose **Options** as shown in *Figure 7.32*:

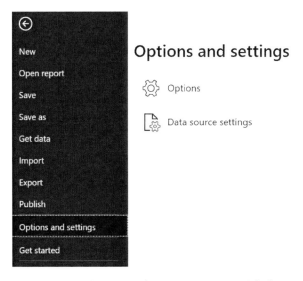

Figure 7.32 – Options and settings in Power BI desktop

3. Next, click on **Security**, and under **Data Extensions**, select the option of **(Not Recommended) Allow any extension to load without validation or warning**. This is shown in *Figure 7.33*. Click **OK**:

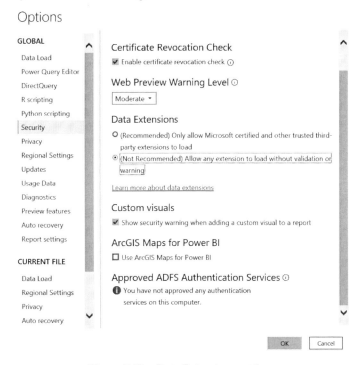

Figure 7.33 – Data Extensions settings

4. Click **OK** when you see the notification in *Figure 7.34* and then restart Power BI Desktop:

Change Requires Restart

Changes to which data extensions are loaded will take effect once
Microsoft Power BI Desktop is restarted.

OK

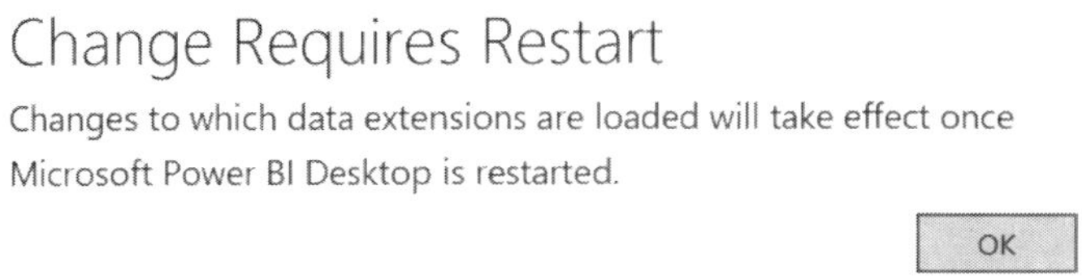

Figure 7.34 – Restart Power BI Desktop

5. Once Power BI Desktop is restarted, choose **Get data**, then click **More...** as shown in *Figure 7.35*:

Figure 7.35 – Connect to a data source

6. Select **Online Services**, then choose **Microsoft Call Quality (Beta)** as shown in *Figure 7.36*. Click **Connect**:

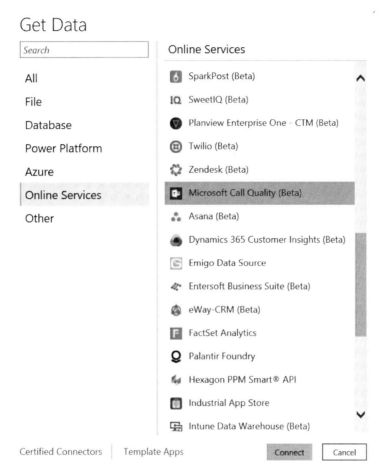

Figure 7.36 – Microsoft Call Quality (Beta)

7. Under **Connecting to a third-party service**, click **Continue** as shown in
    Figure 7.37:

Connecting to a third-party service

The Microsoft Call Quality connector relies on a third-party service and is still under development. Please try it out and give us feedback. We can't guarantee it will work the same way in the final version. Future changes may cause your queries to be incompatible.

Learn more about the service used for the Microsoft Call Quality connector

Figure 7.37 – Connecting to a third-party service

8.   Next, click on **Connect**:

Figure 7.38 – Connect to the Microsoft Call Quality service

9.   You will now see the screen shown in *Figure 7.39*. Click **Load**:

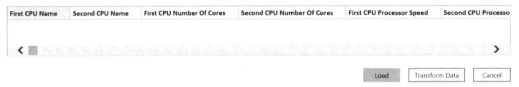

Figure 7.39 – Load the Microsoft Call Quality settings

10. Now select **DirectQuery**, then choose **OK** as shown in *Figure 7.40*:

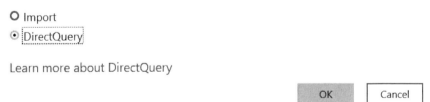

Figure 7.40 – Create the connection

11. The connection will now be created as shown in *Figure 7.41*:

Figure 7.41 – Creating the connection

12. This completes the process of connecting Power BI Desktop to the Call Quality Dashboard. You may now open the templates that you saved in *Step 1* of this process, as shown in *Figure 7.42*, where we have double-clicked to open the CQD Teams Usage Report.pbit file:

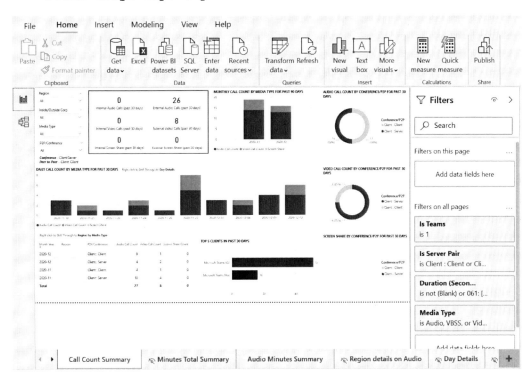

Figure 7.42 – Teams usage report opened in Power BI Desktop

In this section, we showed you how to open up Call Quality Dashboard reports in **Power BI Desktop**. This will be useful to administrators who wish to carry out a more in-depth analysis of data gathered in the Call Quality Dashboard.

Summary

In this chapter, we showed you how the Microsoft Teams admin center contains several usage reports that can help administrators to gain insights into Microsoft Teams usage within their organization and troubleshoot any issues. We also looked at some usage reports for Microsoft Teams that are available in the Microsoft 365 admin center.

In addition, you learned that **Call analytics** within Microsoft Teams can be analyzed on a per-user basis to view and optimize quality for users in calls and meetings and that the **Call Quality Dashboard** provides built-in reports and the ability to create new or imported reports that can be used to monitor and interpret call quality.

Finally, we showed you how Call Quality Dashboard reports can also be viewed and interpreted by using **Power BI Desktop**.

In the next chapter, we will examine the principles of collaboration in Microsoft Teams. We will show you how Teams administrators may control chat features for users in Microsoft Teams by configuring **messaging policies**. We will also examine how you can control external access to your Microsoft Teams environment, and explain how to create channels within Microsoft Teams, which includes private channels. Finally, we will demonstrate how email integration and cloud file storage settings work within Microsoft Teams.

Questions

As we conclude, here is a list of questions for you to test your knowledge regarding this chapter's material. You will find the answers in the *Assessments* section of the *Appendix*:

1. Which of the following is not a report available in the Microsoft Teams admin center?

    a. Teams live event usage

    b. Teams usage

    c. Teams meeting usage

    d. Teams user activity

2. Where in the Microsoft 365 admin center would you go to view the available usage reports?

    a. **Reports | Statistics**

    b. **Reports | Activity**

    c. **Reports | Usage**

    d. **Reports | Overview**

3. True or false – Call Analytics Dashboard activity can also be viewed from within Power BI Desktop.

    a. True

    b. False

4. Which of the following are two possible URLs to reach the Call Analytics Dashboard?

    a. `https://cqd.teams.microsoft.com`

    b. `https://cqd.microsoft.com`

    c. `https://teams.microsoft.com`

    d. `https://admin.teams.microsoft.com`

5. True or false – Teams call and meeting quality can be analyzed on a per-user basis from the Microsoft Teams admin center.

    a. True

    b. False

6. Which of the following is not one of the date range options available for the Teams user activity report in the Microsoft Teams admin center?

    a. 7 days

    c. 30 days

    d. 60 days

    e. 90 days

7. Where in the Microsoft Teams admin center would you go to view per-user call analytics data?

    a. **Users | Username | Call History**

    b. **Users | Username | Account**

    c. **Users | Username | Voice**

    d. **Users | Username | Policies**

8. True or false – Power BI Desktop is not a requirement for using Power BI to analyze Call Quality Dashboard statistics.

    a. True

    b. False

9. Which folder must the Power BI query templates be downloaded to in order for Power BI to be used to view Call Quality Dashboard statistics?

    a. N/A

    b. `[Documents]\Power BI Desktop\Custom Settings`

    c. `[Documents]\Power BI Desktop\Custom Templates`

    d. `[Documents]\Power BI Desktop\Custom Connectors`

10. True or false – Summary reports are an available feature within the Call Quality Dashboard.

    a. True

    b. False

Further reading

Here are links to more information on some of the topics that we have covered in this chapter:

- Monitor usage and feedback in Microsoft Teams: `https://docs.microsoft.com/en-us/microsoftteams/get-started-with-teams-monitor-usage-and-feedback`

- Microsoft Teams Analytics and Reporting: `https://docs.microsoft.com/en-us/microsoftteams/teams-analytics-and-reports/teams-reporting-reference`

- Microsoft Teams usage report: `https://docs.microsoft.com/en-us/microsoftteams/teams-analytics-and-reports/teams-usage-report`

- Microsoft Teams live event usage report: `https://docs.microsoft.com/en-us/microsoftteams/teams-analytics-and-reports/teams-live-event-usage-report`

- Microsoft Teams PSTN usage report: `https://docs.microsoft.com/en-us/microsoftteams/teams-analytics-and-reports/pstn-usage-report`

- Microsoft Teams user activity report: `https://docs.microsoft.com/en-us/microsoftteams/teams-analytics-and-reports/user-activity-report`

- Microsoft Teams device usage report: `https://docs.microsoft.com/en-us/microsoftteams/teams-analytics-and-reports/device-usage-report`

- Microsoft Teams PSTN blocked users report: `https://docs.microsoft.com/en-us/microsoftteams/teams-analytics-and-reports/pstn-blocked-users-report`

- Microsoft Teams PSTN minute pools report: `https://docs.microsoft.com/en-us/microsoftteams/teams-analytics-and-reports/pstn-minute-pools-report`

- Microsoft Teams App usage report: `https://docs.microsoft.com/en-us/microsoftteams/teams-analytics-and-reports/app-usage-report`

- User activity reports for Microsoft Teams: `https://docs.microsoft.com/en-us/microsoftteams/teams-activity-reports`

- Monitor and improve call quality for Microsoft Teams: `https://docs.microsoft.com/en-us/MicrosoftTeams/monitor-call-quality-qos`

- Set up call analytics for Microsoft Teams: `https://docs.microsoft.com/en-us/MicrosoftTeams/set-up-call-analytics`

- Use call analytics to troubleshoot poor call quality: `https://docs.microsoft.com/en-us/MicrosoftTeams/use-call-analytics-to-troubleshoot-poor-call-quality`

- Set up the Call Quality Dashboard: `https://docs.microsoft.com/en-us/microsoftteams/turning-on-and-using-call-quality-dashboard`

- Dimensions and measurements available in the Call Quality Dashboard: `https://docs.microsoft.com/en-us/MicrosoftTeams/dimensions-and-measures-available-in-call-quality-dashboard`

- Use the Call Quality Dashboard to manage call and meeting quality in Microsoft Teams: `https://docs.microsoft.com/en-us/MicrosoftTeams/quality-of-experience-review-guide`

- Use Power BI to analyze call quality data for Microsoft Teams: `https://docs.microsoft.com/en-us/microsoftteams/cqd-power-bi-query-templates`

Section 2:
Administering the Meeting, Calling, and Chat Features within Microsoft Teams

Here, you will learn how to administer the core communication features of Microsoft Teams, including video meeting, calling, and chat features. We'll cover the management and configuration of each to the extent that they might appear in the exam.

This part of the book comprises the following chapters:

- *Chapter 8, Managing Collaboration and Chat within Microsoft Teams*
- *Chapter 9, Managing Meetings and Live Events in Microsoft Teams*
- *Chapter 10, Managing Phone Numbers in Microsoft Teams*
- *Chapter 11, Managing Phone System in Microsoft Teams*

8
Managing Collaboration and Chat within Microsoft Teams

In this chapter, we will examine the collaboration and chat aspects of Microsoft Teams. We will explore the options available to Teams administrators to control which Teams chat features users can leverage by configuring messaging policies. We will also look at how you can control external access to your Teams environment, as well as to SharePoint and OneDrive specifically, since they're integrated but managed separately. Then we will explain the process of creating channels within Microsoft Teams, including private channels. We will then conclude this chapter by examining how email integration and cloud file storage settings work within Microsoft Teams.

In this chapter, we'll look at the skills that will help you meet the test requirements under *Manage chat and collaboration experiences* in the MS-700 exam:

- Configuring messaging policies
- Managing external access and setting external access options for SharePoint and OneDrive
- Managing Teams' channels and private channel creation
- Managing email integration for Teams
- Managing cloud file storage settings

Technical requirements

In this chapter, you will need to have access to the **Microsoft Teams admin center**, which you can reach at `https://admin.teams.microsoft.com`. You will need to be either a *Global Administrator* or a *Teams Service Administrator* to have full access to the features and capabilities within the Teams admin center.

You will also need access to the **SharePoint admin center** for skills specifically associated with managing external access in SharePoint and OneDrive. You'll need to be a *Global Administrator* or a *SharePoint Administrator* for the steps involved there.

Configuring messaging policies

Messaging policies allow Teams administrators to indicate which messaging features team owners and members are allowed to use. For example, you may wish to prevent the deletion of sent messages for a specific group of users – a messaging policy is what would allow this.

By default, your organization has a global policy assigned to all users. This global policy can be modified, or you can create additional policies to assign to specific groups and users, leaving the global default in place for users to whom the custom messaging policies won't apply.

> **Important note**
> Each user in your organization can only have one messaging policy applied to them at any one time. This affects their experience in all Teams uniformly and cannot differ per team.

Creating messaging policies

To create a new messaging policy, select **Messaging policies** from the left-hand menu of the Microsoft Teams admin center at `https://admin.teams.microsoft.com`. Then, click **Add**.

Messaging policies can be configured to affect the following features in Teams:

Setting	Options
Owners can delete sent messages	On or Off
Delete sent messages	On or Off
Edit sent messages	On or Off
Read receipts	User controlled, off for everyone, on for everyone
Chat	On or Off
Use Giphys in conversations	Strict, moderate, no restriction
Giphy content rating	On or Off
Use memes in conversations	On or Off
Use stickers in conversations	On or Off
Allow URL previews	On or Off
Translate messages	On or Off
Allow immersive reader for viewing messages	On or Off
Send urgent messages using priority notifications	On or Off
Create voice messages	Allowed in chats and channels, allowed in chats only, disabled
On mobile devices, display favorite channels above recent chats	Disabled/enabled
Remove users from group chats	On or Off
Suggested replies	On or Off

> **Important note**
>
> To delete a messaging policy, you must first reassign all users currently assigned to it to a different policy before deletion is allowed.

Once the policy is configured and saved, it can be assigned.

Assigning messaging policies

Messaging policies can be assigned to specific users and groups (such as security groups or distribution lists), overriding the current policy assigned to them. This can be done by selecting the new policy, followed by **Manage users** from the menu. This allows manual assignment of a policy, but can be labor-intensive for large numbers of groups and users:

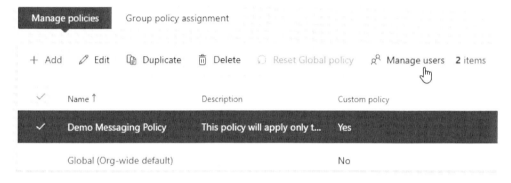

Figure 8.1 – Options available for a selected messaging policy in the Messaging policies section of the Microsoft Teams admin center

For assigning policies to larger batches of users, you can go to **Microsoft Teams admin center** and then click **Users** from the left-hand menu. Here you can use the checkmark above the selection column to select all users, or you can filter/search as needed to select the larger group of users for whom you'll be adjusting policy settings:

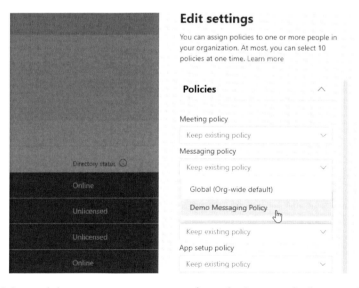

Figure 8.2 – Side panel showing assignment process for multiple types of policies to a large group of users selected in the Users page of the Microsoft Teams admin center

In the event a user is part of multiple groups where each have policies assigned to them, you configure the rank for policies under **Group Policy Assignment** on the **Messaging policies** page of the Microsoft Teams admin center. As seen in *Figure 8.3*, you select a group, enter a numeric rank, and then select the policy assigned to that group:

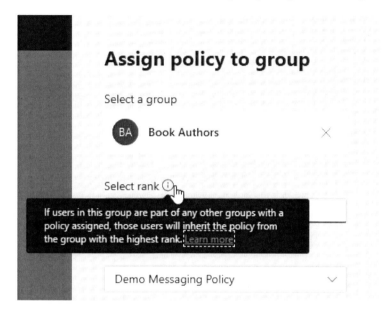

Figure 8.3 – Side panel for assigning a policy and its rank to members of a specific group

In some cases, the Microsoft Teams admin center may prove too hands-on for large-scale operations. In those circumstances, we turn to PowerShell.

Assigning messaging policies via PowerShell

Using the `SkypeForBusiness` PowerShell module, you can assign messaging policies to one or more users using the `Grant-CsTeamsMessagingPolicy` PowerShell cmdlet rather than the Microsoft Teams admin center. In many cases, this would be much more efficient:

- If assigning a messaging policy to one user, you would use something like the following:

```
Grant-CsTeamsMessagingPolicy -identity "Nate Chamberlain"
-PolicyName ITAdminPolicy
```

- And if assigning to many users, you might filter all users by department or another attribute. That PowerShell command would resemble the following:

```
Get-CsOnlineUser -Filter {Department -eq 'IT
Administration'} | Grant-CsTeamsMessagingPolicy
-PolicyName "ITAdminPolicy"
```

You can also use the `MicrosoftTeamsPowerShell` module's `New-CsBatchPolicyAssignmentOperation` cmdlet with the `-PolicyType` `TeamsMessagingPolicy` parameter and value to assign a messaging policy to users in bulk. A batch can contain up to 5,000 users. The following example demonstrates how this might look, where users are referenced using SIPs in an array (though it could also be a reference to a text file of SIPs or otherwise):

```
$users_ids = @("nate@natechamberlain.com","harry@
natechamberlain.com","bertha@natechamberlain.com")

New-CsBatchPolicyAssignmentOperation -PolicyType
TeamsMessagingPolicy -PolicyName ITAdminPolicy -Identity
$users_ids -OperationName "Batch assign ITAdminPolicy"
```

> **Tip**
>
> Replace the `-PolicyName` parameter's value with $null to unassign the specified policy type for the specified users. The affected users would then fall back to the default (global) policy.

Also located in the `MicrosoftTeamsPowerShell` module is the `New-CsGroupPolicyAssignment` cmdlet. This allows a policy to be assigned to a security group or members of a distribution list. Note that group policy assignment is only recommended for groups with no more than 50,000 users. In the following example, using the HR department group's SIP, we use this cmdlet to assign the `AllOn` policy to its members:

```
New-CsGroupPolicyAssignment -GroupId hr@natechamberlain.com
-PolicyType TeamsMeetingPolicy -PolicyName AllOn
```

Next, we'll cover external access in Teams, as well as SharePoint and OneDrive as they relate to Teams.

Managing external access and setting external access options for SharePoint and OneDrive

For admins more familiar with external access settings in SharePoint and OneDrive, it may be confusing to differentiate between guest access and external access.

External access allows the users of Teams in other domains to find you and use the *communication* features of calling, chatting, and setting up meetings with you. They do not have individual team or channel access, or access to the SharePoint content in the backend. It's strictly communication and meeting abilities. External users do not have to sign out of their own domain/organization in order to be able to communicate with you in yours.

Guest access is the ability to allow a user from another organization to be a member of a team. In addition to communication features, guest access members can also *collaborate in Teams, channels, and on files*. They have mostly the same team capabilities as internal members (unless a guest policy has been adjusted to make them more restricted). Guests may have to switch organizations within the Teams client so that they can sign in to your Team(s) using the email address that included the invitation to join. Guests added to Teams (by owners or admins) are added to your organization's Azure Active Directory as guests.

> **Tip**
> To see a full comparison of the abilities granted to external access versus guest access, check out `https://docs.microsoft.com/en-us/microsoftteams/communicate-with-users-from-other-organizations#compare-external-and-guest-access`.

In this section, we are focusing on external access. To explore guest access more, review *Chapter 4, Configuring Guest Access in Microsoft Teams*.

Configuring external access settings in Microsoft Teams

To get to external access settings for Microsoft Teams, go to **Microsoft Teams admin center** at `https://admin.teams.microsoft.com` and select **Org-wide settings** from the left-hand menu. Then, choose **External access**.

External access settings include the following:

Setting	Options
Users can communicate with other Skype for Business and Teams users	On or off
Users can communicate with Skype users	On or off
Domains	Specify domains individually that should either be allowed or blocked

If you block a domain, all others will be allowed unless you list others explicitly. For example, if you block external access for users in the `contoso.com` domain, users from any other domain (unless also listed as blocked) are still allowed.

If you allow a domain, all others will be blocked. For example, if you choose to allow external access to `contoso.com`, no other domains will be allowed to be used with external access unless they're also explicitly listed as allowed in the **External access** settings.

> **Important note**
> Allowed/blocked domains only apply to meetings if the anonymous access setting for meetings is set to *off*. If it is *on*, allowed/blocked domains listed in the **External access** settings will be disregarded for meetings.

When allowing/blocking domains, the settings are quite simple. You enter the domain, followed by your decision to allow or block it, as seen here:

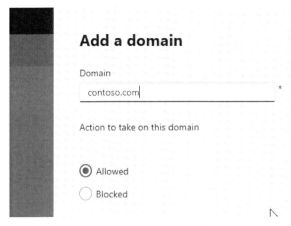

Figure 8.4 – The right panel when adding a domain to be allowed or blocked in the External access settings of the Microsoft Teams admin center

You would not mix allowed and blocked domains as that configuration would conflict with itself. Typically, you'd decide that you want to either allow a specific list of domains or block a specific list of domains.

Configure external access for SharePoint and OneDrive for Business

Teams uses SharePoint for Teams channel file storage, and OneDrive for Business for 1:1 and group chat file storage. The external sharing settings applied to SharePoint and OneDrive for Business (which are shared settings) do affect users' experiences in Teams since Teams' **External access** settings do not override them. You should configure both (Teams and SharePoint) external access/sharing settings so that they work well together and do not conflict or restrain users unintentionally.

You find the **External sharing** settings for SharePoint by going to the SharePoint admin center at `https://YOURTENANT-admin.sharepoint.com` and selecting **Policies** > **Sharing** from the left-hand menu.

SharePoint admin center adds the following **External sharing** settings to content stored in SharePoint and OneDrive, but accessed via Teams. Note that SharePoint's external sharing settings apply to guest users (those invited as team members), but not those simply with external access (to communicate via Teams chat and meetings, for example):

Setting	Options
Content sharing level for SharePoint	Anyone; New and existing guests; Existing guests; Only people in your organization
Content sharing level for OneDrive	Anyone; New and existing guests; Existing guests; Only people in your organization
Limit external sharing by domain	On/Off, with option to specify domains if On
Allow only users in specific security groups to share externally	On/Off, with option to manage security groups if On
Guests must sign in using the same account to which sharing invitations are sent	On/Off
Allow guests to share items they don't own	On/Off
People who use a verification code must reauthenticate after this many days	Enter a numeric value to represent the number of days

You can see these options in *Figure 8.5*:

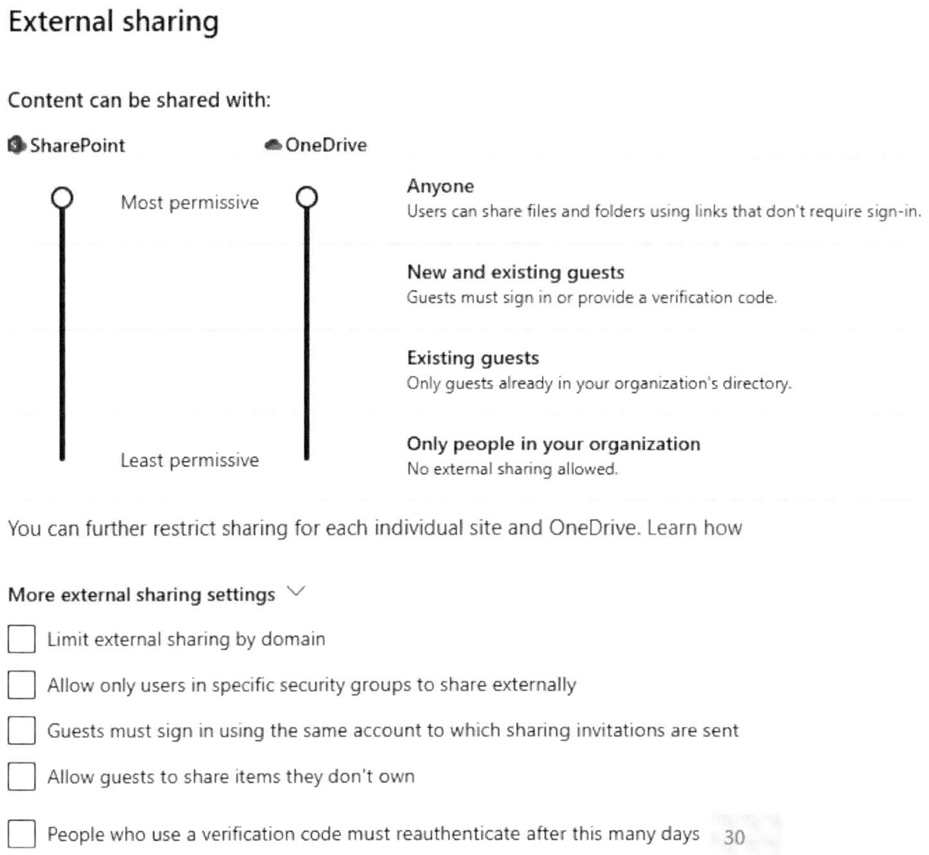

External sharing

Content can be shared with:

SharePoint   **OneDrive**

Most permissive

Anyone
Users can share files and folders using links that don't require sign-in.

New and existing guests
Guests must sign in or provide a verification code.

Existing guests
Only guests already in your organization's directory.

Only people in your organization
No external sharing allowed.

Least permissive

You can further restrict sharing for each individual site and OneDrive. Learn how

More external sharing settings ∨

☐ Limit external sharing by domain

☐ Allow only users in specific security groups to share externally

☐ Guests must sign in using the same account to which sharing invitations are sent

☐ Allow guests to share items they don't own

☐ People who use a verification code must reauthenticate after this many days   30

Figure 8.5 – The External sharing settings section of the SharePoint
admin center's Policies > Sharing section

> **Important note**
> Any changes made in the SharePoint admin center's External sharing settings
> are global throughout your SharePoint environment, but should be considered
> the baseline policy. Individual sites can have unique, stricter (but not more
> permissive) settings that could affect Teams sharing experiences.

So even if your Teams' settings for guest users are most permissive, if SharePoint has restricted sharing settings, those will apply to SharePoint content despite its usage via the Teams interface.

Next, let's look at managing Teams channels.

Managing Teams' channels and private channel creation

In this section, we're going to cover management of Teams channels, but also policies that enable or disable your team owners' ability to create private channels.

Microsoft Teams channels allow for a team's separation of conversations and collaboration activities by task, subgroup, product, topic, and so on. Each team channel has a **Files** tab that mirrors a folder sharing the channel's name in a document library on the team's affiliated SharePoint Online site collection. If you had six channels in a team, there would be six folders in the affiliated site's document library, for example.

Each channel always has its own conversation thread, its own unique set of tabs along the top, and some channels can also be private, with a unique subset of members from the parent team.

To see all the channels in an existing team via the client, look in the Team's settings (click the ellipsis next to the team name, and then **Manage team**). There's a tab in the Team settings for **channels**. For each team, you can choose to show or hide each channel for you, for members, or both by selecting the **Show for me** and/or **Show for members** checkboxes. If hidden, the channel is just included in an expandable list of hidden channels. This allows you to make higher priority or important channels always readily available/visible, while less important channels can be collapsed and placed out of sight.

From the **Channels** tab, you can also perform the following actions:

- Search for channels
- See all the channel names, grouped by active and deleted
- See channel types (standard/open or private)
- See the latest activity by channel
- Create new channels
- Manage individual channels via their ellipses

Under **Manage individual channels** via their ellipses, we have the following options:

- Channel notifications
- Pin/Unpin
- Manage channel (see next section)
- Get email address

- Get link to channel

- Edit the channel

- Connectors

- Delete this channel

Managing channels for a team

Each channel in a team has its own **Channel** settings. These are found by selecting the three dots/ellipsis next to a channel's name and selecting **Manage channel**:

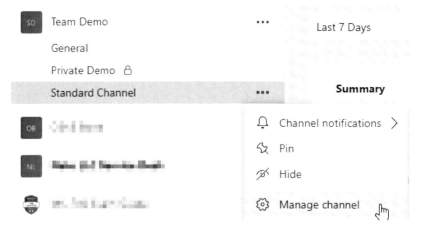

Figure 8.6 – The location of the Manage channel option for a specific channel is found on its ellipsis menu in the left-hand Teams navigation panel

Let's now look at some of the options for managing the channel.

Channel moderation

As a team owner, you can enable channel moderation for a team. This means an owner can select an individual in the team who can start new posts and reply to existing posts. Channel moderation is different for a team's general channel than it is for additional channels.

For *general* channels' moderation settings, an owner can choose one of the following:

- Anyone can post messages

- Anyone can post; show an alert that posting will notify everyone (recommended for large teams)

- Only owners can post messages

For *standard* (additional) channels, owners can choose whether **Channel moderation** is **On** or **Off**. If it's **Off**, the owner chooses whether **everyone** (selected by default) or **everyone except guests** can start new posts. If it's **On**, the owner specifies the following:

- Moderators (the list of moderators is set to Team Owners by default, but additional members can be added. Team owners cannot be removed, however.)

- Team member permissions (multi-select)

The options that appear under Team member permissions are as follows:

- **Allow members to reply to channel messages**

- **Allow members to pin channel messages**

- **Allow bots to submit channel messages**

- **Allow connectors to submit channel messages**

You can see an example of a standard channel's settings in the following screenshot:

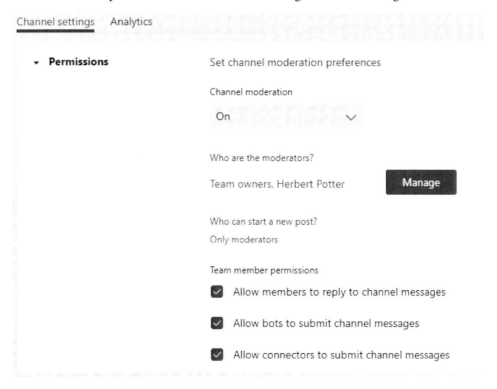

Figure 8.7 – The channel settings (not general or private)

Let's now move on to the next option – channel analytics.

Channel analytics

Team owners can also see analytics for each channel for the last 7, 30, or 90 days. Analytics include the following:

- **Summary**: The number of users and the number of apps
- **Engagement**: The number of posts, replies, mentions, and reactions

Private channel difference

Because private channels have separate membership management and their own separate SharePoint site collection, their settings more closely resemble a full Team's settings. In addition to the **Settings** and **Analytics** tabs, a private channel has members for the management of members from the parent team that also need access to the private channel:

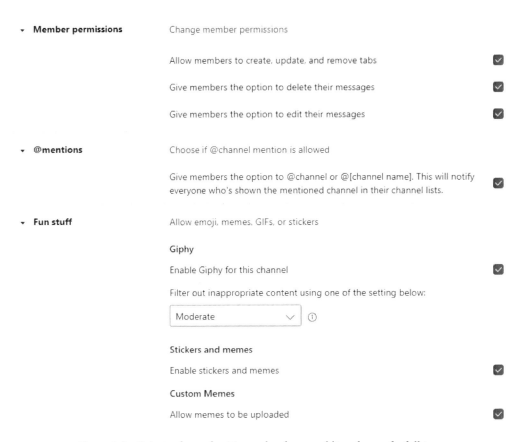

Figure 8.8 – Private channel settings, closely resembling those of a full team

Because private channels do provision a new site collection in SharePoint, governance over the ability to create private channels should be considered thoughtfully. Next, we'll cover how to restrict the ability to create private channels (and therefore separate SharePoint site collections).

Managing private channel creation policies

Private channels only appear for members of that private channel within a team. While all team members see the standard/general channels, you have to be made a member of private channels within that team separately. Private channels do not share a SharePoint site collection with its parent team – they are provided with a new, separate SharePoint site collection to maintain the security boundary of the parent team.

Important note

Private channels can have a maximum of 250 members. A team can have up to 30 private channels, including deleted private channels deleted in the previous 30 days. After 30 days, these *soft deleted* channels will no longer count toward the 30 max figure.

Team owners can restrict private channel creation from Team settings: **Settings** > **Member permissions** > **Allow members to create private channels**. But you, as a *Teams Service Administrator*, can restrict specific users and groups from creating private channels regardless of individual team settings. To manage who can create private channels, you'll create a Teams policy in the Microsoft Teams admin center.

You may wish to simply use the default global policy to set private channel creation to on or off for all users. In other cases, you'll want to create a new Teams policy to turn it on for some users and off for others.

To create a new Teams policy, perform the following steps:

1. Click **Teams** > **Teams policies** from the left-hand menu of the Microsoft Teams admin center.

2. Then, click **Add**.

3. To restrict the creation of private channels, you'll simply give the policy a name, description, and toggle off the **Create private channels** option.

4.   Save the policy, and then apply it to users or groups using the **Manage policies** or **Group policy assignment** tabs, respectively:

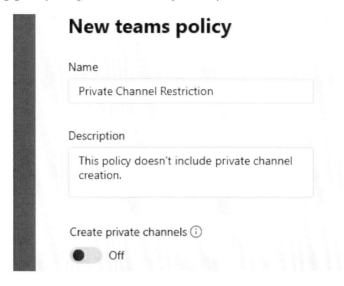

Figure 8.9 – A new Teams policy in which private channel creation has been disabled

You could also create this policy via PowerShell using the `New-CsTeamsChannelsPolicy` cmdlet with the `-AllowPrivateChannelCreation` parameter set to `$false`. For example, a full command might be as follows:

```
New-CsTeamsChannelsPolicy -Identity RestrictPrivateChannels
 -AllowPrivateChannelCreation $false
```

Now, let's explore email integration in Teams.

Managing Email integration in Teams

Email integration in Teams allows users to email channels in order to post. You can find a channel's unique email address by clicking the ellipsis button (three dots) next to a channel name and then **Get email address**. Emails sent to this address post like any other post in the channel conversation, and replies to the post do not get sent back to the emailer – they act as a normal reply to a normal post.

From the Microsoft Teams admin center, you can find the org-wide **Email integration** settings by choosing **Org-wide settings** > **Teams settings** from the left-hand menu. Scroll down on the Teams settings page until you find the **Email integration** section:

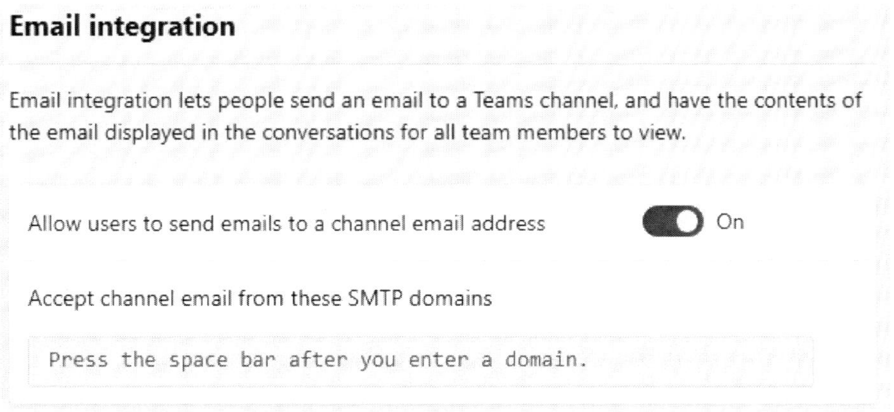

Email integration

Email integration lets people send an email to a Teams channel, and have the contents of the email displayed in the conversations for all team members to view.

Allow users to send emails to a channel email address   On

Accept channel email from these SMTP domains

Press the space bar after you enter a domain.

Figure 8.10 – Org-wide Email integration settings in the Microsoft Teams admin center

Here, you can choose whether users can email unique channel email addresses as a method of posting in the channel. You can restrict allowed domains to make sure users are only emailing from your organization(s), or leave this option blank to allow any email address to post to the channel.

You can also adjust email integration settings per team, rather than at the tenant level. To adjust your individual team's email integration settings, choose the ellipsis next to a channel name and choose **Get email address**. Then, choose **Advanced settings**. Here, you can see (and remove) the channel's email address as well as choose one of the following:

- **Anyone can send emails to this address**

- **Only members of this team**

- **Only email sent from these domains** (and specify those domains in the accompanying textbox, comma-delimited)

> **Important note**
>
> Troubleshooting successful email delivery to channels: In addition to the settings previously mentioned being configured, an email must satisfy certain criteria in order to be delivered and posted to a channel. Emails must have fewer than 51 inline images, have fewer than 21 attachments, and have no attachment greater than 10 MB. If the email meets these criteria, the feature is enabled, the sender's domain is allowed, and the email will be delivered. You should also check to make sure the channel's associated folder in SharePoint hasn't been deleted or renamed.

Lastly, we'll take a look at the cloud file storage settings within Teams.

Managing cloud file storage settings

Each team (and channel) can have unique cloud storage options configured for its members. A team member might do this when they have pre-existing storage in Google Drive that they intend to use alongside their channel's auto-provisioned SharePoint document library folder.

To add cloud storage to a channel's **Files** tab, perform the following steps:

1. Go to the **Files** tab and select **Add cloud storage**.

2. From here, you can select which cloud storage provider you'd like to add to the channel's **Files** tab.

    This doesn't grant permission to the cloud storage location. Users must individually have access to the third-party provider location in order to be able to view it integrated in Teams:

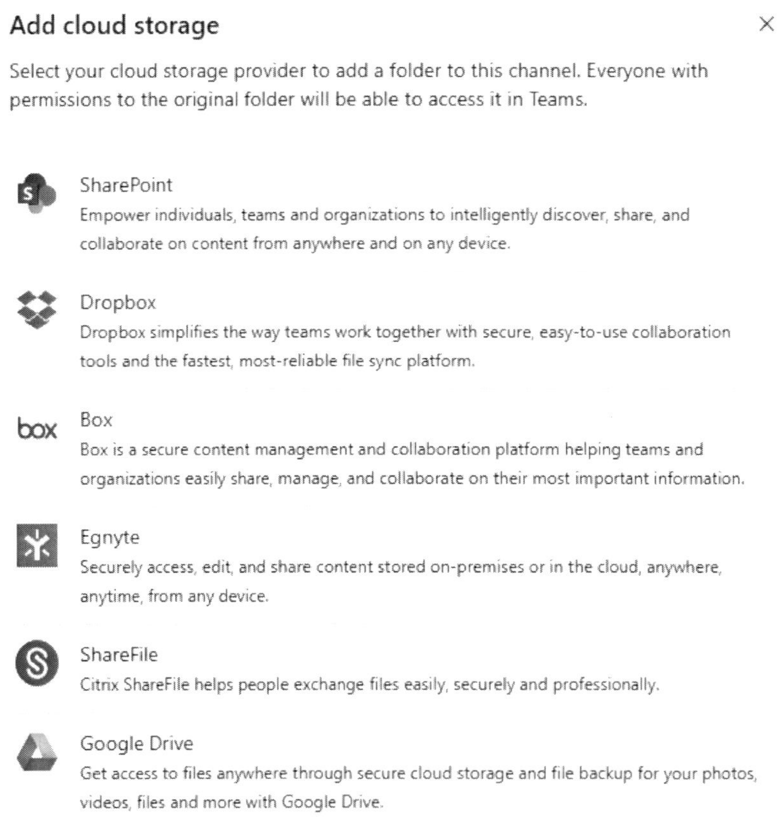

Figure 8.11 – Cloud storage options for team members adding cloud storage to their channel's Files tab

Once a location has been added, it appears as a folder on the **Files** tab alongside content stored in the default SharePoint location.

In the Microsoft Teams admin center, you can enable or disable specific cloud storage providers, as seen in the following screenshot, from the configuration options available in the Microsoft Teams admin center: **Org-wide settings** > **Teams settings** > **Files**. The options you can enable or disable correspond to the cloud storage options presented to team members seen previously:

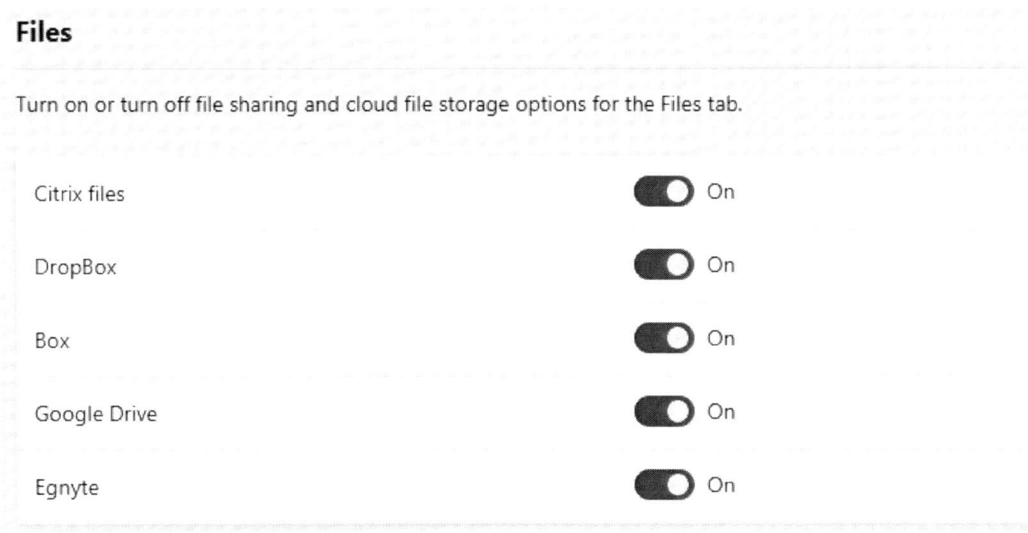

Files

Turn on or turn off file sharing and cloud file storage options for the Files tab.

Citrix files	⬤	On
DropBox	⬤	On
Box	⬤	On
Google Drive	⬤	On
Egnyte	⬤	On

Figure 8.12 – Cloud storage options are found under the Files section of the
Teams settings in the Microsoft Teams admin center

Since SharePoint is required for Teams' file storage in the backend, it cannot be disabled.

Summary

In this chapter, we covered the configuration and assignment of Microsoft Teams messaging policies to users via the Microsoft Teams admin center and PowerShell. This allows us to customize the messaging experience of our users to meet compliance, governance, or user experience requirements.

We then covered external access to Microsoft Teams, as well as SharePoint and OneDrive as they relate to our usage of Microsoft Teams. Understanding how these apps share responsibility access to content helps us protect our teams and the related business processes from potential vulnerabilities.

Next, we covered channel creation, both standard and private, followed by email integration in Teams, and lastly managing cloud file storage settings. Each of these aspects come together to create a robust collaboration environment that exists within our specifications.

In the next chapter, we'll begin exploring the management of meetings and live events in Microsoft Teams.

Questions

As we conclude, here is a list of questions for you to test your knowledge regarding the material covered in this chapter. You will find the answers in the *Assessments* section of the *Appendix*:

1. You've determined that a messaging policy is no longer needed in the organization and should be deleted. The users who are currently assigned to it need to be reverted to the global default policy. What course of action should you take?

    a. Use PowerShell to delete the unnecessary policy.

    b. Use the Teams admin center or PowerShell to reassign the global policy to affected users, and then delete the unneeded policy.

    c. Email team owners with a request to assign the affected members to the global policy.

    d. Delete the unnecessary policy from the Teams admin center. The assigned policy of affected users will automatically fall back to the default global setting.

2. True or false? Users can have up to three messaging policies assigned to them at any one time. In the event of conflicting policy settings, the last to be assigned takes precedence.

    a. True

    b. False

3. True or false? Users can have one messaging policy assigned to them at any one time. In the event that they are a member of multiple groups that have conflicting messaging policies assigned to them, the group with the higher numeric rank in **Group messaging policies** will take precedence.

    a. True

    b. False

4. You need to prevent your `tailspintoys.com` users from messaging external recipients in the `contoso.com` domain. You create a messaging policy. Does this accomplish your objective?

    a. Yes

    b. No

5. You need to prevent your `tailspintoys.com` users from communicating with `contoso.com` users in chats and meetings. Guest users are not allowed in your organization, so the solution just needs to address communication between organizations. What should you modify?

    a. Guest access

    b. Messaging policies

    c. Meeting policies

    d. External access settings

6. You don't want to restrict `contoso.com` users from external access calls and meetings, but you do want to ensure that they aren't sent share links to content found in Teams (but stored in SharePoint). You therefore change the Microsoft Teams External access settings. Could this accomplish the goal?

    a. Yes

    b. No

7. You don't want to restrict `contoso.com` users from external access calls and meetings, but you do want to ensure that they aren't sent share links to content found in Teams (but stored in SharePoint). You change the SharePoint External sharing settings. Could this accomplish your goal?

    a. Yes

    b. No

8. You're receiving support tickets saying guest users cannot access files or shared notebooks in Teams that they are members of. There are no issues with communication features such as chats or channel conversations. Where should you configure external sharing to ensure that these users can also get to the files and notebooks?

   a. SharePoint Online admin center

   b. Azure AD admin center

   c. OneDrive for Business admin center

   d. Microsoft Teams admin center

9. You've been asked to restrict a group of users who haven't completed Teams training from creating private channels. What should you create in the Microsoft Teams admin center that you can apply to those users/groups so as to prevent private channel creation?

   a. Messaging policy

   b. Meeting policy

   c. Teams policy

   d. Setup policy

10. An email sent to a channel in Teams wasn't delivered. Which of the following should you check?

   a. Message characteristics (attachment count, image count, and so on)

   b. Whether the sender's domain is allowed

   c. Whether the feature is enabled at tenant and/or Team level

   d. All of the above

Further reading

Here are a number of links to more information on some of the topics that we have covered in this chapter:

- Managing messaging policies in Teams: `https://docs.microsoft.com/en-us/microsoftteams/messaging-policies-in-teams`

- Grant-CsTeamsMessagingPolicy: `https://docs.microsoft.com/en-us/powershell/module/skype/grant-csteamsmessagingpolicy?view=skype-ps`

- New-CsBatchPolicyAssignmentOperation: `https://docs.microsoft.com/en-us/powershell/module/teams/new-csbatchpolicyassignmentoperation`

- Managing Teams policies in Microsoft Teams: `https://docs.microsoft.com/en-us/microsoftteams/teams-policies`

- Managing external access in Microsoft Teams: `https://docs.microsoft.com/en-us/microsoftteams/manage-external-access`

- External sharing overview: `https://docs.microsoft.com/en-us/sharepoint/external-sharing-overview`

- Communicating with users from other organizations in Microsoft Teams: `https://docs.microsoft.com/en-us/microsoftteams/communicate-with-users-from-other-organizations`

- Setting up and managing channel moderation in Microsoft Teams: `https://docs.microsoft.com/en-us/microsoftteams/manage-channel-moderation-in-teams`

- Overview of teams and channels in Microsoft Teams: `https://docs.microsoft.com/en-us/microsoftteams/teams-channels-overview`

- Seeing all the channels in a team: `https://support.office.com/en-us/article/see-all-channels-in-a-team-15bb047f-a20e-4774-8718-8cd14161b6d0`

- Creating a channel in Teams: `https://support.office.com/en-us/article/create-a-channel-in-teams-fda0b75e-5b90-4fb8-8857-7e102b014525`

- Managing the life cycle of private channels in Microsoft Teams: `https://docs.microsoft.com/en-us/microsoftteams/private-channels-life-cycle-management`

- Private channels in Microsoft Teams: `https://docs.microsoft.com/en-us/microsoftteams/private-channels`

- Managing teams' policies in Microsoft Teams: `https://docs.microsoft.com/en-us/MicrosoftTeams/teams-policies`

- New-CsTeamsChannelsPolicy: `https://docs.microsoft.com/en-us/powershell/module/skype/new-csteamschannelspolicy`

- Managing Microsoft Teams settings for your organization: `https://docs.microsoft.com/en-us/microsoftteams/enable-features-office-365`

- Sending an email to a channel in Teams: `https://support.office.com/en-us/article/send-an-email-to-a-channel-in-teams-d91db004-d9d7-4a47-82e6-fb1b16dfd51e`

- Managing who can send email to a channel in Teams: `https://support.office.com/en-us/article/manage-who-can-send-email-to-a-channel-in-teams-4f1a1224-e71b-45de-8f68-8e08f7874fa9`

- Managing Microsoft Teams settings for your organization: `https://docs.microsoft.com/en-us/microsoftteams/enable-features-office-365`

9
Managing Meetings and Live Events in Microsoft Teams

In this chapter, we will introduce you to the principles of meetings and live events within Microsoft Teams. You will learn how to distinguish between settings and policies for both meetings and live events, and how these are applied to your users and groups within Microsoft Teams. We will demonstrate the effects of the features made available via these settings and policies, and how you can manage these effectively. In addition, we will also explain the process of configuring audio conferencing licenses to set up conference bridges within your Microsoft Teams environment. You will learn how conference bridges can contain one or more telephone numbers, which can be included in meeting invites in Teams.

In this chapter, we're going to cover the following main topics that align with measured exam skills:

- Configuring Teams meeting settings
- Configuring Teams meeting policies
- Configuring Teams live events settings

- Configuring Teams live events policies
- Configuring conference bridge settings

Technical requirements

In this chapter, you will need to have access to the **Microsoft Teams admin center**, which you can reach at `https://admin.teams.microsoft.com`. You will need to be either a **Global Administrator** or a **Teams Service Administrator** to have full access to the features and capabilities within the Teams admin center.

For the conference bridge settings, you will need to have purchased a separate add-on subscription if you're not an E5 subscriber. To make purchases, you will specifically need to be a *Global Administrator*.

Configuring Teams meeting settings

The Microsoft Teams admin center has a **Meeting settings** page, found by choosing **Meetings** > **Meeting settings** from the left-hand menu. It includes the following configuration options:

Section	Setting	Options
Participants	Anonymous users can join a meeting	On/Off
Participants	Anonymous users can interact with apps in meetings	On/Off
Email invitation	Logo URL	Hyperlink field
Email invitation	Legal URL	Hyperlink field
Email invitation	Help URL	Hyperlink field
Email invitation	Footer	Text field
Network	Insert **Quality of Service (QoS)** markers for real-time media traffic	On/Off
Network	Select a port range for each type of real-time media traffic	Specify port ranges, Automatically use any available ports

In the **Email invitation** section, you can also choose to **Preview invite** to see how recipients of Teams meeting invites from your organization will see the invite incorporating your changes to URLs and footer content. *Figure 9.1* shows the pop-up preview when this is selected, while *Figure 9.5* shows how an actual email invite might look:

Email invite preview

Organization logotype email preview

Join Microsoft Teams Meeting

+1 234-567-8901 Country or region, City (Toll)

Conference ID: 123 456 78#

Local numbers | Reset PIN | Learn more about Teams.

Help | Legal

We're excited to collaborate with you.

Note: The preview shown here is for representation purpose only. The actual invitation may vary based on the version of Teams client and Teams plugin for Outlook being used by the users.

Figure 9.1 – The dialog shown when users opt to preview Teams invites

Teams meeting settings apply to your entire organization and cannot differ by user.

Editing meeting settings with PowerShell

You can use the SkypeForBusiness PowerShell module's `Set-CsTeamsMeetingConfiguration` cmdlet to modify your organization's meeting settings. In the following example, the `Help URL` is being set with PowerShell:

```
Set-CsTeamsMeetingConfiguration -HelpURL "https://
natechamberlain.com/MeetingHelp"
```

Now that you're familiar with available options for the configuration of Teams meeting settings, we'll configure Teams meeting policies.

Configuring Teams meeting policies

Meeting policies control the Teams meeting features that users are able to utilize when working in your organization's Teams environment.

Unlike Teams meeting settings, Teams meeting policies can differ by user. Each user can have a maximum of one policy per policy type applied to them at any one time. In the case of conflicting policies (due to membership of multiple groups with varying policies assigned), you will have configured a policy ranking per group to determine which applies to the user.

Meeting policies are configured in the Microsoft Teams admin center by selecting **Meetings** > **Meeting policies** from the left-hand menu.

By default, your tenant comes with a global meeting policy applied to all users. By creating additional policies, you essentially create different Teams meeting experiences for different users and/or groups. Users with no custom policy assigned remain in the global/default policy group.

A meeting policy comprises the following sections, each with its own settings:

- **General**
- **Audio and video**
- **Content sharing**
- **Participants and guests**

Let's look more closely at these sections and the settings available within each.

General

General settings determine whether **Meet now** is a meeting option (an instant, impromptu meeting), whether the Outlook add-in is made available (for easier scheduling), and whether channel and private meeting scheduling is allowed for the users to whom this policy will be applied:

Setting	Options
Allow Meet now in channels	On/Off
Allow the Outlook add-in	On/Off
Allow channel meeting scheduling	On/Off
Allow scheduling private meetings	On/Off

> **Important note**
> Conference bridge dial-in options are not available for *Meet Now* meetings in Teams. They only apply to scheduled meetings.

The next section is Audio & video.

Audio & video

Audio & video settings specify whether the users to whom this policy applies can have transcription and cloud recording abilities. They also include the IP audio and video modes, whether IP video and NDI streaming are allowed, and specify the media bit rate:

Setting	Options
Allow transcription	On/Off
Allow cloud recording	On/Off
Mode for IP audio	Disabled, Outgoing and incoming audio enabled
Mode for IP video	Disabled, Outgoing and incoming audio enabled
Allow IP video	On/Off
Allow NDI streaming	On/Off
Media bit rate (Kbs)*	Number of Kbs with a minimum of 30 Kbs. 10 Mbps (10,000 Kbs) is recommended for the best quality if changing the value. The default value is 50,000 Kbs, which is more than will ever be needed and can just be considered unlimited.

*For the **Media bit rate (Kbs)** policy setting, Microsoft shares the following information regarding bandwidth usage during different Teams scenarios. The following table gives a good idea of the consumption of various features in Teams. Even if you don't use this information to plan and implement meeting policies, it may be helpful in preparing your network for Teams activity:

Bandwidth(up/down)	Scenarios
30 Kbps	Peer-to-peer audio calling
130 Kbps	Peer-to-peer audio calling and screen sharing
500 Kbps	Peer-to-peer quality video calling 360p at 30 fps
1.2 Mbps	Peer-to-peer HD quality video calling with a resolution of HD 720p at 30 fps
1.5 Mbps	Peer-to-peer HD quality video calling with a resolution of HD 1080p at 30 fps
500 kbps/1 Mbps	Group video calling
1M bps/2 Mbps	HD group video calling (540p videos on 1080p screen)

Microsoft's bandwidth usage table from `https://docs.microsoft.com/en-US/microsoftteams/prepare-network#bandwidth-requirements`.

The third section is Content sharing.

Content sharing

Content sharing specifies what sort of content the users assigned this policy can share. These settings include how much of a screen users can share, whether control can be shared, and whether PowerPoint, whiteboard, and shared notes are allowed:

Setting	Options
Screen sharing mode	Entire screen, Single application, Disabled
Allow a participant to give or request control	On/Off
Allow an external participant to give or request control	On/Off
Allow PowerPoint sharing	On/Off
Allow whiteboard	On/Off
Allow shared notes	On/Off

The last section of the meeting policy settings is Participants & guests.

Participants & guests

These settings are specific to the roles and responsibilities of attendees and presenters this policy applies to. Specifically, this section determines whether anonymous users can start a meeting before the presenter/owner, who can be a presenter, whether attendees are automatically admitted, lobby behavior for dial-in users, Meet Now for private meetings, live captioning, and chat during meetings:

Setting	Options
Let anonymous people start a meeting	On/Off
Roles that have presenter rights in meetings	Organizers, but users can override; Everyone in the organization, but user can override; Everyone, but user can override
Automatically admit people	Everyone, Everyone in your organization, Everyone in your organization and federated organizations, Organizer only
Allow dial-in users to bypass the lobby	On/Off
Allow Meet now in private meetings	On/Off
Enable live captions	Disabled but the user can override, Disabled
Allow chat in meetings	Enabled, Disabled

As you can see, policies are much more customizable than the org-wide Teams meeting settings. With multiple policies configured differently, you can get quite granular in how specific groups of users interact with Teams.

For each policy type in Teams, you can assign a policy to individual users (by selecting it and then **Manage Users**) or use the policy page's **Group policy assignment** tab to assign the policy to groups and specify the rank for each as shown in *Figure 9.2*:

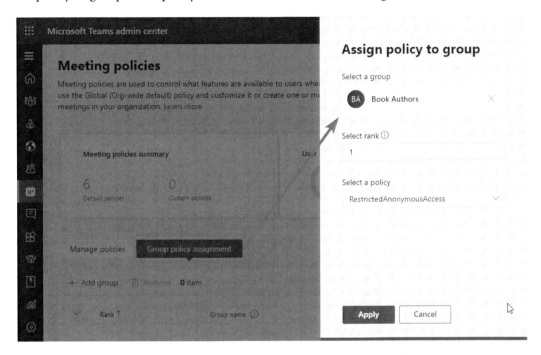

Figure 9.2 – The right panel that appears when selecting Add group from the Group policy assignment tab of Teams policies pages

For all Teams policy types, you can also make bulk policy changes (multiple types of policies at once) for all or some users by going to the Microsoft Teams admin center's **Users** node, selecting individual or all users, and choosing **Edit settings**.

Meeting policy actions with PowerShell

You can assign meeting policies to users, groups, or via policy packages using cmdlets in the MicrosoftTeamsPowerShell module.

To assign a policy to one user, you'd use `Grant-CsTeamsMeetingPolicy`, as seen in the following example where we assign user Bertha the `HRMeetings` Teams meeting policy:

```
Grant-CsTeamsMeetingPolicy -Identity bertha@natechamberlain.com
-PolicyName HRMeetings
```

To assign a policy via group policy assignment, you'd use `New-CsGroupPolicyAssignment`, as shown in the following example, where we assign the `HRMeetings` Teams meeting policy to the HR department:

```
New-CsGroupPolicyAssignment -GroupId hr@natechamberlain.com
-PolicyType TeamsMeetingPolicy -PolicyName HRMeetings
```

And to take it one step further, you can apply multiple types of policies (not just Teams meeting policies) in a policy package to users (a maximum of 5,000 per batch). This uses `Grant-CsGroupPolicyPackageAssignment`, as seen in the following example where we assign multiple policies to the HR department group, including the policy rankings in case more than one group policy applies to an individual user:

```
Grant-CsGroupPolicyPackageAssignment -GroupId hr@
natechamberlain.com -PackageName "HR Members" -PolicyRankings
"TeamsAppSetupPolicy, 1", "TeamsMessagingPolicy, 1",
"TeamsMeetingPolicy, 2"
```

You can also modify existing meeting policy settings using the SkypeForBusiness PowerShell module's `Set-CsTeamsMeetingPolicy` cmdlet. In the following example, a policy named `ITAdminPolicy` is being modified to enable transcription and disable Meet Now for the policy's assignees:

```
Set-CsTeamsMeetingPolicy -Identity ITAdminPolicy
-AllowTranscription $True -AllowMeetNow $False
```

Now let's change focus from Teams meetings to Teams live events and configure their settings and policies.

Configuring Teams live events settings

The Microsoft Teams admin center has a **Live events settings** page, found by choosing **Meetings** > **Live events settings** from the left-hand menu.

> Tip
> Teams meetings are limited to 300 participants, while live events can have up to 10,000 attendees. The Advanced Communication add-on for Microsoft Teams increases these limits to 1,000 and 20,000 respectively. With the add-on, Teams meetings participants that join after the 1,000th (overflow) are view-only participants up to 20,000. You can also use the Microsoft live events assistance program to plan events with up to 100,000 attendees.

For users to be able to create live events, they'll need to be licensed for Office 365 (E1, E3, E5, A3, or A5), Microsoft Teams, and Microsoft Stream (if planning to share recordings to external apps or devices). If not planning to share recordings externally or to other devices, live event recordings are saved to Azure Media Services for 180 days by default and a Stream license is not required. These recordings can then be uploaded to Stream later (with a license) if you wish to retain them longer.

Teams live events settings apply to your entire organization and cannot differ by user. The **Live events settings** page includes the following configuration options.

Support URL

Like the Help URL for meeting settings, the **Support URL** is a hyperlink field where you can specify the page to which users needing help during a live event can find assistance or resources. This is shown to users during the live event, whereas the meeting settings Help URL is provided in email invites.

Third-party video distribution providers

This option is a yes or no toggle button. If **Use a third-party distribution provider** is set to **On**, you can also configure the following:

- SDN/eCDN provider name (Hive, Kollective, or Riverbed are pre-integrated options)

- Provider license key or API token

- SDN API template URL

> **Important note**
> Choosing an SDN/eCDN provider and integrating it with Teams will significantly decrease your network's bandwidth strain from live events without affecting the quality of the stream. This essentially sets up a peer-to-peer network using a shared stream. Without a third-party SDN/eCDN provider, each user viewing gets their own stream individually directly from servers, which increases the bandwidth strain.

Now let's configure Teams live events policies.

Configuring Teams live events policies

Live events policies control the features that users are able to utilize when working in your organization's Teams live events environment.

Unlike Teams live events settings, Teams live events policies can differ by user. Each user can have a maximum of one policy per policy type applied to them at any one time. In the case of conflicting policies (due to membership of multiple groups with varying policies assigned), you will have configured a policy ranking per group to determine which applies to the user.

> **Important note**
> Up to 15 live events can occur simultaneously in your organization. With the Advanced Communication add-on, this increases to 50.

Live events policies are configured in the Microsoft Teams admin center by selecting **Meetings** > **Live events policies** from the left-hand menu.

By default, your tenant comes with a global live events policy applied to all users. By creating additional policies, you essentially create different live event experiences for different users and/or groups. Users with no custom policy assigned remain in the global/default policy group.

When creating a new live event policy, you can configure the following settings:

Setting	Options
Allow scheduling	On/Off
Allow transcription for attendees	On/Off
Who can join scheduled live events	Everyone, Everyone in the organization, Specific users, or groups
Who can record an event	Always record, Never record, Organizer can record

As with meeting policies, you can assign individual users or use the policy page's **Group policy assignment** tab to assign the policy to groups and specify the rank for each.

Next, we'll cover the configuration of conference bridge settings.

Configuring conference bridge settings

To use audio conferencing in Microsoft Teams, you'll need to first be licensed appropriately. **Audio conferencing** is available as an add-on subscription and included in Office 365 E5 subscriptions.

To buy the add-on (if you don't have an E5 subscription), you'll go to the **Microsoft 365 admin center** at `https://admin.microsoft.com`. From here, choose **Billing** > **Purchase services**. Then follow these steps to purchase the add-on:

1. Search for *audio*.

2. Scroll to the bottom and select **Add-ons category**.

3. Choose **Microsoft 365 Audio Conferencing**.

4. Complete the purchase for the number of users needed.

> **Important note**
> Users don't need an Audio Conferencing license to be able to call the conference bridge. Only the users who will be scheduling meetings with a conference bridge dial-in option need the license.

Once you've acquired the Audio Conferencing license (or if you already had it via an E5 subscription) and assigned it to users who will be scheduling meetings with dial-in options, you're ready to begin configuring conference bridge settings.

By default, your conference bridge settings are configured so that they'll use a shared, regional number depending on users' locations. However, you may wish to create a more local, dedicated number exclusive to your organization. For example, in Kansas City our invite's dial-in number might be the shared Chicago phone number by default but we'll create a phone number with a Kansas City area code instead.

Creating a dedicated, local call-in number

To create a local, dedicated conference bridge call-in number, choose **Voice** > **Phone Numbers** from the left-hand menu of the Microsoft Teams admin center. Then click **Add**.

The first settings screen for new numbers will ask for your location, number type, area code, and quantity as shown in *Figure 9.3*:

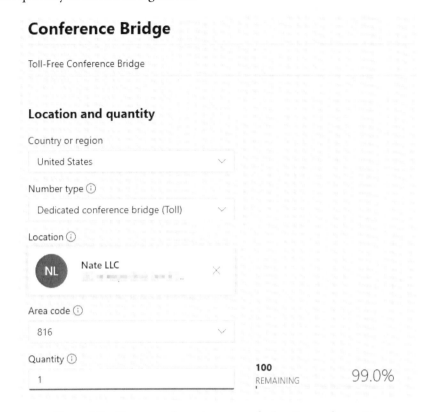

Conference Bridge

Toll-Free Conference Bridge

Location and quantity

Country or region

United States

Number type ⓘ

Dedicated conference bridge (Toll)

Location ⓘ

NL   Nate LLC   ✕

Area code ⓘ

816

Quantity ⓘ

1   **100**
                                          REMAINING   99.0%

Figure 9.3 – Phone number setup screen for location and quantity

If you choose **Toll** for **Number type**, you'll specify a **Location** you've likely already set up previously in the Microsoft Teams admin center. This can be updated in **Locations** > **Emergency addresses** as described in *Chapter 10, Managing Phone Numbers in Microsoft Teams*. There is no additional charge for creating a Toll number type.

If you choose **Toll-Free** it will require that you've set up **Communication Credits** (an additional add-on purchase in the Microsoft 365 admin center). This is essentially an amount of money you fund regularly (automatically or manually) for toll-free number data usage as well as international and other dial-in calling needs.

The second configuration screen for your new number is confirmation of the number order. Click **Place Order** to finalize it.

Now, back on the **Phone numbers** screen, select the new number and choose **Edit**. This is where you'll assign the number as your conference bridge as seen in *Figure 9.4*:

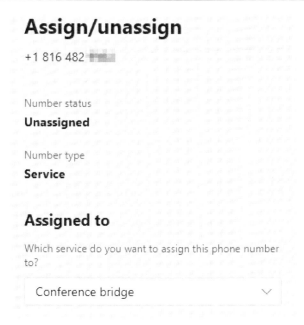

Figure 9.4 – Edit options for a new phone number. This number is being assigned as a conference bridge

So far, we've purchased the Audio Conferencing add-on and assigned it to users whose meetings need dial-in options, then we created and assigned a new phone number as the conference bridge number. That's all you need for those licensed users' Teams meeting invites to include conference bridge dial-in numbers, similar to the example shown in *Figure 9.5*:

Figure 9.5 – An example of a meeting invite sent from a user licensed for Audio Conferencing after you've set up the number and assigned it as a conference bridge

Now let's look at how we can change the dial-in experience.

Changing the conference bridge user experience

To change the user experience when calling into conference bridges, select **Bridge settings** from the **Meetings** > **Conference Bridges** page of the Microsoft Teams admin center. You can configure the following settings:

Setting	Options
Meeting entry and exit notifications	On/Off
Entry/exit announcement type	Names or phone numbers, Tones
Ask callers to record their name before joining a meeting	On/Off
Pin length	Number from 4-12
Automatically send emails to users if their dial-in settings change	On/Off

This is shown in *Figure 9.6*:

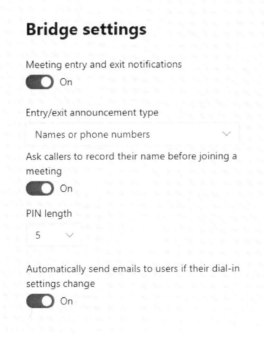

Figure 9.6 – Bridge settings in the Microsoft Teams admin center

This makes it possible to change the experience for different types of calls. For example, you may wish for larger meetings to use a designated conference bridge number that will not have entry/exit notifications to prevent disruption or distraction. Then for smaller groups, you might wish to use a different conference bridge number that has the entry/exit notifications to remain well aware of who is present throughout the more intimate meeting.

Summary

This chapter covered the configuration of settings for Teams meetings as well as meeting policies. These allow us to customize user experiences differently per individual or group. We also explored how to achieve these assignments and policy modifications via PowerShell. We then looked at settings for live events as well as their policies. Through these polices, we are able to change permissions for accessing our live events as well as transcription, scheduling, and recording abilities. Lastly, we reviewed the pre-requisites and setup of conference bridges. We learned that each conference bridge number can have its own unique settings that affect the user experience.

In the next chapter, we'll cover the management of phone numbers in Microsoft Teams.

Questions

As we conclude, here is a list of questions for you to test your knowledge regarding this chapter's material. You will find the answers in the *Assessments* section of the *Appendix*:

1. You need to disallow the usage of the camera during meetings for a subset of your users. Which two actions should you take in the Microsoft Teams admin center?

   a. Modify meeting settings

   b. Create a meeting policy

   c. Assign the policy to the subset of users

   d. Create a setup policy

2. Your security team has required that guests should not be allowed to invite other guests to Teams meetings created in your organization. You create a meeting policy. Could this satisfy the requirement?

   a. Yes

   b. No

3. You want Teams meeting invite emails sent from your organization's users to include a link to a specific help page where users can quickly find support for audio, video, or other Teams meeting-related needs. Where do you configure this setting to include the Help URL in invites?

    a. **Meetings > Meeting settings**

    b. **Meetings > Meeting policies**

    c. **Meetings > Live events settings**

    d. **Teams > Teams policies**

4. Attendees of your organization's live events get the join link from your intranet and not from an email. During the event, attendees may need technical support. Where do you configure the Support URL for live events so it's available to attendees during the event?

    a. **Meetings > Meeting settings**

    b. **Meetings > Meeting policies**

    c. **Meetings > Live events settings**

    d. **Teams > Teams policies**

5. You've been given a requirement that some Microsoft Teams presenters must be able to choose whether or not they record live events. Currently, live events are always recorded automatically for all users. Where do you change this for the presenters?

    a. **Meetings > Live events settings**

    b. **Meetings > Meeting policies**

    c. **Meetings > Live events policies**

    d. **Meetings > Meeting settings**

6. Specific users in your organization shouldn't be allowed to share their entire screen, but rather just one app at a time. Where do you configure this?

    a. **Meetings > Live events settings**

    b. **Meetings > Meeting policies**

    c. **Meetings > Live events policies**

    d. **Meetings > Meeting settings**

7. Your IT administration has said that anonymous users should be prevented from joining Microsoft Teams meetings in your organization. Where is this configured?

    a. **Meetings > Live events settings**

    b. **Meetings > Meeting policies**

    c. **Meetings > Live events policies**

    d. **Meetings > Meeting settings**

8. Your organization is regularly going to have town halls as live events in Teams. The expected attendance will surpass 7,500 attendees. What should be part of your recommendation to decrease bandwidth usage during these regular, large events?

    a. Cap attendance at 5,000

    b. Purchase a third-party SDN/eCDN solution

    c. Purchase a third-party encoder

    d. Create a QoS audio policy

9. Which of the following eCDN providers are NOT pre-integrated with Stream?

    a. Vimeo Enterprise eCDN

    b. Kollective Technology

    c. Hive eCDN

    d. Riverbed

10. A user reports that meeting invites for meetings they've scheduled in Microsoft Teams are being sent without dial-in options/conference bridge information, and users are unable to call in after joining as well. What's the likely cause?

    a. The user isn't licensed for Microsoft Teams

    b. The user isn't licensed for Audio Conferencing

    c. A local, dedicated conference bridge number hasn't been set up

    d. The user isn't licensed for Advanced Communications

Further reading

Here are links to more information on some of the topics that we have covered in this chapter:

- Manage meeting settings in Microsoft Teams: `https://docs.microsoft.com/en-us/microsoftteams/meeting-settings-in-teams`

- Change participant settings for a Teams meeting: `https://support.microsoft.com/en-us/office/change-participant-settings-for-a-teams-meeting-53261366-dbd5-45f9-aae9-a70e6354f88e`

- Meetings in Microsoft Teams: `https://docs.microsoft.com/en-us/microsoftteams/tutorial-meetings-in-teams`

- Schedule a meeting in Teams: `https://support.microsoft.com/en-us/office/schedule-a-meeting-in-teams-943507a9-8583-4c58-b5d2-8ec8265e04e5`

- Manage meeting policies in Teams: `https://docs.microsoft.com/en-us/microsoftteams/meeting-policies-in-teams`

- Limits and specifications for Microsoft Teams: `https://docs.microsoft.com/en-us/microsoftteams/limits-specifications-teams`

- Set-CsTeamsMeetingConfiguration: `https://docs.microsoft.com/en-us/powershell/module/skype/set-csteamsmeetingconfiguration`

- Microsoft Teams PowerShell Overview: `https://docs.microsoft.com/en-us/microsoftteams/teams-powershell-overview`

- Set-CsTeamsMeetingPolicy: `https://docs.microsoft.com/en-us/powershell/module/skype/set-csteamsmeetingpolicy`

- Meetings and conferencing in Microsoft Teams: `https://docs.microsoft.com/en-us/microsoftteams/deploy-meetings-microsoft-teams-landing-page`

- Grant-CsTeamsMeetingPolicy: `https://docs.microsoft.com/en-us/powershell/module/skype/grant-csteamsmeetingpolicy`

- Get started with Microsoft Teams live events: `https://support.microsoft.com/en-us/office/get-started-with-microsoft-teams-live-events-d077fec2-a058-483e-9ab5-1494afda578a`

- Configure live event settings in Microsoft Teams (including Set up event support URL): `https://docs.microsoft.com/en-us/microsoftteams/teams-live-events/configure-teams-live-events`

- Set up for live events in Microsoft Teams: `https://docs.microsoft.com/en-us/microsoftteams/teams-live-events/set-up-for-teams-live-events`

- Prepare your organization's network for Microsoft Teams: `https://docs.microsoft.com/en-us/microsoftteams/prepare-network`

- Change the settings for an Audio Conferencing bridge: `https://docs.microsoft.com/en-us/microsoftteams/change-the-settings-for-an-audio-conferencing-bridge`

- Manage the Audio Conferencing settings for your organization in Microsoft Teams: `https://docs.microsoft.com/en-us/microsoftteams/manage-the-audio-conferencing-settings-for-my-organization-in-teams`

- Set up Audio Conferencing for Microsoft Teams: `https://docs.microsoft.com/en-us/microsoftteams/set-up-audio-conferencing-in-teams`

10

Managing Phone Numbers in Microsoft Teams

This chapter will introduce the principles of enabling Microsoft Teams for **Public Switched Telephone Network (PSTN)** connectivity. You will learn how to choose a PSTN solution, how to order phone numbers, and acquire and manage Teams service numbers, which are toll or toll-free phone numbers for services such as audio conferencing, auto attendants, and call queues. We will show you how to configure your organization's emergency addresses in the Teams admin center, manage the phone numbers that are assigned to users, and configure the voice settings for your users in Microsoft Teams.

In this chapter, we're going to cover the following main topics:

- Choosing a PSTN connectivity solution
- Ordering phone numbers
- Managing service numbers
- Configuring emergency addresses for your organization
- Managing phone numbers for users
- Configuring voice settings for users
- Configuring emergency calling

Technical requirements

In this chapter, you will need to have access to the **Microsoft Teams admin center**, which you can reach at `https://admin.teams.microsoft.com`. You will need to be either a *Global Administrator* or a *Teams Service Administrator* to have full access to the features and capabilities within the Teams admin center.

For the majority of the chapter, you'll need either an Enterprise E5 license or a Business Voice add-on. You'll also need to license users with Phone System licenses (if not included in your current subscription stack) when adding numbers for users. Lastly, depending on your needs and existing subscriptions, you may also need to purchase Communication Credits or a Calling Plan license before a user can make or receive calls. To make these sorts of purchases, you'll need to be a *Global Administrator*.

Choosing a PSTN connectivity solution

There are a few configurations available for your PSTN connectivity solution. PSTN allows your users to make calls outside your company to any number in the world.

The easiest telephony solution to implement with Microsoft Teams is **Microsoft 365 Business Voice**. This is a cloud-based solution in which Microsoft is your PSTN carrier and provides **Private Branch Exchange** (**PBX**) capabilities so your users can make calls within the organization as well as globally. Microsoft 365 Business Voice is available as a separate add-on subscription but limited to 300 users or is included in Microsoft 365 E5 subscriptions (300 or more users).

As for your complete solution, all organizations will require Phone System (included in Business Voice). For connectivity to PSTN for global calling, you can choose Microsoft for the carrier or connect your existing carrier with Direct Routing.

Microsoft supports different configurations that might work better for certain geographies and business structures. At its simplest, you're choosing **Phone System** (base) with either **Calling Plan** (simplest infrastructure deployment) or **Direct Routing** (for existing on-premises carrier solution integration). Your options include the following:

- Phone System with Calling Plan (easiest if Calling Plan is available in your region; you don't need to keep your current PSTN provider, and you want Microsoft to manage your organization's access to the PSTN)

- Phone System with your current PSTN provider with Direct Routing for the integration of your on-premises environment with Teams

- A combination solution of Phone System with Calling Plan and Phone System with Direct Routing

If you're looking for the simplest deployment, you should choose Phone System with Calling Plan. But if you need to use SIP trunks from your current provider, connect a supported **Session Border Controller** (**SBC**) or analog devices, or integrate a certain number range from your on-premises IP-PBX, you'll want to use Direct Routing. Direct Routing can be set up with your own SBC or a hosted solution in which the carrier sets up and manages the SBC.

In the event that you have an on-premises deployment with Direct Routing, you'll likely be interested in configuring voice routing policies as well.

Voice routing policies

Voice routing policies allow calls to be sent to specific SBCs and only apply if you have an on-premises telecom deployment/direct routing. The policy can be set to base the routing on the called number pattern alone, or the pattern and the user who makes the call.

The entire process of implementing voice routing policies can be thought of in four basic steps that can all be done in the Microsoft Teams admin center:

1. Add an SBC.
2. Create a PSTN usage.
3. Configure voice routes.
4. Create and assign a voice routing policy.

Now let's learn in more depth about these four basic steps.

Adding an SBC

If you don't already have any SBCs added, you'll need to do this from the Microsoft Teams admin center (`https://admin.teams.microsoft.com`). Select **Voice** > **Direct Routing**, then select **Add** from the SBC tab you're on by default.

SBCs need a **Fully Qualified Domain Name** (**FQDN**) and have several settings for you to configure. As these likely won't come up on the MS-700 exam, we've just provided a screenshot of the SBC configuration options in *Figure 10.1*:

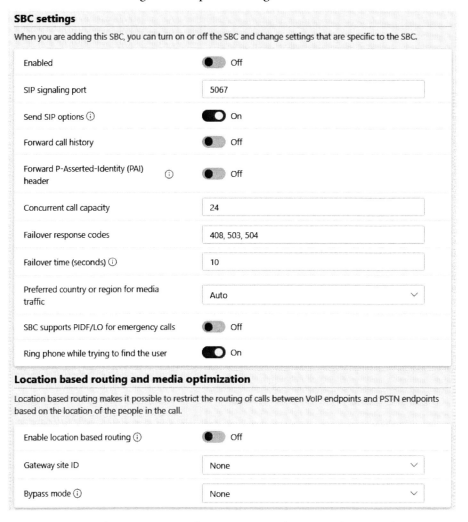

Figure 10.1 – Configuration options for a new SBC in the Microsoft Teams admin center

Once you have at least one SBC added, you can continue to the next step, creating a PSTN usage.

Creating a PSTN usage

From the Microsoft Teams admin center (`https://admin.teams.microsoft.com`), select **Voice** > **Direct Routing**, then **Manage PSTN usage records** from the upper-right corner.

Click **Add**, give the record a name (such as a region, perhaps), and then click **Apply**, as shown in *Figure 10.2*:

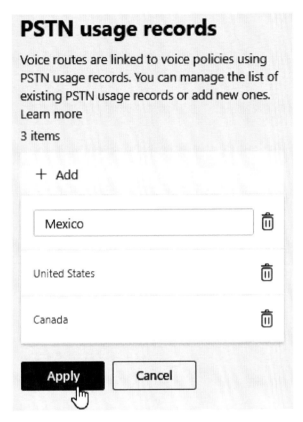

Figure 10.2 – A PSTN usage record for Mexico being added

Next, let's configure voice routes.

Configuring voice routes

From the Microsoft Teams admin center (`https://admin.teams.microsoft.com`), select **Voice** > **Direct Routing**, then select the **Voice routes** tab.

Click **Add** and begin by giving the route a name and description (for a city or section, perhaps).

The rest of the voice route configuration page has the following configuration options:

Settings	Options
Priority (if the pattern matches multiple routes, which should be tried first?)	Numeric value.
Dialed number pattern	Regular expression.
SBCs enrolled	Select/add SBCs to which you'll route calls for this voice route. Those that you add to this route will be tried in random order.
PSTN usage records	Add usage record(s) you created previously in the first step. These can be ordered.

Now we're ready to create the actual policy.

Creating and assigning a voice routing policy

Now that we have our SBC, usage record, and route set up, we can create the policy that will be assigned to specific users. We'll do this from **Voice** > **Voice routing policies**. Click **Add**, then enter your new voice routing policy's name and description. Lastly, add the PSTN usage records you wish to be used by the users to whom this policy will apply.

Click **Save** when finished, then apply the policy as you do with all other Teams policies (by using the policy page assign/unassign option, or by using the **Users** node with bulk policy updates).

Let's next look at how we order phone numbers for usage in Microsoft Teams.

Ordering phone numbers

When ordering numbers, you may be doing so for users, service numbers, or audio conferencing purposes (as shown in the previous chapter, *Chapter 9, Managing Meetings and Live Events in Microsoft Teams*). There are three ways you might add new or existing numbers to your Microsoft Teams deployment:

- Add *new* numbers via the Microsoft Teams admin center (restricted to certain countries and regions).

- Port *existing* numbers.

- Use a request form for *new or existing* numbers (for those countries/regions unsupported by ordering via the Teams admin center or organizations that are otherwise unable to complete their order via the Teams admin center).

You can order different types of numbers via the Teams admin center. They're either **Toll** (user pays for call cost via their own phone plan) or **Toll Free** (you prepay for usage). You can choose from the following options:

- **User (subscriber)**: Regular user numbers. Requires a Phone System license for each user.

- **Dedicated conference bridge (Toll)**: Allows dial-in capabilities for meetings. Requires a Business Voice subscription.

- **Dedicated conference bridge (Toll Free)**: Allows dial-in capabilities for meetings. Requires a Business Voice subscription.

- **Call queue (Toll)**: Used on resource accounts for call queue. Requires a Business Voice subscription.

- **Call queue (Toll Free)**: Used on resource accounts for call queue. Requires a Business Voice subscription.

- **Auto attendant (Toll)**: Assigned to a resource account. Requires a Business Voice subscription.

- **Auto attendant (Toll Free)**: Assigned to a resource account. Requires a Business Voice subscription.

Let's review the steps for placing an order for new user numbers.

Adding numbers via the Teams admin center

This is the easiest and fastest method of adding numbers for your users if you don't need to use existing numbers. You will need a Phone System license assigned to each user receiving a number, and either Calling Plan or Communication Credits licenses assigned to them before they'll be able to make or receive PSTN calls.

To purchase numbers for users specifically, follow these steps:

1. Go to the Teams admin center at `https://admin.teams.microsoft.com`.

2. Choose **Voice** > **Phone numbers** from the left-hand menu.

3. Click **Add**.

4. Enter a name and description for the order.

5. Complete the order fields:

    a. Fill in **Country or region** (drop-down selection).

    b. Choose **User (subscriber)** for **Number type** (not available in all regions).

    c. Under **Location**, select a location or create a new one.

    d. Based on the location, you'll choose an appropriate area code for the next field, **Area code**.

    e. Enter a quantity of numbers to purchase (limited to your subscription's max), then click **Next** to select your specific numbers.

6. Select your numbers and complete the order (click **Place Order**) within 10 minutes of having clicked **Next** in *step 5*, or the numbers are returned to the available pool of numbers.

Figure 10.3 shows the previously mentioned fields completed for *steps 1-5*:

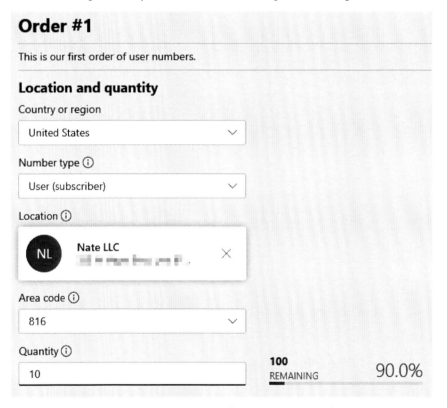

Figure 10.3 – A new number order form in the Teams admin center

Next, we'll look at how to port your existing numbers.

Porting/transferring existing numbers

Porting numbers starts similarly to how you order new numbers via the Teams admin center. For countries/regions not eligible to submit via Teams, see the next sub-section on manually submitting a request. Otherwise, to port your numbers, follow these steps:

1. Go to the Teams admin center at `https://admin.teams.microsoft.com`.

2. Choose **Voice** > **Phone numbers** from the left-hand menu.

3. Click **Port**.

There are several notices and conditions that must be acknowledged before continuing. They are as follows:

- You need your account information from your current service provider for the phone numbers you are trying to transfer.

- Don't disconnect or cancel any of the phone numbers with your current provider.

- All of your phone numbers being transferred must all be from the same service provider.

- You can't transfer phone numbers for broadband lines that are used for the internet or dedicated numbers used for faxing.

- The transfer date is controlled by your current service provider and is set by them.

- To continue with your porting request, you must sign and upload a **Letter of Authorization** (**LOA**).

- All numbers must be submitted using the E.164 format.

After reviewing these and meeting each of them (where applicable), continue with these steps:

1. Click **Next**.

2. Complete the order fields, choosing **Geographic** and **Users** for fields b and c:

   a. Fill in **Country or region** (drop-down selection).

   b. You can choose either **Geographic** or **Toll free** for **Type of phone numbers**.

    c. Next, you can choose **Users**, **Voice features**, or **Conferencing features** for **Numbers assigned to**. Your options in this dropdown depend on your selection in the previous field, b: **Type of phone numbers**:

    i) **Geographic** allows the selection of **Users**, **Voice features**, and **Conferencing features**.

    ii) **Toll free** applies to just **Voice features** and **Conferencing features**.

3. Click **Next**.

4. Name your port order.

5. Add **Notification emails** (who should be kept informed of order progress?).

6. Choose **Desired transfer date and time** (knowing it's just a preference and will depend on your current provider's chosen date).

7. For **Port Type**, choose **All of your numbers** or **Some of your numbers**.

8. Then, enter the relevant contact details for **Authorizing person on account**.

9. Next, enter your current service address and carrier details, including your **Billing Telephone Number** (**BTN**).

10. Click **Next**.

11. Upload your existing numbers as a CSV file with a single column named **PhoneNumber**. The numbers listed must match the requested country/region selected in *step 5*, and at least one of the numbers must be the BTN specified in *step 12*.

12. Click **Next**.

13. Upload an LOA. You can download a template for this step, complete it, then upload it. It must be signed by a person who can make changes to the account.

14. Once your LOA is uploaded, click **Submit**. Microsoft will contact your current provider to continue and complete the process of porting.

> **Important note**
>
> You can only have a single active porting request for each BTN (entered in *Step 12*). If you have multiple requests for the same BTN, porting the numbers won't work.

Lastly, we'll review the steps involved for countries and regions that aren't listed in either of the previous two methods' **Country or region** dropdowns.

Requesting numbers or transfers by PDF form

If your country or region is not listed under **Country or region**, or you were otherwise unsuccessful in ordering or porting numbers using the Microsoft Teams admin center, you can still order new or transfer existing numbers by manually completing your request via PDF and submitting it to Microsoft:

1. Go to `https://docs.microsoft.com/en-us/MicrosoftTeams/manage-phone-numbers-for-your-organization/`.

2. Select your country from the drop-down menu in the first section.

3. Find the action you're attempting to complete (order new, transfer existing, change a user to service, and so on) and follow the steps unique to your country or region listed in the table. Your specific actions will likely involve downloading and completing a form(s) and sending it to a provided Microsoft address.

> **Important note**
>
> LOAs are required if you have any of the following being ported to Microsoft from another provider: users, services (toll), audio conference bridges, auto attendants, call queues, and toll-free numbers. You'll also need an LOA completed and uploaded if requesting more than 999 user numbers and the Microsoft Teams admin center's porting wizard isn't working for them.

In the next section, we'll review the management of service numbers.

Managing service numbers

As mentioned earlier in this chapter, there are several types of numbers you can order via the Teams admin center. In addition to user (subscriber), there are service types such as call queues and auto attendants. We'll take a closer look at these non-user number types in this section (not conference bridges, as that was covered in *Chapter 9, Managing Meetings and Live Events in Microsoft Teams*).

As a reminder, you can order **Toll** (user pays for call cost via their own phone plan) or **Toll Free** (you prepay for usage) service numbers. We'll specifically focus on call queues and auto attendants:

- **Call queue (Toll)**: Used on resource accounts for call queue. Requires a Business Voice subscription.

- **Call queue (Toll Free)**: Used on resource accounts for call queue. Requires a Business Voice subscription.

- **Auto attendant (Toll)**: Assigned to a resource account. Requires a Business Voice subscription.

- **Auto attendant (Toll Free)**: Assigned to a resource account. Requires a Business Voice subscription.

As with users in the previous section, you can port/transfer existing service numbers following the same steps. You can also order new, again following the same order processes mentioned previously. In *Chapter 11*, *Managing Phone System in Microsoft Teams*, we'll take a closer look at the features of the two service options we haven't yet covered: call queues and auto attendants.

In the next section, we'll configure the emergency addresses associated with phone numbers in our organization.

Configuring emergency addresses for your organization

Emergency addresses are associated with phone numbers in your organization so that emergency first responders can receive accurate location information for the phone numbers you've deployed to users in your organization.

You can (and should) create multiple emergency addresses so that you have one for each office location to which you're deploying associate phone numbers.

To create an emergency address, go to the Teams admin center at `https://admin.teams.microsoft.com` and select **Locations** > **Emergency addresses** from the left-hand menu. You might already see a default location added for the one you used when setting up your tenant. To create a new address, click **Add**.

For each emergency address, you'll name it and specify the location by lookup or manual entry as seen in *Figure 10.4*:

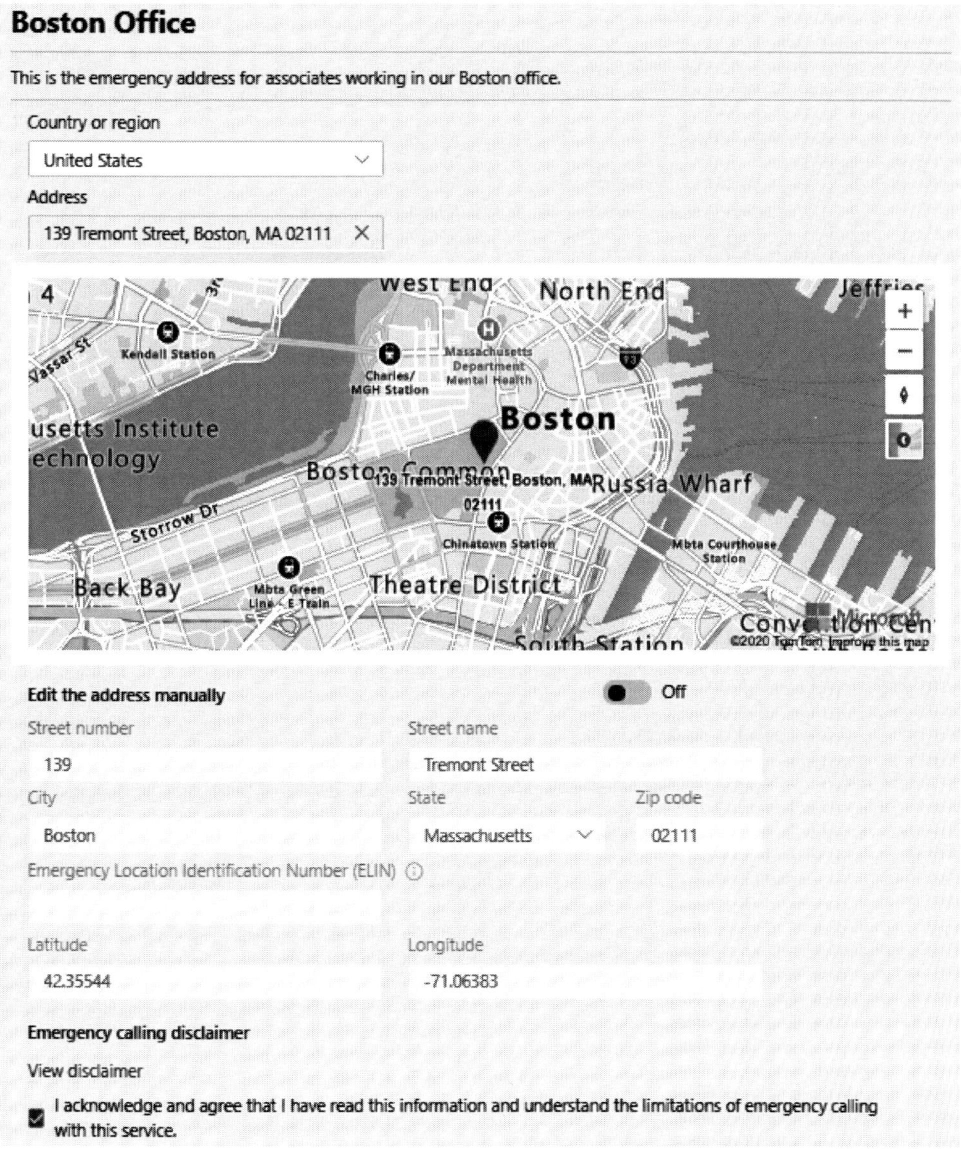
Boston Office
This is the emergency address for associates working in our Boston office.
Country or region
United States
Address
139 Tremont Street, Boston, MA 02111
West End
North End
Kendall Station
Charles/ MGH Station
Massachusetts Department Mental Health
Boston
Boston Common
139 Tremont Street, Boston, MA 02111
Russia Wharf
Chinatown Station
Mbta Courthouse Station
Storrow Dr
Back Bay
Mbta Green Line - E Train
Theatre District
©2020 TomTom Improve this map
Edit the address manually
Off
Street number
139
Street name
Tremont Street
City
Boston
State
Massachusetts
Zip code
02111
Emergency Location Identification Number (ELIN)
Latitude
42.35544
Longitude
-71.06383
Emergency calling disclaimer
View disclaimer
I acknowledge and agree that I have read this information and understand the limitations of emergency calling with this service.

Figure 10.4 – A new emergency address being created in the Teams admin center

As part of setting up a new emergency address, you'll be required to acknowledge and urged to share the following disclaimer with all users of the emergency calling service:

IMPORTANT INFORMATION

Emergency Services calling operates differently with this service than on traditional telephone services. It is important that you understand these differences and communicate them to all users of this service. You acknowledge and agree that you have read and understand the differences in our Emergency Services calling and will provide this notice to each user of this service. The differences in our Emergency Services calling capabilities include the following:

1. the service may not know the actual location of a caller making an Emergency Services call, which could result in the call being routed to the wrong Emergency Services call center and/or emergency services being dispatched to the wrong location;

2. if the user's device has no power, is experiencing a power outage or, for any reason, cannot otherwise access the Internet, the user cannot make an Emergency Services call through the service; and

3. although this service can be used anywhere in the world where an Internet connection is available, users should not make an Emergency Services call from a location outside their home country because the call likely will not be routed to the appropriate call center in that country.

After creating an emergency address, it can be used to order new numbers and (more importantly, as it pertains to this section) assign emergency locations to specific phone numbers. An emergency address also *can't be changed once it's been validated*. It will need to be deleted and recreated.

An emergency address can have more specific places within the address, such as buildings on campus, floors of a building, and so on, to be more specific and helpful to first responders. To customize an existing emergency address, you'll select its name from the **Locations** > **Emergency addresses** screen.

Each top-level emergency address (or location) can have the following:

- Places (more specific locations within an address)
- Voice users
- Subnets
- Wi-Fi access points
- Switches
- Ports

All of these additional data points are used elsewhere in Teams administration, except for places, which can be used as more specific emergency addresses associated with phone numbers.

Each place within a location can also have the following:

- Voice users
- Subnets
- Wi-Fi access points
- Switches
- Ports

Again, these are used elsewhere in Teams administration, but not for emergency purposes.

As shown in *Figure 10.5*, each user type phone number (**Voice** > **Phone numbers** in the Teams admin center) can be assigned to a user and have its own **Emergency location** setting, which may differ from the location used to order the number originally. For example, you may order 10 numbers for Kansas City, Missouri but you may have four more specific emergency locations created in the Teams admin center for your four different Kansas City offices to which users will be assigned. And inside each unique address, you can add unique places as seen in *Figure 10.5,* where the single Boston address has two more specific places to choose from within it:

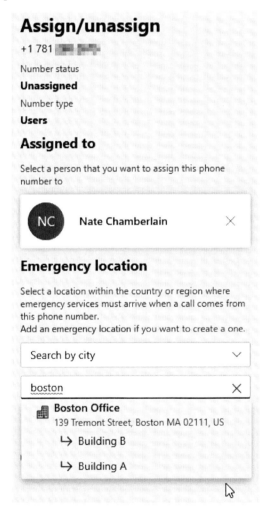

Figure 10.5 – A phone number's settings, showing it is assigned to Nate Chamberlain and options to set a specific place within an emergency address as that number's emergency location

Next, we'll cover managing phone numbers for users in the Teams admin center.

Managing phone numbers for users

So far in this chapter, we've already covered ordering numbers and setting up service numbers with resource accounts and voice apps (such as call queues and auto attendants). This section will focus specifically on managing user type phone numbers and assigning them to users. Note that we can only manage numbers we got from Microsoft and not those assigned via Direct Routing.

To view your user type phone numbers, go to the Teams admin center (`https://admin.teams.microsoft.com`) and select **Voice** > **Phone numbers** from the left-hand menu. Here, you'll see all phone numbers in your organization that have been ordered or ported.

Assigning phone numbers to users

You can assign phone numbers to users in the Teams admin center by either going to **Voice** > **Phone numbers** or **Users**.

The more straightforward method might be selecting a user from the Teams admin center **Users** page, then updating the user's **General information** settings and assigning an available number as shown in *Figure 10.6*:

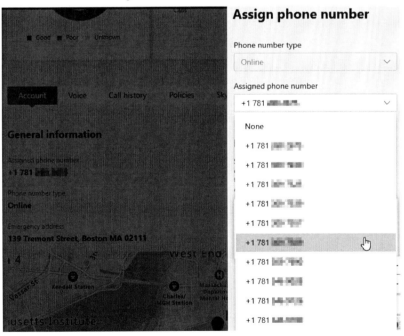

Figure 10.6 – The General information side panel for choosing a user's phone number from available, unassigned user type phone numbers

From **Voice** > **Phone numbers**, you can also view unassigned phone numbers by clicking the filter icon and setting **Status** to equal **Unassigned**, as seen in *Figure 10.7*. Click **Apply** and you'll be looking at only the numbers available to be assigned to users and service accounts:

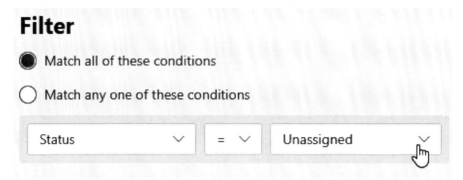

Figure 10.7 – Phone number list filter set to only show unassigned numbers

Since as of the writing of this book there isn't a filter for **Number type**, you'll want to just keep an eye on the **Number type** column to see whether the unassigned number is of the **User** type or not.

From there, just select a number and choose **Edit**. Then, you can assign the number to a user and choose that number's emergency location.

Releasing/deleting a phone number

Releasing a phone number back to Microsoft's pool of available phone numbers for order is straightforward. You must first unassign it if it is assigned (edit the number's settings from **Voice** > **Phone numbers** and delete the assignment). Then, simply select the number and click **Release** from the menu.

Now, let's configure voice settings for users.

Configuring voice settings for users

In this section, we'll review possibilities for changing the Teams user voice experience.

One of the most essential settings for voice solutions is **voicemail**. For cloud-only solutions, voicemail is automatically set up for users once they're assigned a Phone System user license. Voicemail includes transcription (voice-to-text) by default as well.

Users may wish to perform a number of administrative actions for their voicemail and phone line that you won't need to do for them as an administrator, but it might be helpful to know about it. These actions are done from the Teams client by individual users and include the following:

- Adding and removing delegates (**Profile picture** > **Settings** > **General** > **Delegation**)
- Changing audio device settings (**Profile picture** > **Settings** > **Devices**)
- Making a test call (**Profile picture** > **Settings** > **Devices** > **Make a test call**)
- Call answering rules (**Profile picture** > **Settings** > **Calls**)
- Voicemail settings (**Profile picture** > **Settings** > **Calls** > **Voicemail**)

Figure 10.8 shows the **Calls** settings dialog, which users can configure for themselves. This specific figure shows the settings for call forwarding, simultaneous, or chain ringing, as well as voicemail configuration and ringtones:

Figure 10.8 – Calls settings for an individual Teams user

There are several opportunities in the Microsoft Teams admin center's **Voice** node where admins can create policies that enhance and change the Teams user experience for calls as well. In addition to caller ID, calling, and call park policies (all covered in *Chapter 11, Managing Phone System in Microsoft Teams*), you can configure dial plans to enhance the user experience and save users time dialing.

Dial plans

Dial plans are sets of rules that can convert partial dial pad entries into a standard (E.164) phone number format. E.164 is the international public telecommunication numbering plan, or international standard, that is used globally and ensures that every number worldwide is unique.

We want to use a dial plan to make our users' dialing experiences as simple as possible while still utilizing full E.164 format numbers. For example, when users dial 700 from within your organization, it could direct them to the Help Desk. Another common example is letting users dial within the organization just by the extension (the last 3-4 digits of assigned numbers). You could pair this with a dial plan setting that requires a **9** to be dialed before users can dial an external number so it doesn't attempt to translate a full, external number into an extension translation.

Dial plans can be configured with the following settings:

Setting	Options
External dialing prefix	1-4 digits
Optimized device dialing	On/Off
Normalization rules	A section where translation details are specified, such as completing the internal number only if an extension is entered

The plan configuration page also includes a section where you can test the dial plan by entering a number and seeing how it performs based on the rules and details configured in the plan. Before you can use the test feature, you have to save and return to editing the plan.

You can have multiple normalization rules per dial plan. For each normalization rule within the plan, you can configure it as basic or advanced.

Basic normalization rules are best for those unfamiliar with regular expressions and include the following configuration options (where X represents an integer):

Settings	Options
Name	Text
Description	Text
Basic/Advanced	(set to Basic in this table)
If all selected conditions match	The number dialed begins with X and/or the length of the number being dialed is exactly or at least X.
Then do this	Remove X digits from the start and/or add X to the beginning (such as "+1816").
Test this rule (optional)	Enter a dial pad entry to see if the rule fires and how it translates the entry if so.

Advanced normalization rules use regular expressions and include the following configuration options.

In *Figure 10.9*, you can see an advanced normalization rule being created that will allow 4-digit dialing, automatically translating the extension to a full number:

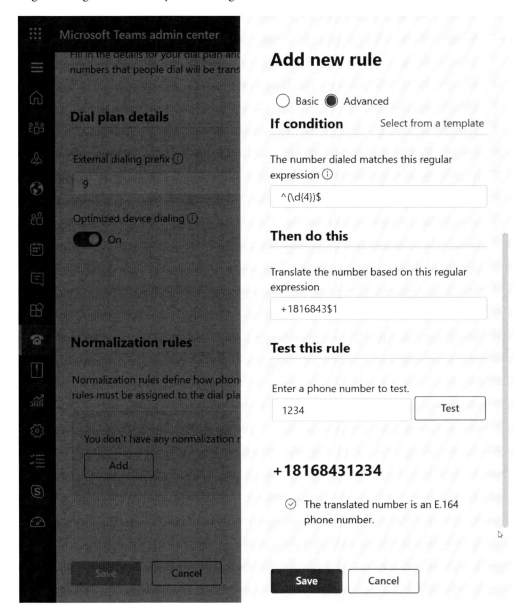

Figure 10.9 – A normalization rule in progress that translates a 4-digit dialpad entry into a full E.164 number

As with other Teams policies, you can create dial plans using PowerShell (though there are certainly more parameters to deal with given the inclusion of normalization rules). The cmdlet for creating a new dial plan is `New-CsTenantDialPlan` and an example of doing this might be as follows:

```
New-CsTenantDialPlan -Identity ExternalDialing -Description
"Dial Plan for External Calling"  -ExternalAccessPrefix 9
-OptimizeDeviceDialing $true -SimpleName "Dial-Plan-for-
External-Calls"
```

> **Important note**
> Optimized device dialing must be enabled if configuring an external dialing prefix.

Lastly, let's cover emergency calling.

Configuring emergency calling

In the Teams admin center, you'll find **Emergency policies** in the left-hand menu under **Voice**. There are two types we'll cover in this section:

- Emergency calling policies
- Emergency call routing policies

As with other Teams policies, your tenant comes with a default, global policy for each type that can either be customized or supplemented by additional, custom policies. Also, as with other policies, a user can have a maximum of one policy per type applied to them at any one time.

We'll start with reviewing emergency calling policies.

Emergency calling policies

Emergency calling policies specify the emergency numbers for Direct Routing and then the actions that occur when a call to one of those numbers is made, such as notifications to a security team in your organization.

These calling policies specify who in the organization call routing policies apply to.

Emergency call routing policies

Emergency call routing policies control how users can use dynamic calling features. These policies can have the following settings configured:

Setting	Options
Dynamic emergency calling	On/Off
Emergency numbers	Emergency numbers your users might use, such as 911, 999, 112, and so on.

If you enable dynamic emergency calling, users to whom the policy is applied will be able to use emergency call routing features when they move from one location to another.

Summary

This chapter was all about phone numbers in Microsoft Teams. We began by choosing a PSTN solution for our telephony needs.

Then, we ordered and managed our phone numbers and service numbers. We learned that users need their own Calling Plan license or Communication Credits licenses assigned, and that we can create audio conferencing, auto attendant, or call queue service numbers.

Then, we configured emergency addresses to associate with our user phone numbers, so that when our users call from our environment, that address information can be made available to responders.

After that, we covered the management of user phone numbers and configured voice settings for users such as voicemail configuration and dial plans to help us transform abbreviated entries, such as extensions, into full phone numbers.

Lastly, we learned about emergency calling policies and call routing policies.

In the next chapter, we'll be looking at managing Phone System in Microsoft Teams.

Questions

This chapter's practice questions will consist of a scenario with three associated questions all related to that single scenario (*Question set 1*). The remaining seven questions will all be multiple-choice questions (*Question set 2*).

Question set 1

You must choose PSTN connectivity solutions for your organization's international deployments. You currently have offices in Sweden, Denmark, and the United States. When implementing Phone System at each, you must consider the following:

- You must minimize the work and required infrastructure for your new Sweden office.

- Denmark needs to use the analog devices they currently have, as well as the existing SIP trunks provided by a pre-existing carrier.

- The United States office needs to integrate the existing phone number range and their on-premises PBX.

What do you suggest for each? Choose either Calling Plans or Direct Routing for each:

1. Sweden's office:

   a. Calling Plans

   b. Direct Routing

2. Denmark's office:

   a. Calling Plans

   b. Direct Routing

3. The United States' office:

   a. Calling Plans

   b. Direct Routing

Question set 2

1. A user type phone number can be assigned to more than one user. True or false?

    a. True

    b. False

2. You want to make sure that emergency responders have the correct address for emergency calls made from one of your offices. What should you do to make sure phone numbers associated with a certain address are providing the correct information automatically to emergency services when called, and not just your headquarters' address?

    a. Create and assign a calling policy to each affected user.

    b. Create and assign a configuration profile to each affected user.

    c. Add an emergency address for the office, then update each user's profile to use it.

    d. Add an emergency address for the office, then update each phone number to use it.

3. You have an on-premises telecom solution and need to direct calls to specific SBCs for certain users. What do you create?

    a. Caller ID policy

    b. Call park policy

    c. Calling policy

    d. Voice routing policy

4. Rather than having users dial entire numbers within your organization, you want them to be able to just dial a 4-digit extension internally and dial 9 before a full number to dial externally. What do you create?

    a. Dial plan

    b. Call park policy

    c. Calling policy

    d. Voice routing policy

5. Voicemail is set up automatically when a cloud-only organization's user is assigned a Phone System user license. True or false?

    a. True

    b. False

6. Only an admin can set up a user's phone delegation settings. True or false?

    a. True

    b. False

7. You're setting up emergency locations for your tenant. You have two cities with offices, and three buildings on each city's campus. How should you add these locations to the Microsoft Teams admin center?

    a. Six locations

    b. Two locations with three places each

    c. Six locations with one place each

    d. Two locations with three subnets each

Further reading

Here are links to more information on some of the topics that we have covered in this chapter:

- Plan your Teams voice solution: `https://docs.microsoft.com/en-us/microsoftteams/cloud-voice-landing-page`

- Microsoft telephony solutions: `https://docs.microsoft.com/en-us/skypeforbusiness/hybrid/msft-telephony-solutions`

- What is Phone System?: `https://docs.microsoft.com/en-us/MicrosoftTeams/what-is-phone-system-in-office-365`

- Phone System Direct Routing: `https://docs.microsoft.com/en-us/MicrosoftTeams/direct-routing-landing-page`

- Getting phone numbers for your users: `https://docs.microsoft.com/en-us/microsoftteams/getting-phone-numbers-for-your-users`

- Getting service phone numbers: `https://docs.microsoft.com/en-us/microsoftteams/getting-service-phone-numbers`

- Phone numbers for Audio Conferencing in Microsoft Teams: `https://docs.microsoft.com/en-us/microsoftteams/phone-numbers-for-audio-conferencing-in-teams`

- Manage phone numbers for your organization: `https://docs.microsoft.com/en-us/microsoftteams/manage-phone-numbers-for-your-organization/manage-phone-numbers-for-your-organization`

- Add, change, or remove an emergency location for your organization: `https://docs.microsoft.com/en-us/microsoftteams/add-change-remove-emergency-location-organization`

- Add, change, or remove a place for an emergency location in your organization: `https://docs.microsoft.com/en-us/microsoftteams/add-change-remove-emergency-place-organization`

- Assign, change, or remove a phone number for a user: `https://docs.microsoft.com/en-us/microsoftteams/assign-change-or-remove-a-phone-number-for-a-user`

- Understand calling in Microsoft Teams: `https://docs.microsoft.com/en-us/microsoftteams/tutorial-calling-in-teams`

- Manage voice mail settings for a user in Exchange Online: `https://docs.microsoft.com/en-us/exchange/voice-mail-unified-messaging/set-up-voice-mail/manage-voice-mail-settings`

- Set up Cloud Voicemail: `https://docs.microsoft.com/en-us/microsoftteams/set-up-phone-system-voicemail`

- Manage audio settings in a Teams meeting: `https://support.microsoft.com/en-us/office/manage-audio-settings-in-a-teams-meeting-6ea36f9a-827b-47d6-b22e-ec94d5f0f5e4`

- Calling policies in Microsoft Teams: `https://docs.microsoft.com/en-us/microsoftteams/teams-calling-policy`

11
Managing Phone System in Microsoft Teams

In this chapter, we will explain the principles of managing Phone System within Microsoft Teams. You will learn how to manage resource accounts, which may be required for call queues, and configure auto attendants. We will also demonstrate how to set up policies to control the behavior of features such as call park, calling, and caller IDs in Microsoft Teams. Finally, we will show you how to access and interpret Health Dashboard for Direct Routing, which allows you to monitor connections between your session border controllers and the Direct Routing interface.

In this chapter, we're going to cover the following main topics:

- Managing resource accounts
- Creating and managing call queues
- Creating and managing auto attendants
- Managing call park, calling, and caller ID policies
- Understanding and accessing Health Dashboard for Direct Routing

Technical requirements

In this chapter you will need to have access to the **Microsoft Teams admin center**, which you can reach at `https://admin.teams.microsoft.com`. You will need to be either a *Global Administrator* or a *Teams Service Administrator* to have full access to the features and capabilities within the Teams admin center.

To create resource accounts, you'll need a phone system license. Call queues and auto attendants will also need to be assigned Phone System – Virtual User licenses (these are free).

Managing resource accounts

Resource accounts are Azure **Active Directory** (**AD**) objects (specifically disabled user objects) that can have phone numbers assigned to them. These could be for conference rooms, call queues, auto attendants, equipment, and so on.

When working with Teams, we will use resource accounts specifically for our call queues and auto attendants. Having a resource account designated for these allows us to assign call queues and auto attendant phone numbers. We'll cover the setup of call queues and auto attendants in detail later in this chapter.

First, let's look at the process of creating a new resource account.

Creating and editing a resource account

To create a resource account, do the following:

1. Go to the Microsoft Teams admin center at `https://admin.teams.microsoft.com`.

2. Select **Org-wide settings** > **Resource accounts** from the left-hand menu.

3. Click **Add**.

4. Provide the following information for the new resource account:

   Display name (how it'll show up in Azure AD and lookups).

   Username (for instance, `AutoHelpDesk@contoso.com`).

   Resource account type (how it will be used). This can be **Auto attendant** or **Call queue**.

5. Click **Save**.

Later, you can edit your resource account by repeating *Steps 1-2* and selecting the display name of the account you wish to edit. You can only edit some settings if the account is currently not assigned to a voice application (a call queue or an auto attendant). If it's assigned to something, you'll need to unassign the resource account, make changes, and then reassign it.

> **Tip**
> Once created, you cannot edit a resource account's username in the Microsoft Teams admin center. You can only modify the display name and resource account type if the account is unassigned, and you can also change the phone number type and assignment.

You can also create resource accounts using PowerShell.

Creating a resource account using PowerShell

The Skype for Business PowerShell module's cmdlet for creating a new resource account is New-CsOnlineApplicationInstance. This is paired with one of two application IDs that indicate whether **Resource account type** is **Auto attendant** or **Call queue**. They are as follows:

- Auto attendant: ce933385-9390-45d1-9512-c8d228074e07

- Call queue: 11cd3e2e-fccb-42ad-ad00-878b93575e07

Here's an example of using this cmdlet with an application ID to provision a new resource account:

```
New-CsOnlineApplicationInstance -UserPrincipalName
AutoHelpDesk@contoso.com -ApplicationId "ce933385-9390-45d1-
9512-c8d228074e07" -DisplayName "Auto Attendant - Help Desk"
```

Now let's assign a phone number to our new resource account.

Assigning a phone number to a resource account

Once your account is created, you can assign a phone number to it that will be used to reach the call queue or auto attendant associated with the account. To assign or unassign a phone number, follow these steps:

1. Go to the Microsoft Teams admin center at `https://admin.teams.microsoft.com`.

2. Select **Org-wide settings** > **Resource accounts** from the left-hand menu.

3. Select the display name of an existing resource account.

4. Click **Assign/unassign**.

5. Select options for each of the settings:

   a. Choose a **Phone number type** option (**None**, **Online**, **Toll-free**, or **On-premises**).

   b. For **Assigned phone number**, choose an available phone number to associate with the account. If none is available, you may need to get additional numbers of the correct type (auto attendant or call queue). See *Chapter 10, Managing Phone Numbers in Microsoft Teams*, for assistance.

   c. If you already have your auto attendant set up, you can assign it under **Select an auto attendant** here as well.

6. Click **Save**.

You'll want to make sure a license is assigned to the resource account (use the free Phone System – Virtual User license) before it can be used.

To unassign numbers, simply repeat *Steps 1-4* and remove the assigned number from the settings.

Assigning/unassigning Direct Routing numbers to/from resource accounts

You will need to use PowerShell when assigning a Direct Routing (on-premises) number to a resource account (see *Chapter 10, Managing Phone Numbers in Microsoft Teams*, for more information on Direct Routing). You could accomplish this by using the following cmdlet and parameters, for example:

```
Set-CsOnlineApplicationInstance -Identity AutoHelpDesk@contoso.
com -OnpremPhoneNumber +11234567890
```

To unassign a Direct Routing number, you'd use something similar to the following:

```
Set-CsOnlineApplicationInstance -Identity  AutoHelpDesk@
contoso.com -OnpremPhoneNumber ""
```

Next, we'll cover deleting a resource account.

Deleting a resource account

Before a resource account can be deleted, you must first unassign any numbers assigned to it. Once unassociated with a service number, you can delete the resource account from the **Users** node of the Microsoft Teams admin center as you would with a user.

In the next sections, we'll be covering call queues and auto attendants, which can be associated with resource accounts.

Creating and managing call queues

Before we create a call queue or auto attendant, there are steps that need to be taken to make the process simple. Let's look at those steps first.

Preparing to create and manage call queues and auto attendants

Before you can use call queues and auto attendants, you must follow these steps:

1. You must have purchased or transferred the phone numbers to be used.

2. You'll then need a resource account created in Azure AD for each of the lines (both queues and auto attendants). A resource account can be assigned more than one service number if needed.

3. Each resource account for call queues and auto attendants must be assigned a Phone System – Virtual User license, and each user who will receive calls from a call queue must have a calling plan.

4. Next, you'll create the holidays your auto attendants should be aware of for off-hours call handling.

5. You may choose to also configure call park and retrieval if you wish to implement that in your solution.

6. Create the groups (security, distribution list, team membership, or M365 group) to be used in call handling, such as a team for Service Desk members who will answer call queue calls (this is optional, as you can directly assign individual members if you wish).

7. If you're allowing dial-by-extension, you'll need to make sure each user to be reached by extension has that property populated in their Azure AD profile.

> **Tip**
> Use Microsoft Teams team membership for call queue agent population so that those agents also have a space for collaboration, shared storage, and more to help standardize their responses, work, and internal collaboration.

It's important that you order or transfer service numbers and then create resource accounts to which you'll assign those numbers *prior* to creating auto attendants and call queues. During the configuration of auto attendants and call queues, you'll have the chance to attach the resource account (with an assigned number already) to the new voice app, saving you a significant amount of backpedaling.

Now you've completed the steps necessary to begin creating and using auto attendants and call queues.

Call queues

Call queues are like virtual lobbies that allow you to configure the following:

- A greeting
- Hold music
- Call routing (first in, first out)
- Options for overflow and timeout

You might combine an auto attendant with a call queue so that users *press 1* to speak with the Service Desk, then are placed in the Service Desk call queue until a representative/agent can take their call:

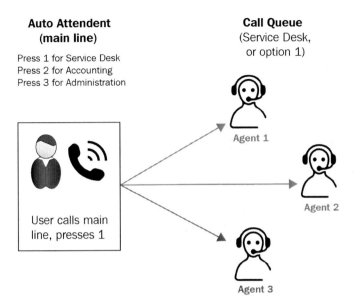

Auto Attendent (main line)

Press 1 for Service Desk
Press 2 for Accounting
Press 3 for Administration

User calls main line, presses 1

Call Queue (Service Desk, or option 1)

Agent 1

Agent 2

Agent 3

Figure 11.1 – Call queues

Call queues can have users waiting for the first available of a group of users, send them to voicemail, or redirect users to other queues and auto attendants.

Call queues can be created in multiple languages, similar to auto attendants, but cannot handle off-hours calls like auto attendants. You'd want to use an auto attendant as the greeting and handler, then only redirect to call queues during appropriate hours.

An excellent feature of call queues is the ability to integrate with Teams presence indicators. This means that if a representative of the Service Desk is unavailable, they won't receive call queue calls until they're available again.

Creating a call queue

It's important that you've completed the prerequisites mentioned in the *Managing resource accounts* section. You'll save time by already having ordered the service number for your call queue and already having assigned it to a resource account (which you'll create if there isn't one before creating this call queue).

You'll also save time by already having created the group or team whose membership will make up the agent/associate pool of those who will be responsible for answering calls waiting in this queue.

When ready, you'll follow these steps to create the call queue:

1. Go to the Teams admin center at `https://admin.teams.microsoft.com`.

2. Select **Voice** > **Call queues** from the left-hand menu.

3. Click **Add**.

4. Name your call queue.

5. Select or create the resource account(s) to associate with this call queue.

6. Set the **Language** setting for this call queue to be used for voicemail transcription, system prompts, and greetings.

7. Set **Greeting** to either **No greeting** or **Play an audio file** (which you'll upload here).

8. Either set **Music on hold** to the default Teams-provided music or upload your own audio file.

9. Add users (individually) and/or groups to the **Call answering** section. These are the agents who will receive calls from this queue. Individuals that are listed are prioritized higher than groups. The specific individuals and groups are ordered within each category based on the routing method you'll specify in *Step 11*.

10. Choose whether this call queue should be in conference mode. When this is enabled, agents will get calls more quickly and directly. If **Off**, calls are redirected traditionally via a transfer.

11. Choose the **Routing method** setting to use to prioritize who receives calls from those listed in *Step 9*. You can choose **Attendant routing** (all available agents ring, and the first to pick up stops the ringing for the rest), **Serial routing** (this will work down the list one by one until someone answers, prioritizing individuals before groups), **Round robin** (evenly distribute call volume to agents), or **Longest idle** (whoever has been set to Available the longest).

12. Choose to enable **Presence-based routing** (where someone's Teams presence determines their availability to take a call), as well as **Agents can opt out of taking calls** (agents can reject a call).

13. Choose a number of seconds for **Agent alert time**, which determines how long the phone rings before moving on to its next course of action, such as trying another agent according to the **Routing method** settings.

14. Next, you can specify **Call overflow handling**, which either disconnects or redirects callers if the queue reaches a certain number of users (up to 200).

15. Choose **Call time out handling** settings for the maximum caller wait time (up to 45 mins) and whether to disconnect or redirect the caller at that specified time.

16. Click **Save**.

When choosing overflow and timeout handling in *Steps 14-15*, you can choose to redirect callers to another user, voicemail, a voice app (another auto attendant or call queue), or an external phone number.

> **Important note**
>
> Agents who use Skype for Business instead of Teams will not receive calls from the queue if **Conference mode**, **Longest idle**, or **Presence-based routing** are enabled, as shown in *Figure 11.2*:

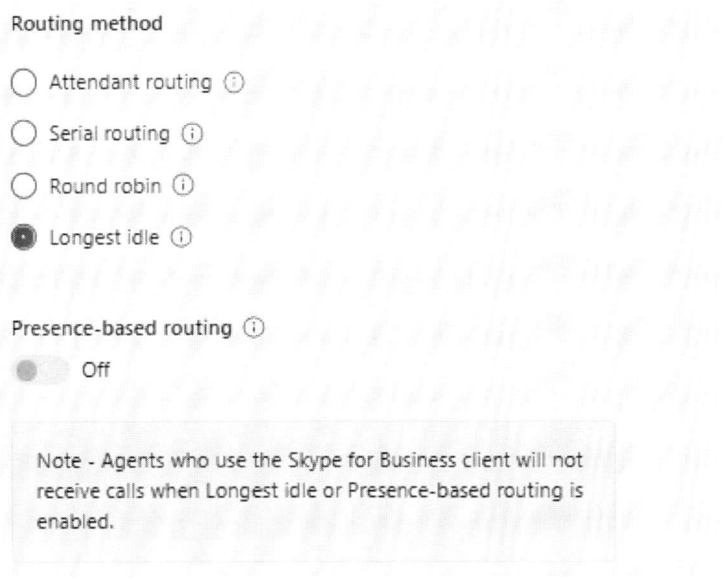

Figure 11.2 – Routing method settings for a call queue with the conditional disclaimer about agents who may be using Skype for Business that won't receive calls if the setting are saved as-is

Now that we've prepared for auto attendants and call queues and configured call queues, let's change our focus to auto attendants.

Creating and managing auto attendants

Auto attendants are the bot-like operators for calls that provide numeric button options for users to get to the right department or person. You can either record and upload the audio used by the auto attendant or use text-to-speech technology (system-generated prompts) for the greeting and menu.

Each auto attendant has its own language and time zone, making it easy for it to assist in business needs during local business hours in the most appropriate language. Being available during business hours is helpful, as is the counterpart of configuring it to respond during off-hours, weekends, holidays, and so on in a way that's most appropriate for the context.

Each auto attendant can optionally be configured with a specific person in your organization set as the operator. This allows someone to speak personally with a professional in your organization who is familiar with the business processes or structure of the business area in which the auto attendant is meant to work.

Users can use auto attendants to search the company directory by name or extension. You configure the dial scope to note who should be included in the searchable directory available to callers. This would be useful to make sure your C-suite executives' direct lines aren't directly reachable by callers, for example.

Creating an auto attendant

Creating auto attendants involves a few more steps than creating a call queue. You'll follow these steps to create an auto attendant in the Microsoft Teams admin center:

1. Go to the Teams admin center at `https://admin.teams.microsoft.com`.

2. Select **Voice** > **Auto attendants** from the left-hand menu.

3. Click **Add**.

4. Name your auto attendant.

5. Choose an operator (optional) for the auto attendant if you want users to be able to opt to speak with an associated individual instead of the auto attendant. This can be set to **No operator**, **Person in organization**, **Voice app** (another auto attendant or call queue), or **External phone number**.

6. Choose the auto attendant's assigned **Time zone** and **Language** settings from the drop-down menus.

7. Choose whether to enable voice inputs or stick with strictly numeric button inputs.

So far, you should have completed the steps shown in *Figure 11.3*:

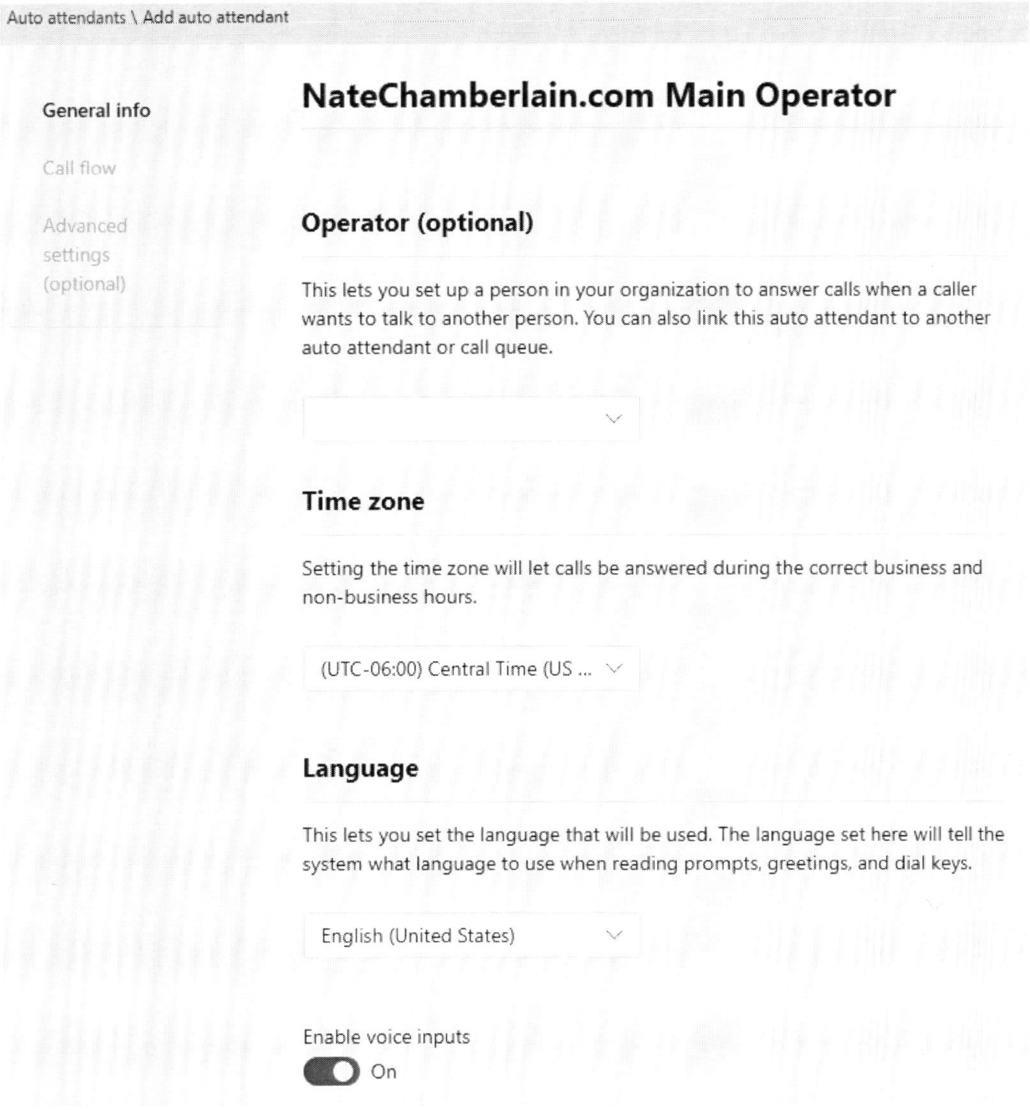

Figure 11.3 – The General info section of creating a new auto attendant

8. Click **Next** to proceed to **Call flow** settings.

9. Set the greeting message to **No greeting**, **Play an audio file** (you'll upload this if selected), or **Type in a greeting message** (for text-to-voice narration).

10. Choose either **Disconnect**, **Redirect call** (to a person, voice app, external number, or voicemail), or **Play menu options**.

11. If you choose **Play menu options**, you'll need to either upload a recording of the options being read aloud with their corresponding numbers or type in the message to be narrated with text-to-voice technology. You'll click **Assign a dial key** for each number that will be configured to redirect to a person, voicemail, app, operator, or external account as seen in *Figure 11.4*:

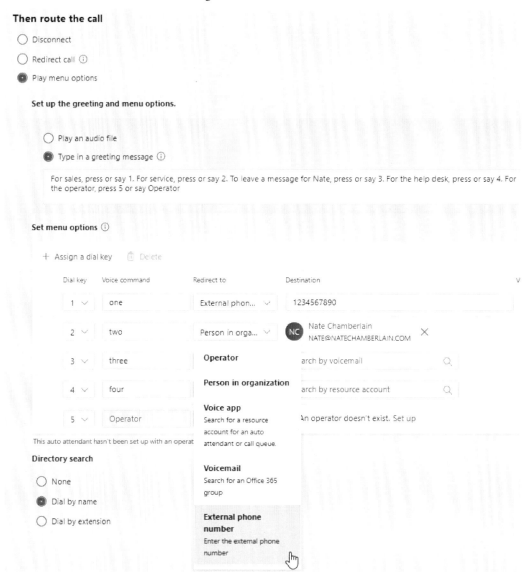

Figure 11.4 – Call flow settings for a new auto attendant where menu options are being configured

12. Click **Finish** if you're done, or **Next** if you want to configure the following optional settings:

    a. **Business hours** (days and times to consider the *default* in terms of call flow)

    b. **After hours call flow** (repeat of *Steps 9-11* but for the special handling of off-hours calls)

    c. **Holiday call flow** (repeat of *Steps 9-11* but for the handling of calls during holiday breaks that you specify)

    d. **Dial scope** (who is searchable by name or extension in the directory, specified individually or by group for inclusion or exclusion)

    e. **Resource accounts** (add an existing or new resource account to associate with the auto attendant)

In order for your auto attendant to have a number, you need to be sure to complete optional *Step 12e*. You will have ordered or transferred a service number(s) in advance and assigned the number(s) to the resource accounts that you created as mentioned in the *Preparing for call queues and auto attendants* sub-section earlier this chapter.

Important note

If you choose to create a new holiday during *Step 12c*, you'll be redirected away from your auto attendant setup to create the org-wide holiday in the Teams admin center and will need to start the auto attendant creation from scratch. Save your auto attendant, then edit it later to include holiday details if the holiday isn't created in advance.

After your auto attendant is created, you'll find it listed among the rest you've created by repeating *Steps 1-2*. You can come back here to edit the auto attendant's settings at any time.

Now let's review the call park, calling, and caller ID settings available to us.

Managing call park, calling, and caller ID policies

In this section, we'll take a close look at call park, calling, and caller ID policies in the Microsoft Teams admin center under the **Voice** node.

With all of these policies, there are PowerShell options. Each is prefixed with New- (create), Set- (modify), or Grant- (assign to users/groups). Even if not all three are explicitly mentioned in the following subsections, just remember that each type has these three cmdlets.

Let's start by reviewing call park policies.

Call park policies

Call park enables users to place calls on hold and transfer them to other users. As with other Teams policies, only one call park policy can be applied to a single user.

Call park policies can be configured with the following settings:

Setting	Options
Allow call park	On/Off
Call pickup start of range	Numeric value (10 by default)
Call pickup end of range	Numeric value (99 by default)
Park timeout (seconds)	Numeric value (300 by default)

In these settings, only the first (**Allow call park**) can be changed in the policy creation/modification page. The other three numeric value fields are disabled regardless of the first setting's configuration.

> **Important note**
> Call park and retrieve is only available if your tenant is in Teams Only deployment mode. You cannot implement this ability for Skype for Business IP phones.

You can modify an existing call park policy by using PowerShell. Use the Set-CsTeamsCallParkPolicy cmdlet with -Identity (policy name) and -AllowCallPark parameters such as in the following example, disabling call park for the **Global** policy:

```
Set-CsTeamsCallParkPolicy -Identity Global -AllowCallPark
$false
```

You can also create new policies using the same PowerShell parameters but with the New-CsTeamsCallParkPolicy cmdlet instead of the Set cmdlet.

Now let's review calling policies.

Calling policies

Calling policies determine which calling features users in your organization are allowed to use. You might, for example, create a custom policy to prevent a group of users from being able to use call forwarding. As with all other Teams policies, only one calling policy can be assigned to a user. If a policy isn't explicitly applied to a user, the default global policy will apply.

To create a custom calling policy, go to the Microsoft Teams admin center at `https://admin.teams.microsoft.com` and choose **Voice** > **Calling policies** from the left-hand menu. Once there, click **Add**.

Each calling policy can be configured with the following settings:

Setting	Options
Make private calls	On/Off
Call forwarding and simultaneous ringing to people in your organization	On/Off
Call forwarding and simultaneous ringing to external phone numbers	On/Off
Voicemail is available for routing inbound calls	User-controlled, enabled, or disabled
Inbound calls can be routed to call groups	On/Off
Allow delegation for inbound and outbound calls	On/Off
Prevent toll bypass and send calls through the PSTN	On/Off
Busy on busy is available when in a call	On/Off
Allow web PSTN calling	On/Off

Busy on busy is a newer setting whose name can be a bit confusing. It simply means you will (if the policy is applied to you) provide a busy signal to callers when you're already on a call (whether actively, or one placed on hold) and you won't be distracted by a notification of another call. In the global policy, this is disabled by default, meaning users can still receive and make calls even if they're already on a call.

When each setting for your custom policy is configured as you wish, click **Save**. You'll be redirected back to the **Calling policies** page.

As with other Teams policies, you can assign a policy to users by selecting it on its page then choosing **Manage users** from the menu.

You can alternatively use the **Users** node to assign policies to users in bulk (select all users to whom you're applying policy changes, then choose **Edit settings**). This bulk option allows you to set not only calling policies, but multiple policies in one action. *Figure 11.5* shows the pane that appears when editing multiple policy settings for users on the **Users** node of the Microsoft Teams admin center:

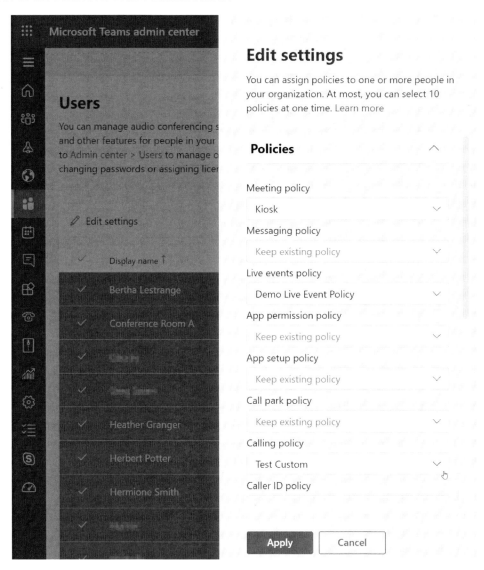

Figure 11.5 – The Edit settings pane of the Users node for bulk policy modification

You can also update calling policy settings via PowerShell using the
`Set-CsTeamsCallingPolicy` cmdlet. An example might be the following, in which
we're disallowing call forwarding on the **Global** policy:

```
Set-CsTeamsCallingPolicy -Identity Global
-AllowCallForwardingToPhone $false
```

Replace `Set` with `New` in order to create a policy rather than modifying an existing policy.

Lastly, let's look at caller ID policies.

Caller ID policies

Caller ID policies either modify or block the caller ID experience for users in your
organization. By default, recipients of your users' calls see the user's assigned phone
number displayed when they're calling.

You can change the number that displays, which might be helpful when callers from help
desk environments don't want personal lines shown but would rather people call a shared
queue for the group.

In some scenarios, it may also be helpful to replace all users' phone numbers with an
auto attendant for the whole organization if a user makes an external outgoing call to the
PSTN. This would make sure returned calls go through a dedicated process rather than
calling users directly and having individual lines.

Caller ID policies can be configured with the following settings:

Setting	Options
Block incoming caller ID	On/Off
Override the caller ID policy	On/Off
Replace the caller ID with	User's number, Service number, Anonymous
Replace the caller ID with this service number [if Service number is chosen in the previous setting]	Select from available service numbers in your organization

If you choose to enable **Override the caller ID policy**, users can choose for themselves whether their number or **Anonymous** shows when they make outbound calls. *Figure 11.6* shows a caller ID policy being created that will set the caller ID for its users to **Anonymous** when they make outbound calls. It also allows the individual users to override that setting and choose to show their number instead:

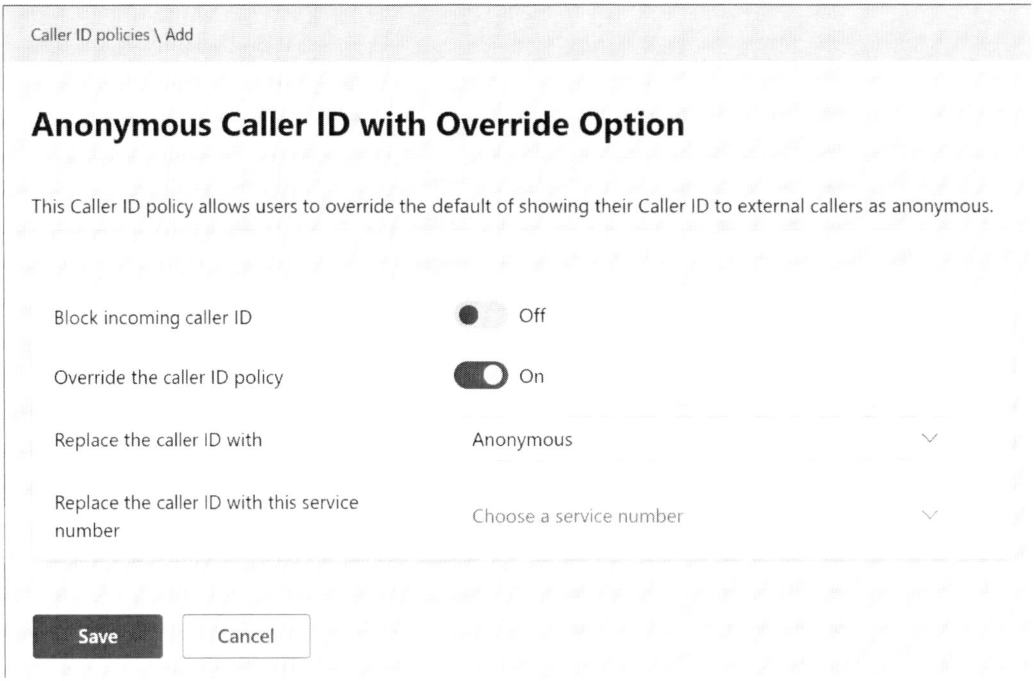

Caller ID policies \ Add

Anonymous Caller ID with Override Option

This Caller ID policy allows users to override the default of showing their Caller ID to external callers as anonymous.

Block incoming caller ID	● Off
Override the caller ID policy	◉ On
Replace the caller ID with	Anonymous ⌄
Replace the caller ID with this service number	Choose a service number ⌄

[Save] [Cancel]

Figure 11.6 – A caller ID policy showing the caller ID as Anonymous but allowing override

Caller ID is also known as Calling Line Identity/ID. This is what's used in the PowerShell cmdlets for Caller ID policies. The cmdlets are `New-CsCallingLineIdentity` (create new), `Set-CsCallingLineIdentity` (modify existing), and `Grant-CsCallingLineIdentity` (assign to users). An example of usage might be the following, where a new caller ID policy is being created that sets the caller ID to display as **Anonymous** for outgoing calls but allows users to override that setting:

```
New-CsCallingLineIdentity  -Identity AnonymousOutgoing
-Description "Anonymous displays for outgoing calls."
-CallingIDSubstitute Anonymous -EnableUserOverride $true
```

Now let's look at how to understand and access Health Dashboard for Direct Routing.

Understanding and accessing the Health Dashboard for Direct Routing

Health Dashboard for Direct Routing measures two main items in your Teams environment when you've deployed an on-premises solution connecting SBCs to your Direct Routing interface. These two measures are as follows:

- The health of connected SBCs

- Information about connected SBCs

For example, this dashboard would be helpful in analyzing dropped call information. This is also the place where, in *Chapter 10, Managing Phone Numbers in Microsoft Teams*, we set up SBCs, PSTN usage records, and voice routes to be used with voice routing policies.

Health Dashboard can be found via the Microsoft Teams admin center (`https://admin.teams.microsoft.com`) > **Voice** > **Direct Routing**. It consists of a Health Dashboard summary, then areas for SBCs, voice routes, and PSTN usage records.

The Health Dashboard summary shows the following:

- Total SBCs

- Voice routes

- SBCs with issues

The SBCs section of the dashboard lists all of your SBCs and shows the network effectiveness, average call duration, TLS connectivity status, SIP options status, concurrent calls capacity, and whether the SBC is enabled. SBCs can be viewed in list format or as a map using the **Map View** icon.

The voice routes section lists the priority, name, description, regex pattern, related PSTN usage, and SBCs enrolled for each voice route. These can be searched, edited, and re-prioritized from this tab.

PSTN usage records can be added and deleted from the **Manage PSTN usage records** panel.

Summary

In this chapter, we covered the management of resource accounts that are used for things such as call queues and auto attendants, which provide a more efficient experience for both the caller and recipient(s).

We then took a deeper dive into the configuration and management of call queues and auto attendants. These are assigned to resource accounts with phone numbers.

We covered three main policies that can alter the Teams calling experience for users: call park, calling, and caller ID. These features enhance user capabilities in your organization and can be configured differently for various users and groups.

Lastly, we explored Health Dashboard for Direct Routing and its components, which only apply to environments that utilize Direct Routing on-premises.

In the next chapter, we'll cover creating and managing teams.

Questions

As we conclude, here is a list of questions for you to test your knowledge regarding this chapter's material. You will find the answers in the *Assessments* section of the *Appendix*:

1. An auto attendant can read typed text aloud for greetings and menu options so that you don't need to record (and re-record) and upload audio files. True or false?

    a. True

    b. False

2. You've been asked to create a general service desk number that features an automated greeting and hold music when users call. The call must not have menu options once the call is received by the service desk. You'll need to create at least three of the following items to accomplish the goal – what are the most appropriate items to create (select all that apply)?

    a. An auto-attendant

    b. A call queue

    c. A call park

    d. A resource account

    e. A service number (call queue type)

    f. A service number (auto-attendant type)

3. Your users need to be able to place a call on hold, then transfer it to other users. What should you create for users who need that ability?

    a. Caller ID policy

    b. Call park policy

    c. Calling policy

    d. Voice routing policy

4. You have a certain set of users in the organization who should not be interrupted during a call with another call coming in. The caller who would otherwise interrupt should be given a busy signal. What do you configure for users who are not to be interrupted during calls and meetings?

    a. Dial plan

    b. Call park policy

    c. Calling policy

    d. Voice routing policy

5. You need to make sure outgoing calls from your organization show up on recipients' phones with a centralized, auto attendant phone number rather than the caller's specific, individual phone number. What should you create?

    a. Caller ID policy

    b. Call park policy

    c. Calling policy

    d. Voice routing policy

6. Your help desk staff are using the longest idle setting in their call queue to determine which agent receives the next call to the queue. One of your agents uses Skype for Business and can communicate with other users and make calls, but they're not receiving any calls from the call queue. What's the cause?

    a. The user needs to update their Skype client.

    b. The user needs an additional license.

    c. Longest idle doesn't work with Skype for Business.

    d. Call queues don't work with Skype for Business.

7. Agents who use Skype for Business will only receive calls from a call queue if which of the following routing methods are used (select all that apply)?

   a. Attendant routing

   b. Serial routing

   c. Round robin

   d. Longest idle

8. Which of the following can be used to specify the agents to receive calls in a particular call queue (select all that apply)?

   a. Security group

   b. Distribution list

   c. Teams team members

   d. M365/O365 group

9. You need auto attendant calls to be handled differently for an upcoming holiday in which most offices will be closed. What two actions should you take?

   a. Create a work schedule in Microsoft Teams Shifts.

   b. Create a holiday (**Org-wide settings** > **Holidays**).

   c. Update the auto attendant's call flows during holidays settings.

   d. Update the auto attendant's call flow for afterhours settings

10. Which of the following is not a Teams voice policy type?

    a. Call queue

    b. Call park

    c. Caller ID

    d. Calling

Further reading

Here are links to more information on some of the topics that we have covered in this chapter:

- What is Phone System?: `https://docs.microsoft.com/en-us/ microsoftteams/what-is-phone-system-in-office-365`

- Manage resource accounts in Microsoft Teams: `https://docs.microsoft.com/en-us/microsoftteams/manage-resource-accounts`

- Create a call queue: `https://docs.microsoft.com/en-us/microsoftteams/create-a-phone-system-call-queue`

- Set up an auto attendant: `https://docs.microsoft.com/en-us/microsoftteams/create-a-phone-system-auto-attendant`

- Answer auto attendant and call queue calls directly from Teams: `https://docs.microsoft.com/en-us/microsoftteams/answer-auto-attendant-and-call-queue-calls`

- Small business example – set up an Auto Attendant: `https://docs.microsoft.com/en-us/microsoftteams/tutorial-org-aa`

- What are Cloud auto attendants?: `https://docs.microsoft.com/en-us/microsoftteams/what-are-phone-system-auto-attendants`

- Call park and retrieve in Microsoft Teams: `https://docs.microsoft.com/en-us/microsoftteams/call-park-and-retrieve`

- Calling policies in Microsoft Teams: `https://docs.microsoft.com/en-us/microsoftteams/teams-calling-policy`

- Manage emergency calling policies in Microsoft Teams: `https://docs.microsoft.com/en-us/microsoftteams/manage-emergency-calling-policies`

- Manage caller ID policies in Microsoft Teams: `https://docs.microsoft.com/en-us/microsoftteams/caller-id-policies`

- Set the caller ID for a user: `https://docs.microsoft.com/en-us/microsoftteams/set-the-caller-id-for-a-user`

- How can caller ID be used in your organization?: `https://docs.microsoft.com/en-us/microsoftteams/how-can-caller-id-be-used-in-your-organization`

- Health Dashboard for Direct Routing: `https://docs.microsoft.com/en-us/microsoftteams/direct-routing-health-dashboard`

- Monitor and troubleshoot Direct Routing: `https://docs.microsoft.com/en-us/microsoftteams/direct-routing-monitor-and-troubleshoot`

Section 3: Planning, Deploying, and Managing Policies for Microsoft Teams, and Apps within Teams

This final part of the book will cover the configuration, deployment, and management of policies that apply to users and groups throughout Microsoft Teams' various features and apps.

This part of the book comprises the following chapters:

- *Chapter 12, Creating and Managing Teams*
- *Chapter 13, Managing Team Membership Settings*
- *Chapter 14, Creating App Policies within Microsoft Teams*

12
Creating and Managing Teams

This chapter will demonstrate how teams in Microsoft Teams can be created, both from scratch and from an existing resource of a Microsoft 365 group. You will also learn how to apply privacy settings to your teams so that not everyone is able to view and join them. In addition, we will demonstrate how creating an organization-wide team is a useful method to communicate with all employees in your organization.

By learning the material in this chapter, you'll add team creation and management skills to your skillset, which will prove useful when taking the MS-700 exam.

In this chapter, we're going to cover the following main topics:

- Creating a team
- Creating a team from an existing M365 group
- Managing the privacy settings for a team
- Managing organization-wide teams

Technical requirements

In this chapter, you will mostly just need to have the ability to create teams in your organization. To create an org-wide team, you'll need to be a *Global Administrator*.

Creating a team

In this section, we're going to create a new Microsoft Teams team from scratch. There are three ways to create a new team:

- Via the Microsoft Teams client application or SharePoint Online site
- From the Microsoft Teams admin center
- Via PowerShell

Let's review each method, beginning with the client option.

Creating a new team from the Microsoft Teams client

As long as you haven't prevented the option as a global admin, users in your organization can create teams themselves using the Teams client. Users will find this option in the lower left-hand corner of the Teams client after selecting the **Teams** option from the left-hand-side navigation menu as shown in *Figure 12.1*:

Figure 12.1 – The Join or create a team option in Teams

Next, you would click **Create team**. From here, you have the option to create a new team from scratch or create one from a group or team. There are also several Teams templates to choose from to pre-load your team with relevant channels and apps. These templates currently include the following:

Template	Category	Description
Adopt Office 365	General	Create a champion community to drive adoption.
Manage a Project	General	Coordinate your project.
Manage an Event	General	Improve your event management and collaboration.
Onboard Employees	General	Create a central experience to onboard employees.
Organize Help Desk	General	Bring resources together to build your Help Desk.
Collaborate on Patient Care	Healthcare	Collaborate on patient care in a hospital ward or department.
Collaborate on a Global Crisis	Financial Services	Create a place for your team to coordinate on a major crisis.
Collaborate within a Bank Branch	Financial Services	Create a place for bank branch collaboration.
Coordinate Incident Response	Government	Centralize resources and communications for incident response.
Hospital	Healthcare	Facilitate collaboration within a hospital.
Organize a Store	Retail	Collaborate with your retail store employees.
Quality and Safety	Manufacturing	Centralize communication and plant operations.
Retail – Manager Collaboration	Retail	Collaborate with managers across stores, regions, and so on.

We'll select **From scratch** (as seen in *Figure 12.2*) to create a blank new team:

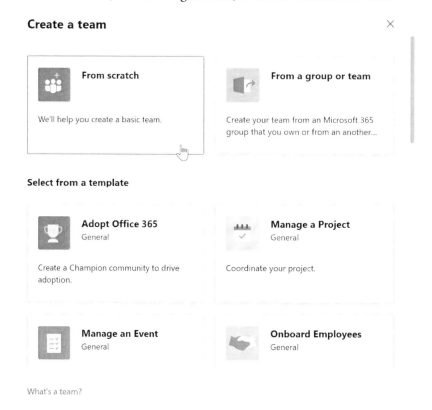

Figure 12.2 – Cursor hovering over the From scratch option in the Create a team dialog

Name and describe your new team, then click **Create**. You'll be prompted to add members (individuals, security groups, or distribution lists) to the team and can upgrade some to owners at this stage. You can also add members and owners later, as shown in *Chapter 13, Managing Team Membership Settings*. If you're not adding any members yet, click **Skip**.

You'll automatically be taken to your new team and its default *General* channel.

> **Tip**
> Keep in mind that once a team is created via the client or SharePoint Online, the creator is automatically the team owner of that team.

Next, let's review the steps for creating a team as a *Teams Service Administrator* or *Global Administrator* via the Microsoft Teams admin center..

Creating a new team from the Microsoft Teams admin center

A nice advantage of creating sites from the admin center or PowerShell is the ability to set the owner as someone other than the creator. This sub-section details the steps to take from the admin center.

From the Microsoft Teams admin center (`https://admin.teams.microsoft.com`), you can create a new team by selecting **Teams** > **Manage teams** from the left-hand menu. Once there, click **Add**.

A side panel floats in with fields for team name, description, owner, and privacy level, as shown in *Figure 12.3*:

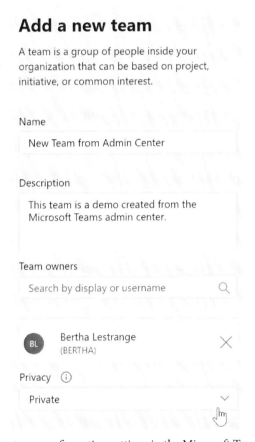

Figure 12.3 – New team configuration settings in the Microsoft Teams admin center

Once you've configured the new team fields as required, click **Apply**.

> **Important note**
>
> Once you've created a team, you can still change its name, privacy level, and even the O365 group name later, without using PowerShell. However, to change the O365 group email address, you'll need to use Exchange PowerShell.

Next, let's look at creating a team via PowerShell.

Creating a new team via PowerShell

Connecting to Microsoft Teams in PowerShell is as simple as importing the Teams PowerShell module (`Install-Module MicrosoftTeams`), then executing the `Connect-MicrosoftTeams` cmdlet. This will prompt you for credentials in a pop-up dialog. You can then use the `New-Team` cmdlet to create a new team. This would be excellent for incorporation into an automated request-and-provision process that helps you adhere to governance guidelines. For example, here's how you would create a team for the Help Desk using PowerShell:

```
New-Team -DisplayName "Help Desk" -Description "Team for
internal collaboration amongst Help Desk agents." -Visibility
"Private"
```

Pair this cmdlet with other parameters and cmdlets to really enhance the provisioning of new teams via PowerShell. For example, add `-Owner`, `Add-TeamUser`, and `New-TeamChannel` to add users and channels at creation time as well. For example, here's how we create the same team in the previous example but with a unique owner other than the person running the script, and adding two members and two channels:

```
$group = New-Team -MailNickname "HelpDesk" -displayname
"Help Desk" -Description "Team for internal collaboration
amongst Help Desk agents." -Visibility "Private" -Owner "nate@
natechamberlain.com"

Add-TeamUser -GroupId $group.GroupId -User "bertha@
natechamberlain.com"

Add-TeamUser -GroupId $group.GroupId -User "tyler@
natechamberlain.com"

New-TeamChannel -GroupId $group.GroupId -DisplayName "Open
Tickets"

New-TeamChannel -GroupId $group.GroupId -DisplayName "Everyday
Resources"
```

In the next section, we'll create a group from an existing Microsoft 365 group.

Creating a team from an existing M365 group

Creating a new team from scratch creates a new Microsoft 365 group that helps power its membership from the backend. However, you may already have a Microsoft 365 group if you first had a SharePoint Online site, Planner plan, Stream channel, and so on that used a Microsoft 365 group. Rather than duplicating the groups and doubling your membership management, you can create a team using a pre-existing Microsoft 365 group.

One option for doing this is via a pre-existing SharePoint Online site. Users are presented with a banner message encouraging them to create a team for their site if the site was created in SharePoint (and not as a result of a team being created first). To create a team from a SharePoint Online site, look for this banner message in the lower left-hand corner of a SharePoint Online site that resembles what's shown in *Figure 12.4*:

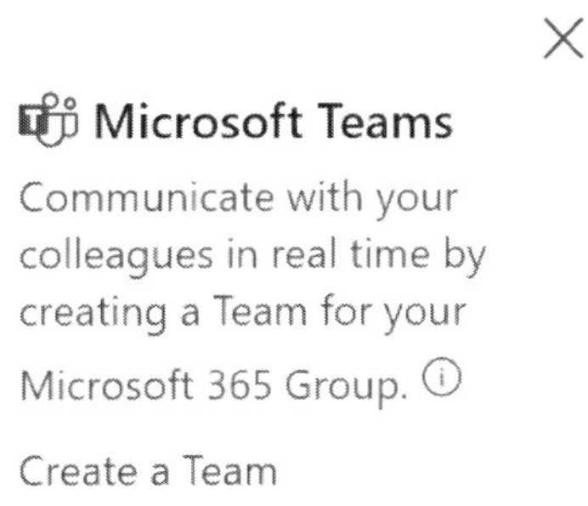

Figure 12.4 – The Microsoft Teams message for team creation on a SharePoint Online site

Because the banner doesn't always appear, and because if closed it won't reappear, the more reliable method is to again use the Microsoft Teams client. Instead of **From scratch**, you'll choose **From a group or team** in the first dialog.

This will present you with the option of either using an existing team or a Microsoft 365 group to create the new team as seen in *Figure 12.5*. If you choose **Team**, you'll see all of your teams and can choose one to base the new team on. If you choose **Microsoft 365 group**, you can select an M365 group that doesn't already have a team to base the new team on:

Figure 12.5 – Dialog when creating a team from an existing team or group

After you make a selection of **Team** or **Microsoft 365 group** and choose the existing asset on which to build the new team, you'll click **Create**.

> **Important note**
> Adding teams to an existing Microsoft 365 group is permanent and can't be undone.

In the next section, we'll manage the privacy settings for our team.

Managing the privacy settings for a team

There are three privacy levels to choose from for your teams. When you're creating a team, you select this as part of the process. You can see an example of this dialog in *Figure 12.6*. After you create a team, however, you're still able to modify this selection, thereby changing a team from private to public, or even org-wide if you haven't hit the organizational max yet.

To change privacy settings for a team, from within the Teams client, select the ellipsis (three dots) next to a team name and select **Edit team**. Once there, your screen will show the dialog seen in *Figure 12.6*:

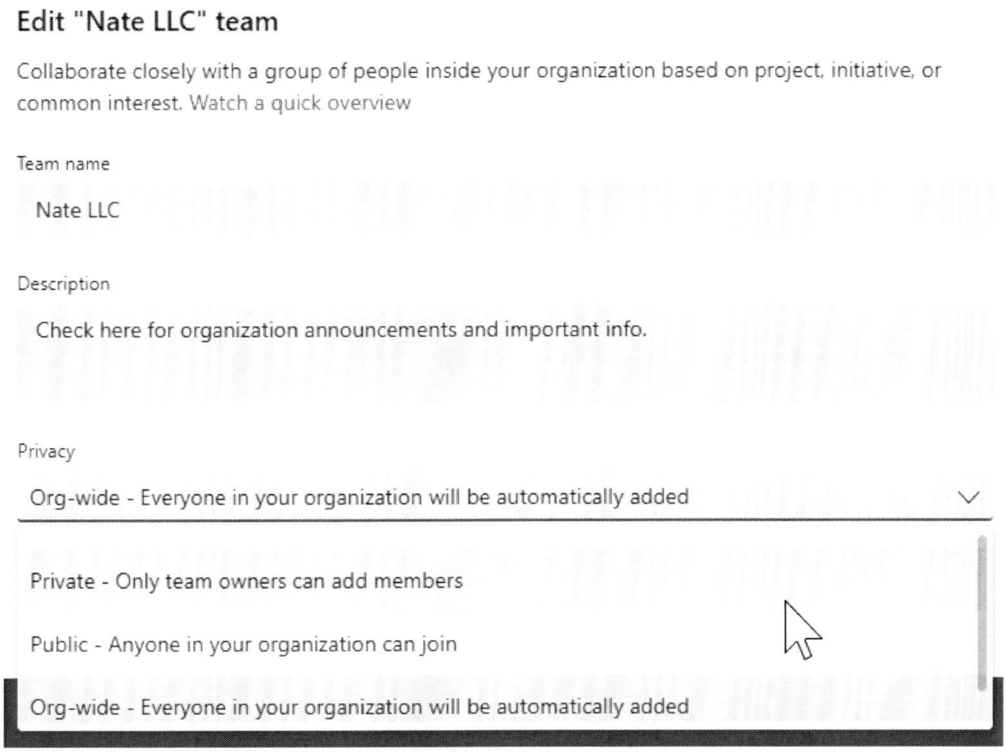

Edit "Nate LLC" team

Collaborate closely with a group of people inside your organization based on project, initiative, or common interest. Watch a quick overview

Team name

Nate LLC

Description

Check here for organization announcements and important info.

Privacy

Org-wide - Everyone in your organization will be automatically added ⌄

Private - Only team owners can add members

Public - Anyone in your organization can join

Org-wide - Everyone in your organization will be automatically added

Figure 12.6 – Privacy setting selection options for a team currently set to Org-wide

Now select the **Privacy** dropdown.

You can choose one of the following:

- **Private** – Only team owners can add members
- **Public** – Anyone in your organization can join
- **Org-wide** – Everyone in your organization will be automatically added

Once you've changed your selection for the team, click **Done**.

When you choose **Private**, users can bypass join approval using a team code generated at **Team settings** > **Team Code** > **Generate**. Otherwise, when a user requests to join, team owners will get requests.

To prevent your private teams from appearing in Teams gallery search results, you can also change your team discoverability setting in **Team settings** > **Team discoverability**.

To change an existing team to **Private** and disable its discoverability, you can also run the following PowerShell. The first line gets a specific team, then everything following `Set-Team` sets that team's visibility to private and removes it from search and suggestions.

```
$team = Get-Team -DisplayName "Nate LLC"
Set-Team -GroupID $team.GroupID -Visibility Private
-ShowInTeamsSearchAndSuggestions $false
```

Once executed, you'll see a confirmation of the action as shown in *Figure 12.7*:

Figure 12.7 – Completed PowerShell script showing privacy setting changes for a team

Now let's look at managing organization-wide teams.

Managing organization-wide teams

To create and configure organization-wide teams, you must be a Global Administrator. Your organization can have a maximum of 5 org-wide teams per tenant. Your organization can also have no more than 5,000 users to be able to create org-wide teams.

If you meet both of those pre-requisites (being a global administrator in an organization with 5,000 users or less), you can proceed with creating an org-wide team following the steps in the *Creating a team* section earlier in this chapter. The only difference will be selecting **Org-wide** after selecting **From scratch**. **Org-wide** will appear as an option as seen in *Figure 12.8* only if you're a global administrator:

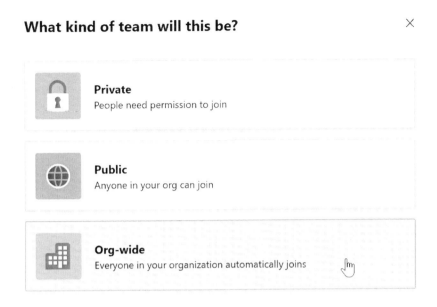

Figure 12.8 – The Org-wide option when creating a new team from scratch

You'll then be asked for a team name and description before clicking **Create**. As with other teams, your org-wide team will come pre-loaded with a **General** channel with **Posts**, **Files**, and **Wiki** tabs.

Team members in org-wide teams are automatically added and removed based on your Azure AD membership. So as new employees join the company, they'll automatically have access to the org-wide team(s) once licensed and in AD, and team owners are automatically set to your Teams administrators.

For the remainder of this book, we'll focus on the management of organization-wide teams.

Summary

In this chapter, we covered the creation of teams both from scratch as well as from existing O365 groups.

We then covered privacy settings for teams, seeing that we can change teams from their original privacy setting to **Public**, **Private**, or **Org-wide**.

Lastly, we reviewed the creation and management of organization-wide teams, keeping in mind that we are limited to 5 per tenant and only in organizations with 5,000 or fewer users.

In the next chapter, we'll cover team membership settings including dynamic security groups for membership, Azure AD access reviews, and membership management using PowerShell.

Questions

As we conclude, here is a list of questions for you to test your knowledge regarding this chapter's material. You will find the answers in the *Assessments* section of the *Appendix*:

1. Currently, members of your team have to invite other members. What is the privacy level of your team?

    a. Private

    b. Public

    c. Org-wide

    d. Hidden

2. You want anyone in your organization to be able to join your team without an invite, but not be automatically added. Which privacy level should you choose for your team?

    a. Private

    b. Public

    c. Org-wide

    d. Hidden

3. Every member of your organization, as soon as they're entered into the system, needs access to a team used for organization announcements and resources. What sort of team privacy level should a team like this have?

    a. Private

    b. Public

    c. Org-wide

    d. Hidden

4. What are the limits for org-wide teams?

    a. <10,001 users and no more than 3 org-wide teams per tenant

    b. <3,001 users and no more than 5 org-wide teams per tenant

    c. <5,001 users and no more than 5 org-wide teams per tenant

    d. <15,001 users and no more than 3 org-wide teams per tenant

5. Which of the following is not true?

    a. You can create a team from the Teams client.

    b. You can create a team with PowerShell.

    c. You can create a team from the Microsoft Teams admin center.

    d. You can create a team from Outlook.

6. Which of the following is true?

    a. All team types can be made non-discoverable.

    b. Any non-org-wide team can be made non-discoverable.

    c. Any private team can be made non-discoverable.

    d. All teams must be searchable, whether private or not.

7. If you create a team based on an existing Microsoft 365 group but choose the wrong group, this action can be undone. True or false?

    a. True

    b. False

8. You can change a team's privacy settings and discoverability via PowerShell. True or false?

    a. True

    b. False

9. Public teams can be made private, and vice versa. True or false?

    a. True

    b. False

10. Which of the following can you change without using PowerShell *after* creating a new team from scratch? Select all that apply.

a. O365 group name

b. O365 group email

c. Team name

d. Team privacy level

Further reading

Here are links to more information on some of the topics that we have covered in this chapter:

- Create a team from scratch: `https://support.microsoft.com/en-us/office/create-a-team-from-scratch-174adf5f-846b-4780-b765-de1a0a737e2b`

- Create your first teams and channels in Microsoft Teams: `https://docs.microsoft.com/en-us/microsoftteams/get-started-with-teams-create-your-first-teams-and-channels`

- Overview of teams and channels in Microsoft Teams: `https://docs.microsoft.com/en-us/MicrosoftTeams/teams-channels-overview`

- Create a team from an existing group: `https://support.microsoft.com/en-us/office/create-a-team-from-an-existing-group-24ec428e-40d7-4a1a-ab87-29be7d145865`

- Enhance existing Microsoft 365 groups with Microsoft Teams: `https://docs.microsoft.com/en-us/MicrosoftTeams/enhance-office-365-groups`

- Manage team settings and permissions in Teams: `https://support.microsoft.com/en-us/office/manage-team-settings-and-permissions-in-teams-ce053b04-1b8e-4796-baa8-90dc427b3acc`

- Create an org-wide team in Microsoft Teams: `https://docs.microsoft.com/en-us/microsoftteams/create-an-org-wide-team`

- Manage Microsoft Teams settings for your organization: `https://docs.microsoft.com/en-us/microsoftteams/enable-features-office-365`

13
Managing Team Membership Settings

In this chapter, we will show you how to manage user access to teams. You will learn that users may be added to a team with either member or ownership permissions, and how this affects the actions they can perform in relation to the team. We will also demonstrate how users may be automatically added to the required teams using Azure AD dynamic group membership settings. Finally, you will learn how Azure AD access reviews may be used to review current Microsoft 365 group memberships that relate to your teams.

In this chapter, we're going to cover the following main topics:

- Managing users within a team
- Configuring dynamic team membership
- Using access reviews to validate team membership

Technical requirements

To manage users, in this chapter, you'll just need to be a team owner to manage your private team's membership via the client. To use the Teams admin center or PowerShell, you'll want to be a *Teams Service administrator* or *Global administrator*.

To configure dynamic team membership, you'll need the *Global administrator* or *User administrator* role and an Azure AD Premium P1 license.

To configure access reviews, you'll want to be assigned the *Global administrator* or *User administrator* role or be assigned an Azure AD Premium P2 license. The P2 license is not required if you have the Global admin or User admin role.

Managing users within a team

Users can be added to a team as either an owner or a member. This can be changed at any time, promoting or demoting owners as needed.

Owners of teams have elevated privileges, including the following:

- Create and delete a team
- Modify a team name and description
- Create and delete private channels
- Add members to a team or private channels (if you're also a member)

Team owners can also modify the settings of a team that change member experiences. For example, a team owner can choose to disable the following abilities for members:

- Create and delete channels
- Modify channel names and descriptions
- Create private channels
- Add apps
- Create/update/delete tabs

Members can add other members to public teams themselves and can request members be added to private teams. Members can also elect to leave a team themselves at any time as long as the team's membership is not populated by a dynamic security group.

If moderation is turned on for a team, its channels can have separate moderators that don't have to necessarily be owners. Each channel can have its own assigned moderators. See *Chapter 8*, *Managing Collaboration and Chat within Microsoft Teams*, for more information on moderation.

To manage users (changing roles, adding, and deleting), you can use any of these methods:

- The **Manage team** option via the client application (team owners)
- Microsoft Teams admin center's **Teams** node (Teams Service or Global Administrator)
- PowerShell (Teams Service or Global Administrator)

Let's look at each of these methods, beginning with the admin center.

Managing users via the Microsoft Teams admin center

To manage users in the Microsoft Teams admin center (`https://admin.teams.microsoft.com`), select the **Teams** > **Manage teams** node from the left-hand menu. Then select the team name for which you'll be managing users. You'll automatically be taken to the **Members** tab by default.

To add a user, select **Add** and search for the user. Select the user to add, then **Apply**.

To remove a user, select their row in the **Members** listing and then **Remove**, as seen in *Figure 13.1*:

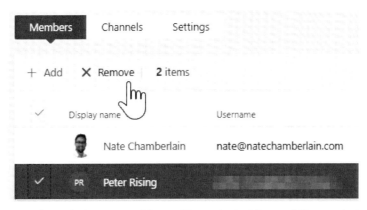

Figure 13.1 – A user being removed from a Team via the Microsoft Teams admin center

To change a user's role, use the drop-down menu in the **Role** column as shown in *Figure 13.2*. You can't promote guests to owners, but regular members can be promoted and demoted:

Figure 13.2 – A user being promoted to Owner via the Microsoft Teams admin center

> **Important note**
> A team must have at least one owner. You cannot demote the last owner of a team to a member until another member has been promoted to owner.

Next, let's review user management in the client app.

Managing users via the Microsoft Teams client app

To manage users in the client, a team owner can select the ellipsis (three dots) next to the team name for which they'll be managing users. The owner then chooses **Manage team**.

Similar to the admin center, the owner can then choose **Add member** to add a new user to the team. This opens a search dialog to find the user(s). As users are added, you can also choose to promote them to **Owner** via the dropdown next to their name, which is set to **Member** by default.

To remove a member, select the **X** next to the user's role as shown in *Figure 13.3*:

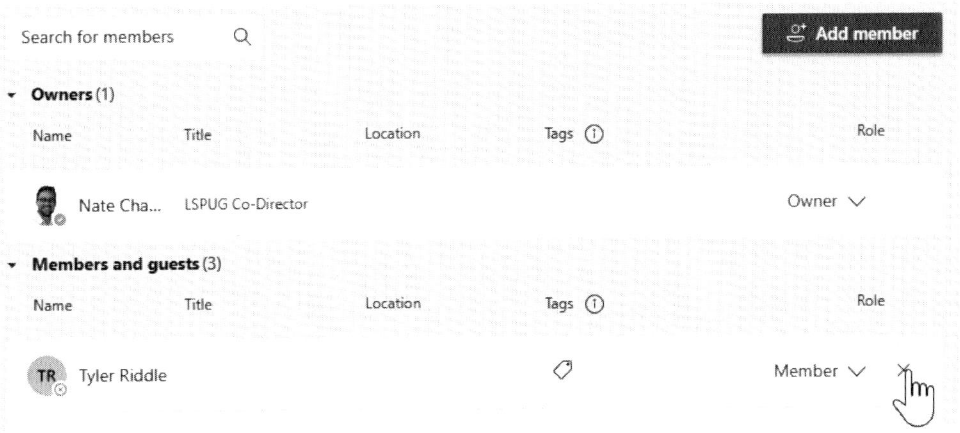

Figure 13.3 – A user being removed from a team via the client application

And to change a user's role (from **Member** to **Owner** or vice versa), use the dropdown in the **Role** column.

Lastly, let's look at user management in PowerShell.

Managing users via PowerShell

Changing user roles via PowerShell isn't intuitive in that there isn't a command for *Set* or *Update* users. Instead, we use `Add-TeamUser` with the `-Role` parameter set to `Owner` to promote a member to an owner even if they've already been added to the team.

And to demote an owner to a member, we use `Remove-TeamUser` with the `-Role` parameter set to `Owner`. This doesn't remove the user as a member as long as the `-Role` parameter is present with a role change.

As an example, Bertha and Tyler are already members of Nate LLC in the following example. Tyler is currently an owner. To promote Bertha to an owner and to demote Tyler from an owner to a member, we'd connect to the `MicrosoftTeamsPowerShell` module (`Connect-MicrosoftTeams`) if not connected already and then run the following set of commands:

```
$team = Get-Team -DisplayName "Nate LLC"
Remove-TeamUser -GroupId $team.GroupID -User tyler@
natechamberlain.com -Role Owner
Add-TeamUser -GroupId $team.GroupID -User bertha@
natechamberlain.com -Role Owner
```

Without the role parameters, the same commands would be used to add/remove new/ existing members. In the following example, Tyler is being removed from the team entirely and Bertha is being added:

```
$team = Get-Team -DisplayName "Nate LLC"
Remove-TeamUser -GroupId $team.GroupID -User tyler@
natechamberlain.com
Add-TeamUser -GroupId $team.GroupID -User bertha@
natechamberlain.com
```

In this section, we managed Teams users via the Microsoft Teams admin center, the client application, and PowerShell. In the next section, we'll configure dynamic team membership to simplify team membership management.

Configuring dynamic team membership

Adding users manually to a team can be time-intensive, particularly teams with a high turnover and number of additions. With the exception of org-wide teams, all teams require that users and groups are added manually. However, we can use dynamic groups as part of a team's membership to help us automatically add users matching certain criteria (for example, department equals Human Resources).

> **Important note**
>
> Dynamic membership rules can make users members of a team but cannot promote members to owners conditionally. That will still need to be done manually.
>
> Because these groups will be dynamically populated, that means members cannot opt to leave if they meet the criteria for the group.
>
> Team owners will also not be able to add or remove users from the dynamic group. They can still add/remove additional team members directly to/from the team (who aren't included in the dynamic group) but cannot change who is added as a member of the team as a result of meeting dynamic group membership criteria. In a situation like this, your *team members* would include the dynamic group plus Bertha and Herbert separately, for example. But you wouldn't be able to modify the dynamic group manually itself.

To create or modify a group with dynamic membership, you'll need to use Azure Active Directory (Azure AD) at `https://aad.portal.azure.com` and must have an Azure AD Premium P1 license assigned to you. If not, your option to use dynamic (instead of assigned) membership will be disabled.

Dynamic membership is a membership type selection you can make for either Microsoft 365 groups or security groups. You can use this feature in multiple scenarios/configurations. For example, you could do the following:

- Create a new Microsoft 365 group with dynamic membership, then create a new team based on that group.

- Modify an existing Microsoft 365 group used for team membership and give it the dynamic membership type (noting that this will remove all current members and replace them only with those matching the dynamic rules).

- Create a security group (or multiple) and make it a member of an existing team (not recommended because it's a one-time extraction of members and won't update until added again).

From Azure AD, you can create either Microsoft 365 groups or security groups. If you use security groups, you can add multiple groups per team, but they will extract upon being added and not update again. Therefore, you'd be adding that security group manually on a regular basis to update membership. If you choose a Microsoft 365 group, you're likely planning on creating a new team based on this group because you cannot add multiple Microsoft 365 groups to a single team.

Let's go over the steps for creating a new Microsoft 365 group, a security group, and then modify an existing Microsoft 365 group to be dynamic. We'll also touch on the conversion of distribution lists to Microsoft 365 groups.

Creating a new Microsoft 365 group with dynamic membership and creating a team

Any single team can have a maximum of one Microsoft 365 group used in its membership. In this section, we'll create a Microsoft 365 group with dynamic membership that we intend to use in the creation of a new team based on this new group.

From Azure AD (`https://aad.portal.azure.com`), select **Groups** > **New Group**, then follow these instructions:

1. Change **Group type** to **Microsoft 365**.

2. Fill in **Group name**, **Group email address**, and **Group description**.

3. Leave **Azure AD roles can be assigned to the group** set to **No**.

4. Change **Membership type** to **Dynamic User**.

5. Select a group owner(s) (optional).

6. Select **Add dynamic query** under **Dynamic user members**.

At this point, the first expression has been started for you. Change the **Property** dropdown, **Operator**, and **Value** to match the conditions on which a user will be added to this group and, by extension, the team for which it's being created. *Figure 13.4* shows an expression configured to add all members of **Human Resources** to this group:

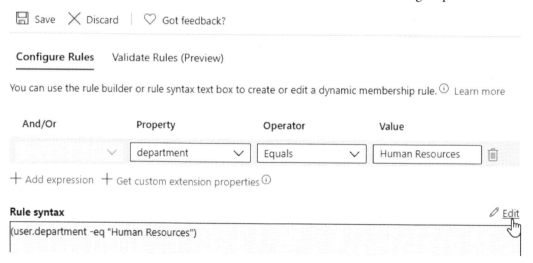

Figure 13.4 – A dynamic expression for getting all members of Human Resources

Notice as you add expressions, the rule syntax is written out as text below the expressions. In our example, this becomes (**user.department -eq "Human Resources"**). You can edit this manually by clicking **Edit** in the upper-right corner of the textbox.

You can add up to five expressions in the rule builder.

When finished, click **Save** to commit your membership rules to the group. Then click **Create** to create the group officially for usage.

Remember that only one Microsoft 365 group can be used in a team's membership, and if the team was created from scratch, it already has a Microsoft 365 supporting it. So, in this case, we would want to create a team from an existing group following the instructions in the *Creating a team from an existing group* section of *Chapter 12, Creating and Managing Teams*. Note that it can take a while for the new group to synchronize with the Microsoft Teams client application.

Next, let's create a security group with dynamic membership.

Creating a new security group with dynamic membership and adding it to a team

We can use security groups for the initial team membership population along with individual members added directly. The following details the creation of a security group with dynamic membership, keeping in mind dynamic membership will only apply to Azure AD and will not dynamically update within Teams.

> **Important note**
> This method is not recommended if you want truly dynamic membership. The rules for membership will always apply to the security group, but once you add a security group as a member of a team, Teams performs a one-time extraction of members and will not update again unless you add the security group as a member again at a later date, and it will add new members (but not remove former/since-removed members).

From Azure AD, select **Groups** > **New Group**. Then follow these instructions:

1. Change **Group type** to **Security**.
2. Fill in **Group name** and **Group description**.
3. Leave **Azure AD roles can be assigned to the group** set to **No**.
4. Change **Membership type** to **Dynamic User**.
5. Select a group owner(s) (optional).
6. Select **Add dynamic query** under **Dynamic user members**.

Just like with the Microsoft 365 group, we'll add expressions as rules for membership in our security group. For this example, we'll look for users with either *Director* or *Manager* in their job title to add them to a management security group. *Figure 13.5* illustrates this multi-expression rule:

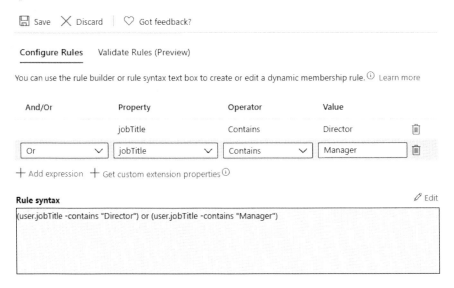

Figure 13.5 – Expressions seeking Director or Manager in job titles for dynamic membership

When finished, again select **Save** then **Create** to complete the process.

Because we chose a security group in this example, we can add it along with other (multiple) security groups for a team's membership, or use it by itself. It'll appear when searched during adding members to a team as seen in *Figure 13.6*:

Figure 13.6 – A new dynamic security group shown as an option when searching for members
to add to an existing team

Now that we have learned how to modify security groups with dynamic membership, let's learn how to modify an existing team's Microsoft 365 group to utilize dynamic membership.

Modifying a team's existing Microsoft 365 group to have dynamic membership

Because we may not always want to create a new team in order to utilize dynamic membership, we do have the option of modifying an existing Microsoft 365 group (even those used to support an existing team) to use dynamic instead of assigned membership. It's important to remember, however, that making this change will remove all members from the group and replace them with only those meeting the criteria added in the expressions.

To modify a team's Microsoft 365 group's membership setting, you'll want to go to Azure AD (`https://aad.portal.azure.com`), then select **Groups**. Then follow these steps:

1. Select the name of the group (it matches the team name).

2. Select **Properties**.

3. Change **Membership type** to **Dynamic User**.

4. Select **Add dynamic query** under **Dynamic user members**.

Then, as with the other two examples, define the criteria for membership in this group and click **Save**. When finished with property adjustments, click **Save** once more to complete the conversion. You'll be prompted with a warning as seen in *Figure 13.7* on the final save to be sure this is the action you want to take. Click **Yes** to proceed:

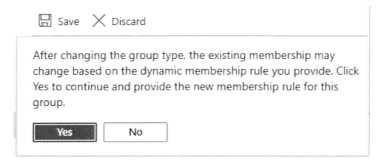

Figure 13.7 – The warning presented to a user when replacing a group's
membership type with dynamic

Once the change is saved, the team(s) that rely on that Microsoft 365 group(s) will have updated membership based on the rule(s) you defined in the expressions.

Upgrading distribution lists to Microsoft 365 groups for membership

Distribution lists may be upgraded to Microsoft 365 groups, but they must meet certain criteria. In order to upgrade a distribution list, it must be the following:

- Cloud-managed (not on-premises)
- Simple (non-dynamic, less than 100 owners, no special characters in the alias, and so on)
- Non-nested

You also cannot upgrade security groups.

To upgrade an eligible distribution list to a Microsoft 365 group, you'll go to the Exchange admin center (`https://outlook.office365.com/ecp/`) > **Recipients** > **Groups** and then click **Get started** on the **UPGRADE DISTRIBUTION LISTS** notice, as shown in *Figure 13.8*:

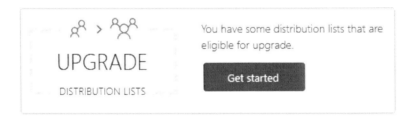

Figure 13.8 – Get started button for upgrading distribution lists in the Exchange admin center

Then you'll select the eligible distribution lists you wish to upgrade and click **Start upgrade**.

This concludes our review of dynamic team membership, and now we will look at using access reviews for team membership validation.

Using access reviews to validate team membership

Access reviews can be configured to allow you the ability to easily review team membership (group membership) on a regular basis. You can choose to regularly recertify memberships for members and guests alike. This helps improve your governance efforts by reporting on access to information regularly to those who have the ability to revoke and adjust those privileges (such as team owners). You can also have members self-certify continued membership as well to make the process more autonomous when appropriate.

Before you can create access reviews, you must be assigned as a Global or User administrator and have an Azure Active Directory Premium P2 license assigned to you. You'll also need to assign P2 licenses to anyone who will perform the following tasks:

- Anyone assigned as reviewers, including group or application owners
- Anyone performing a self-review

Once assigned a proper role or licensed appropriately, you can onboard to be able to use the feature going forward. This section will show how to onboard for your first-time usage, then how to create an access review for team/group membership.

Onboarding to utilize access reviews

To onboard and begin using access reviews, go to the Azure Active Directory admin center at `https://aad.portal.azure.com`. Then follow these instructions:

1. Click on **Azure Active Directory** then choose **Identity Governance**.

2. Click **Onboard** on the left-hand navigation pane as shown in *Figure 13.9*. If you don't see it, you're likely already onboarded:

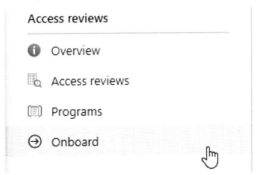

Figure 13.9 – Access review onboarding link in the left-hand menu of AAD Identity Governance

3. Review the information and then click **Onboard Now**.

4. Wait for successful onboarding. You'll receive a notification when finished, as seen in *Figure 13.10*:

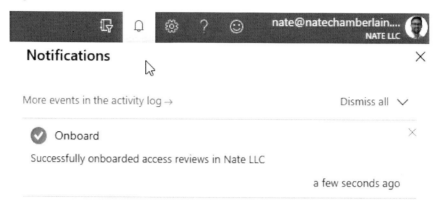

Figure 13.10 – Successful access review onboarding notification

Now let's set up an access review.

Creating an access review for team/group membership validation

Once onboarded, we're ready to utilize access reviews. Follow these steps to create an access review:

1. Go to Azure Active Directory (`https://aad.portal.azure.com` > **Azure Active Directory**) then choose **Identity Governance**.

2. Choose **Access Reviews** from the left-hand menu, then **New access review** as seen in *Figure 13.11*:

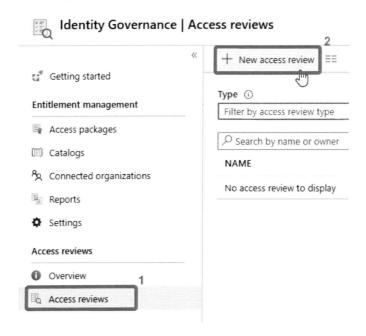

Figure 13.11 – Navigation for adding a new access review in Azure AD Identity Governance

3. Name and describe the access review, then choose a **Start date**, **Frequency**, **Duration (in days)**, and **End** parameters as shown in *Figure 13.12*:

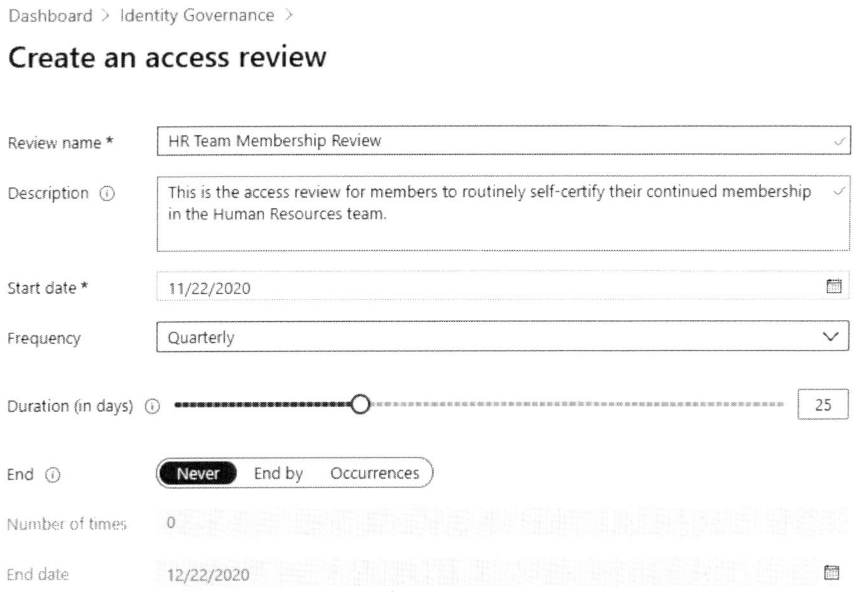

Dashboard > Identity Governance >

Create an access review

Review name *	HR Team Membership Review
Description ⓘ	This is the access review for members to routinely self-certify their continued membership in the Human Resources team.
Start date *	11/22/2020
Frequency	Quarterly
Duration (in days) ⓘ	●———————○·················· 25
End ⓘ	Never End by Occurrences
Number of times	0
End date	12/22/2020

Figure 13.12 – A new access review being created for quarterly HR team membership review

4. Set **Users to review** to **Members of a group**.

5. Set **Scope** to **Everyone**, unless you only want the access review to apply to guest users, then choose **Guest users only**.

6. Click **Select a group**, then search for and select the team's Microsoft 365 group for which you're creating the access review. Click **Select**.

7. For **Reviewers**, you can choose **Group owners**, **Selected users (static)**, or **Members (self)** as shown in *Figure 13.13*. In this example, we'll choose **Members (self)** so that each member of the team self-certifies continued membership:

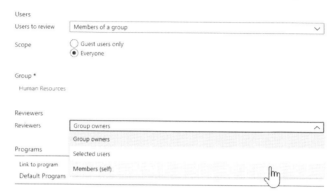

Figure 13.13 – An access review's Users, Group, and Reviewers settings

8. Expand **Upon completion settings** and **Advanced settings** as shown in *Figure 13.14*. Complete the settings here and click **Start** to begin the access review:

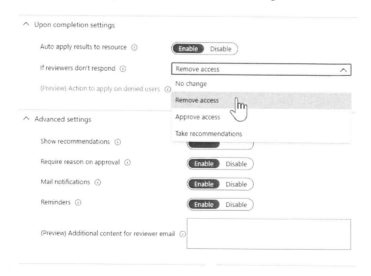

Figure 13.14 – Advanced settings for an access review

Users asked to certify their own membership receive emails like the one shown in *Figure 13.15* asking them to confirm their ongoing membership requirement:

Microsoft Azure <azure-noreply@microsoft.com>
Sun 11/22/2020 4:32 PM
To: Nate Chamberlain

Please review HR Team Membership Review in Nate LLC:

Please review by December 22, 2020 to confirm your continued need for access.

Learn more about reviewing your access.

Review access >

Figure 13.15 – An email received by a team member asking them to review their own access

After the user clicks **Review access >**, they'll be given the opportunity to choose whether or not to remain a member of the team, and if you configured it to require a reason, they can enter that as well, as seen in *Figure 13.16*:

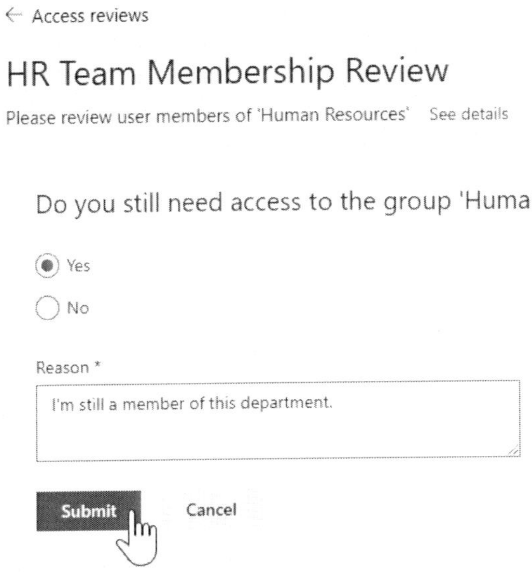

← Access reviews

HR Team Membership Review

Please review user members of 'Human Resources'   See details

Do you still need access to the group 'Human Resources'?

◉ Yes

○ No

Reason *

I'm still a member of this department.

Submit   Cancel

Figure 13.16 – A user's team membership self-approval access review

Or, if you're the reviewer, you'll make decisions for the group (such as whether **Reviewer** is set to team/group owner) and be presented with a recommendation based on previous user activity, as shown in *Figure 13.17*:

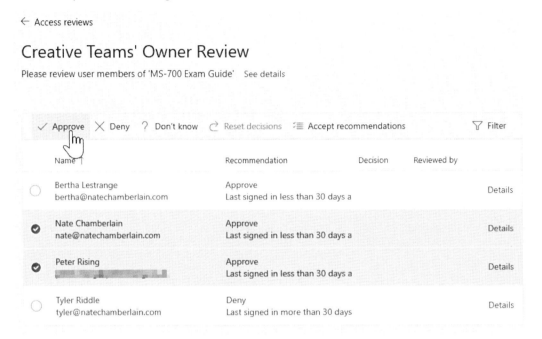

Figure 13.17 – A reviewer's view with responsibility for many users for bulk approval or denial

Access reviews can be created for each team and each can have different actions taken based on the team's content. For example, for more sensitive teams (those containing confidential information, for instance) you might choose to review monthly but have the owners review membership as opposed to letting users self-approve.

You can also select multiple groups instead of selecting them individually, having a whole set of groups' accesses reviewed in the same fashion and saving administrative time in setting up so many access reviews. Even though they were created simultaneously, the different groups will appear as separate access reviews on the dashboard once created but won't notify overlapping reviewers multiple times.

Summary

In this chapter, we covered Microsoft Teams membership configuration. First, we reviewed managing team membership at the user level, including the promotion of members to owners and vice versa.

Then we saw how membership can be automated using Microsoft 365 or security groups with dynamic membership (such as based on a user's department or job title).

Lastly, we learned how to implement access reviews so that users and team owners can be more autonomous in their membership management.

In the next and final chapter of this guide, we'll explore Microsoft Teams app policies.

Questions

This practice questions section consists of four questions related to a scenario (*Question set 1*), and six traditional multiple-choice questions (*Question set 2*)

Question set 1

Of the many departments in your organization, you're working on creating a team for each of the four shown here:

Name	Type
Marketing	Universal security
IT	Distribution
HR - Benefits	Nested distribution list
Sales	Global Security

You need to be sure you can create a team from each group. What should you do, minimizing administrative effort, to be able to create teams from these groups?

1. Marketing (Universal security)

   a. Change the group to an O365 group.

   b. Recreate the group as an O365 group.

   c. Change the group to a security group.

   d. Change the group to a distribution group.

2. IT (Distribution)

   a. Change the group to an O365 group.

   b. Recreate the group as an O365 group.

   c. Change the group to a security group.

   d. Change the group to a distribution group.

3.   HR – Benefits (Nested distribution list)

a. Change the group to an O365 group.

b. Recreate the group as an O365 group.

c. Change the group to a security group.

d. Change the group to a distribution group.

4.   Sales (Global Security)

a. Change the group to an O365 group.

b. Recreate the group as an O365 group.

c. Change the group to a security group.

d. Change the group to a distribution group.

Question set 2

1.   Members of a team must be reviewed monthly to make sure access is still needed by all members and that only active users remain. What solution should you implement?

a. Access reviews in the Azure AD admin center

b. eDiscovery cases in the Security & Compliance center

c. Usage reports in the SharePoint admin center

d. Usage reports in the Microsoft Teams admin center

2.   One of your team's owners has requested that their members are emailed annually to verify their continued interest in membership of the team. This solution should simplify membership management. What solution should you implement?

a. Make the team owner an Azure AD admin

b. Access reviews in the Azure AD admin center

c. Supervision policies in the Security & Compliance center

d. A Power Automate flow on a recurrence trigger

3. You have the following dynamic rule in place for membership:

```
(user.department -contains "HR" -or user.department
-contains "IT") -and (user.country -eq "US") -and (user.
userType -contains "Guest")
Which of the following users will be included in the
group?
```

a. A guest user in IT that has the country attribute set to UK

b. An internal member of IT that has the country attribute set to US

c. An internal member of Marketing that has the country attribute set to UK

d. A guest user in HR that has the country attribute set to US

4. Which of the options should be Line 2, completing a PowerShell command set correctly to promote Bertha from team member to team owner?
Line 1: `$team = Get-Team -DisplayName "Nate LLC"`
Line 2: _____

a. `Set-TeamUser -GroupId $team.GroupID -User bertha@ natechamberlain.com -Role Owner`

b. `Add-TeamUser -GroupId $team.GroupID -User bertha@ natechamberlain.com -Role Owner`

c. `Update-TeamUser -GroupId $team.GroupID -User bertha@ natechamberlain.com -Role Owner`

d. `Remove-TeamUser -GroupId $team.GroupID -User bertha@ natechamberlain.com -Role Member`

5. You're attempting to create a dynamic membership group in Azure AD, and have made it to the new group creation screen, but the option to change membership type from assigned to dynamic is disabled (grayed out). What's the likely cause?

a. You aren't assigned an Azure Active Directory Premium P1 license.

b. You aren't assigned the user administrator role.

c. You aren't assigned the global administrator role.

d. You aren't assigned an Azure Active Directory Premium P2 license.

6. Who needs to be assigned an Azure Active Directory Premium P2 license in the access review process? Assume none of these individuals are Global or User administrators. Select all that apply.

a. The person setting up an access review in Azure AD

b. The person assigned as a reviewer in an access review

c. The member being reviewed by the team owner in an access review

d. The team owner reviewing all members of their team/group in an access review

Further reading

At the following links, you can find more information about the mentioned tools:

- Assign team owners and members in Microsoft Teams: `https://docs.microsoft.com/en-us/microsoftteams/assign-roles-permissions`

- Manage user access to Teams: `https://docs.microsoft.com/en-us/microsoftteams/user-access`

- Manage teams in the Microsoft Teams admin center: `https://docs.microsoft.com/en-us/microsoftteams/manage-teams-in-modern-portal`

- Manage team settings and permissions in Teams: `https://support.microsoft.com/en-gb/office/manage-team-settings-and-permissions-in-teams-ce053b04-1b8e-4796-baa8-90dc427b3acc`

- Overview of dynamic membership for Teams: `https://docs.microsoft.com/en-us/microsoftteams/dynamic-memberships`

- Dynamic membership rules for groups in Azure Active Directory: `https://docs.microsoft.com/en-us/azure/active-directory/enterprise-users/groups-dynamic-membership`

- Create or update a dynamic group in Azure Active Directory: `https://docs.microsoft.com/en-us/azure/active-directory/enterprise-users/groups-create-rule`

- Change static group membership to dynamic in Azure Active Directory: `https://docs.microsoft.com/en-us/azure/active-directory/enterprise-users/groups-change-type`

- What are Azure AD access reviews?: `https://docs.microsoft.com/en-us/azure/active-directory/governance/access-reviews-overview`

- Manage user access with Azure AD access reviews: `https://docs.microsoft.com/en-us/azure/active-directory/governance/manage-user-access-with-access-reviews`

- Create an access review of groups and applications in Azure AD access reviews: `https://docs.microsoft.com/en-us/azure/active-directory/governance/create-access-review`

- Complete an access review of groups and applications in Azure AD access reviews: `https://docs.microsoft.com/en-us/azure/active-directory/governance/complete-access-review`

14
Creating App Policies within Microsoft Teams

In this final chapter, we will show you how to configure and manage Teams app permissions policies and Teams app setup policies from the Teams admin center. You will learn that app permission policies can be used to control which apps are made available to your Teams users, while app setup policies will control the user experience for apps in the Teams app in relation to the ability to upload custom apps to Teams, allow user pinning, choose which apps are installed for groups of users, and determine the order that apps appear in within the Teams app.

In this chapter, we're going to cover the following main topics:

- Setting up and managing app permission policies
- Setting up and managing app setup policies

Technical requirements

In this chapter, you will need to have access to the **Microsoft Teams admin center**, which you can reach at `https://admin.teams.microsoft.com`. You will need to be either a *Global Administrator* or a *Teams Service Administrator* to have full access to the features and capabilities within the Teams admin center.

Setting up and managing app permission policies

Teams app **permission policies** control the apps available to users from the **Apps** node of the left-hand navigation bar in Teams. For example, you may wish to choose to disallow a certain app from being added to Teams in your organization, or perhaps only certain users should be able to utilize a certain third-party app within Teams.

As with the other Teams policies, only one permission policy can be assigned to any single user, whether by individual or group assignment. If no custom policy is explicitly assigned to a user, the **Global** (**Org-wide** default) policy will apply to them.

Each permission policy has three areas that can be configured: **Microsoft apps**, **Third-party apps**, and **Custom apps**. For each area, you can choose one of the following settings:

- **Allow all apps**
- **Allow specific apps and block all others**
- **Block specific apps and allow all others**
- **Block all apps**

If you choose either **Allow specific apps and block all others** or **Block specific apps and allow all others**, you'll also choose the apps that are to be allowed or blocked, respectively.

In *Figure 14.1*, a permission policy is configured to allow all Microsoft apps, block all third-party apps except Adobe Sign and ADP Virtual Assistant, and block all custom apps:

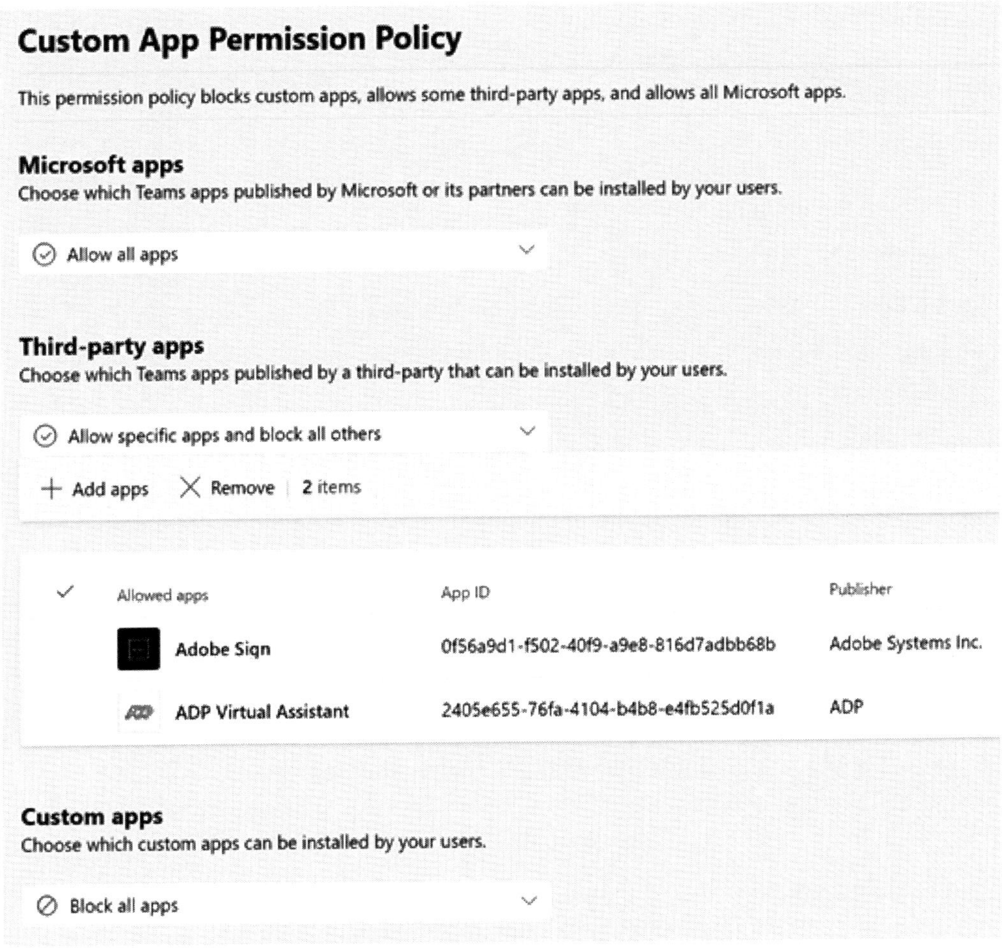

Figure 14.1 – A custom permission policy configured to only allow Microsoft apps
and two specific third-party apps

In the next section, we'll cover setting up and managing app setup policies.

Setting up and managing app setup policies

Teams app **setup policies** are what determine the apps that are installed for users by default, those to be listed in users' left-hand navigation bar in Teams, as well as the order in which they're listed from top to bottom. You can also specify whether the user(s) can upload custom apps and allow user pinning.

Even though you'll determine a base policy for users, they still may be able to install additional apps and re-order their left-hand navigation bar based on the permission policies set up for the user(s).

Each app setup policy features the following configurable settings:

- **Upload custom apps** (on/off)
- **Allow user pinning** (on/off)
- **Installed apps** (add apps you want to be installed for applicable users)
- **Pinned apps** (those apps that should appear in the left-hand navigation bar and the order in which they should be listed)

If you allow users to **upload custom apps** (in ZIP format), they can do so by selecting **Apps** from the left-hand navigation menu in Teams, then choosing **Upload a custom app** from the bottom of the left menu.

Allowing user pinning means that in addition to their apps being pinned how you specify via the app setup policy, users can elect to pin *additional* apps to their own navigation menu. This makes Teams customizable and can improve the user experience for those frequently utilizing other apps not included in your app setup policy.

Installed apps are those that a user would normally have to add manually, such as the Starbucks app, which allows teammates to send each other digital Starbucks cards via Teams chats. You can choose to install this app (or any non-default app) for users so that all users who are assigned the policy have the same set of tools automatically.

Lastly, **pinned apps** are the apps that you want to show permanently in users' left-hand navigation menus and the order in which they should appear (top to bottom).

To create a new app setup policy, choose **Teams apps** > **Setup policies** from the Microsoft Teams admin center, then click **Add**.

Figure 14.2 shows a setup policy configured to pin *Shifts* to the left-hand navigation bar of Teams for assigned users:

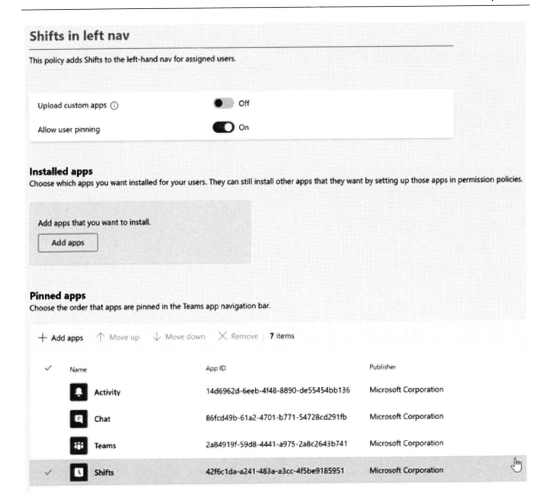

Figure 14.2 – An app policy showing Shifts pinned for users in the fourth nav position

Policies like this can help make user adoption more likely by creating more tailored user experiences requiring less work by users to set up a relevant interface for their daily work.

Summary

In this chapter, we covered the configuration of app permission policies, which specify the apps a user should be able to install for themselves.

We also reviewed app setup policies, which allow us to customize user experiences by pre-installing and pinning certain apps in a particular order for assigned users.

Questions

This practice questions section consists of four questions related to a scenario (*Question set 1*), and six traditional multiple-choice questions (*Question set 2*)

Question set 1

Your organization has a permission policy configured as shown in *Figure 14.3*:

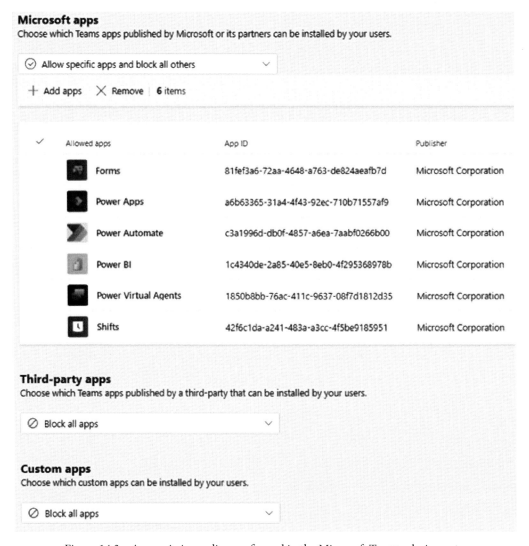

Figure 14.3 – A permission policy configured in the Microsoft Teams admin center

State whether each of the following statements is true or false based on the policy shown in *Figure 14.3*:

1. Users can install Adobe Sign.

   a. True

   b. False

2. Users can install their own custom apps.

   a. True

   b. False

3. Users can install DocuSign.

   a. True

   b. False

4. Users can install Power Virtual Agents.

   a. True

   b. False

Question set 2

1. Which type of policy specifies which apps and in what order they appear in users' left-hand navigation menu?

   a. App permission policy

   b. App setup policy

   c. Meeting policy

   d. Live events policy

2. A group of users uses the Shifts app regularly, but not all users. How can you pin the Shifts app to the left-hand navigation for just a subset of users?

   a. Create a live events policy and assign it to all users

   b. Create a meeting policy and assign it to specific users

   c. Create an app setup policy and assign it to specific users

   d. Create an app setup policy and assign it to all users

3. You need to prevent most users from installing third-party or custom apps in Teams. What should you create?

    a. An app permission policy assigned to a subset of users

    b. An app permission policy assigned to all users

    c. An app setup policy assigned to a subset of users

    d. An app setup policy assigned to all users

4. You've been tasked with creating a solution to allow Marketing department members to install the DocuSign and Adobe Sign apps in Teams to help with their frequent virtual documentation processes. No other users in your organization should be allowed to install these apps. What should you create?

    a. An app permission policy assigned to a subset of users

    b. An app permission policy assigned to all users

    c. An app setup policy assigned to a subset of users

    d. An app setup policy assigned to all users

5. You want to change the order of pinned apps in the Teams left-hand navigation menu for all users in your organization. You have not created any custom app setup policies and want a solution that avoids doing so. What can you do?

    a. Create an app permission policy

    b. Create an app setup policy – it's unavoidable

    c. Adjust the **Global** (**Org-wide** default) app setup policy

    d. Adjust the **Global** (**Org-wide** default) app permission policy

6. Which of the following is not a configurable section of a new app permission policy?

    a. **Microsoft apps**

    b. **Uploaded apps**

    c. **Custom apps**

    d. **Third-party apps**

Further reading

At the following links, you can find more information about the tools mentioned in this chapter:

- Manage app permission policies in Microsoft Teams: `https://docs.microsoft.com/en-us/microsoftteams/teams-app-permission-policies`

- Admin settings for apps in Microsoft Teams: `https://docs.microsoft.com/en-us/microsoftteams/admin-settings`

- Manage app setup policies in Microsoft Teams: `https://docs.microsoft.com/en-us/microsoftteams/teams-app-setup-policies`

Section 4: Mock Exams and Assessments

Each chapter in the book has included review questions. All answers to the review questions and the two mock exams in this part of the book can be found in the *Assessments* section at the end.

This part of the book comprises the following chapters:

- *Chapter 15, Mock Exam*
- *Chapter 16, Mock Exam Answers*
- *Chapter 17, Assessments*

15
Mock Exam

This chapter consists of 25 exam questions that are designed to be as close as possible to the actual test. All of the questions are multiple-choice, and there may be more than one correct answer for each question; you will need to select all of them for each question in order to get the question correct. Some of the questions that follow will be in the form of a case study.

Case study (five questions)

You are the Teams administrator for an organization called Contoso. Here is your current situation:

Offices, group SIPs, and current coexistence modes

- Chicago

  chicago@contoso.com

  150 users

  Uses Skype for Business Online only (SfBOnly)

- London

  `london@contoso.com`

  350 users

  Uses Teams only (`TeamsOnly`)

- New York City

  `newyork@contoso.com`

  500 users

  Uses Skype for Business Online for chats/calls and Teams for collaboration and meetings (`SfBWithTeamsCollabAndMeetings`)

Devices

All locations are using Windows 10 devices.

The Chicago and New York City locations use iOS mobile devices.

The London office uses Android devices.

Voice project

Contoso plans to assign all users in all locations new phone numbers, discarding their current on-premises solution and existing numbers, and use Microsoft 365's Phone System instead.

In addition to making sure each user will have their own number, each geographic location will need a number assigned to a resource account to be used with an auto attendant to assist in call routing.

There are two help desks: one based in New York for both US locations and one for the UK. Each help desk will also need a unique number to be used with a call queue.

Policies and settings

All policies are the **Global (Org-wide default)** option. Settings and policies that have been customized are listed and configured as follows:

Messaging policy

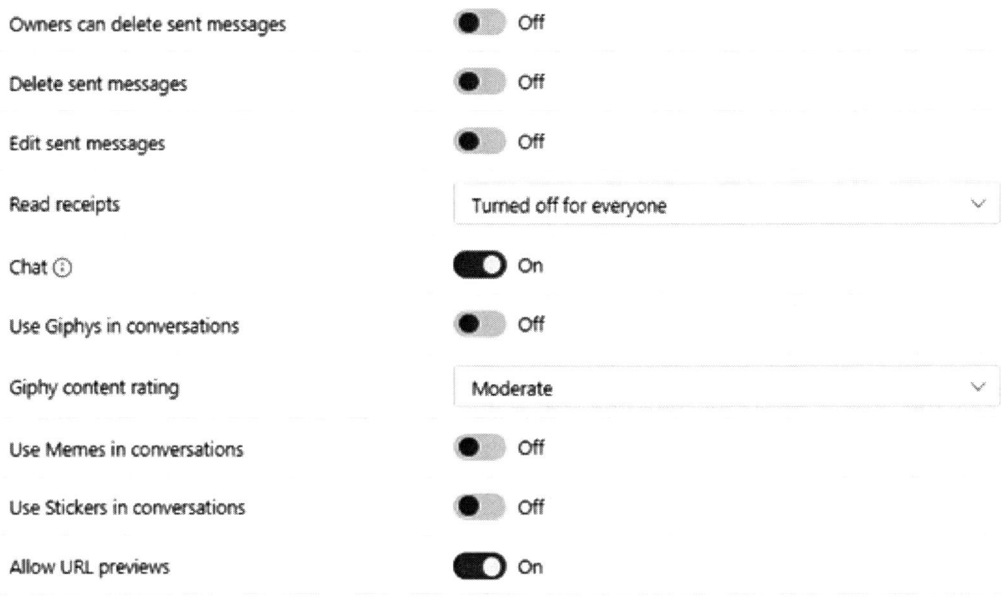

Owners can delete sent messages
Off
Delete sent messages
Off
Edit sent messages
Off
Read receipts
Turned off for everyone
Chat
On
Use Giphys in conversations
Off
Giphy content rating
Moderate
Use Memes in conversations
Off
Use Stickers in conversations
Off
Allow URL previews
On

Figure 15.1 – A messaging policy configuration in the Microsoft Teams admin center

Meeting settings

Participants
Anonymous users can join a meeting
On
Anonymous users can interact with apps in meetings
On

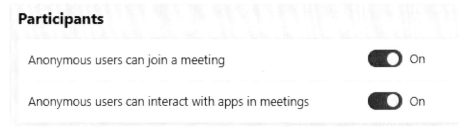

Figure 15.2 – Participants section of Meeting settings

Case study questions

1. You need to set the Microsoft Teams upgrade policy for your Chicago users so that they only use Skype for chats/calls/meetings but will use Teams for collaboration (channels). You have a CSV of the Chicago users you'll be importing. Which two values would complete the following PowerShell script and grant all users in the CSV the correct upgrade policy?

   ```
   import-csv ChicagoUsers.csv{_____
   -PolicyName _____ -Identity $_.upn}
   ```

   a. `Grant-CsTeamsUpgradePolicy`, `SfBWithTeamsCollabAndMeetings`

   b. `Grant-CsTeamsUpgradePolicy`, `SfBWithTeamsCollab`

   c. `Set-CsTeamsUpgradePolicy`, `SfBOnly`

   d. `Set-CsTeamsUpgradePolicy`, `UpgradeToTeams`

2. You've been asked if users from other companies will be able to join meetings created and sent from your organization. Based on the provided information in the case study, how should you respond?

   a. Yes, users from other companies are able to join our meetings.

   b. No, users from other companies are restricted from joining our meetings.

3. How many phone numbers and licenses (at a minimum) will you need to complete the voice project?

   a. 1 calling plan license, 5 Phone System – Virtual User licenses, 1,000 phone numbers

   b. 1,000 calling plan licenses, 5 Phone System – Virtual User licenses, 1,005 phone numbers

   c. 1,000 calling plan license, 5 Phone System – Virtual User licenses, 1,000 phone numbers

   d. 1,005 calling plan licenses, 5 Phone System – Virtual User licenses, 1,005 phone numbers

4. You need to ensure that Microsoft Teams is deployed to all Windows devices in the London office. What is the best way to achieve this?

   a. Go to the **Teams admin center**, choose the option to download the Teams app in the background for Skype for Business users, and set it to **Off**.

   b. Go to the **Teams admin center** and under **Org-wide settings | Teams upgrade**, choose the option to download the Teams app in the background for Skype for Business users and set it to **On**.

   c. Create an **App setup policy** in the Teams admin center.

   d. Use `Set-CSTeamsAppSetupPolicy` in PowerShell.

5. The New York office would like to start using Teams Rooms devices. In order to simplify the configuration of the new Teams Rooms devices, you plan to set up a configuration profile for Teams Rooms devices in the Teams admin center. Does this meet the goal?

   a. Yes

   b. No

Multiple-choice questions (20 questions)

1. What can you use to investigate call quality issues?

   a. Network Planner

   b. Teams client debug logs

   c. Teams usage reports

   d. Call Analytics Dashboard

2. As a Teams admin for your organization, you've been asked to create a hotline that would reach any available help desk associate. How can this be accomplished?

   a. Create a call queue.

   b. Create an auto attendant.

   c. Create a resource account.

   d. Create a conference bridge.

3. As a Teams admin for your organization, you've been asked to help automate some of the work done by the organization's phone operator to reduce their call volume and wait times. You'll need to give callers the ability to press a number corresponding to their request type to make sure they're routed to the right individual or call queue. They should still have the option to speak to the operator if they wish. What should you create to accomplish this?

    a. A call queue

    b. An auto attendant

    c. A call park policy

    d. A conference bridge

4. You want to create a regular, monthly meeting where every member of a team is invited to share best practices and ideas related to your shared goals. What type of meeting should you create?

    a. Private meeting

    b. Channel meeting

    c. Outlook meeting

    d. Live event

5. You want to restrict users from using GIFs in chats and conversations. What should you create?

    a. Calling policy

    b. Teams policy

    c. Meeting policy

    d. Messaging policy

6. Users have been primarily using Dropbox instead of M365 solutions such as OneDrive or SharePoint for their teams' file tabs. You need to modify Microsoft Teams as an administrator to disable third-party storage solution providers including Dropbox to encourage M365 usage. What should you configure to accomplish this?

    a. App permission policy

    b. Teams policy

    c. App setup policy

    d. Teams settings

7. You need to pin a custom app to the left navigation menu for all HR members, but not for any other users in the organization. How can you accomplish this from the Teams admin center?

   a. App setup policy

   b. Teams policy

   c. App permission policy

   d. Messaging policy

8. Your organization wants to use Microsoft 365 for a voice pilot project and you're the Teams administrator. What two actions should you perform?

   a. Deploy a **Session Border Controller (SBC)**.

   b. Purchase a calling plan for each user.

   c. Purchase a calling plan for the organization.

   d. Create a dial plan for the organization.

   e. Assign an additional license and phone number for each user.

   f. Purchase a third-party encoder.

9. Your organization uses Microsoft Teams and has a group named SharePoint Champions. You need to remove inactive users from SharePoint Champions by having the group owner (User1) validate membership on a monthly basis. What two things do you need to accomplish this?

   a. Assign User1 an Azure Active Directory Premium P1 license.

   b. Assign User1 and Azure Active Directory Premium P2 license.

   c. Create an access review in the Azure Active Directory admin center.

   d. Create a usage report in the Microsoft Teams admin center.

   e. Create an eDiscovery case in the Security & Compliance admin center.

10. You've been asked to limit which apps sales department users can install in Teams. You'll need to block all third-party and custom apps and only allow a handful of Microsoft apps. The solution should only affect users in the sales department. What should you configure to accomplish this?

    a. App permission policy

    b. App setup policy

    c. Teams settings

    d. Teams policies

11. As a Teams administrator, you have been asked to grant permissions to a user so they may troubleshoot communications issues using basic tools. Which administrative role should you assign to the user (applying the principle of least privilege)?

    a. Teams Service Administrator

    b. Teams Communications Support Engineer

    c. Teams Device Administrator

    d. Teams Communications Support Specialist

12. You have been asked to enable the users in your organization to use Skype for Business to receive chats and calls but use Microsoft Teams for group collaboration and meeting scheduling. From the Microsoft Teams admin center, you navigate to **Org-wide settings | Teams upgrade** and set **Coexistence mode** to **Skype for Business with Teams collaboration**. Does this meet the goal?

    a. Yes.

    b. No.

13. You have been asked to ensure that only a designated set of users in your organization have the permissions to create teams within Microsoft Teams. What is the first step you need to take to achieve this?

    a. Create a Microsoft 365 group and add the required users to the group.

    b. Create a new distribution group and add the required users as members.

    c. Create a new security group and add the required users to the group.

    d. Create a new dynamic distribution group and add the required users as members.

14. You need to configure your Teams and Skype for Business users to be able to communicate with users outside of your organization. You go to the Teams admin center and navigate to **Org-wide settings | Guest access** and set the option for **Allow guest access to Teams** to **On**. Does this meet the goal?

    a. Yes.

    b. No.

15. You have been asked to create retention policies for all workloads within your Microsoft 365 environment, including Teams. What is the minimum number of retention policies that you will need to create in the Microsoft Compliance center to achieve this?

    a. 1

    b. 2

    c. 3

    d. 4

16. You have a group naming policy in place to ensure that when a team is created, a suffix is added to the team name. You note that some new teams that are being created are not created with the required suffix. What could be a possible reason for this?

    a. The group naming policy is set up with a fixed string instead of a user attribute.

    b. You have not added any custom blocked words to your group naming policy.

    c. The user who created the team is a Global Administrator.

    d. The user who created the team is a Teams Service Administrator.

17. You have been asked to ensure that an administrator is notified whenever a new team is created. You create an alert policy in the Security & Compliance Center. Does this meet the goal?

    a. Yes.

    b. No.

18. You need to assign a user the ability to view the Teams user activity report with the principle of least privilege applied. Which role should you assign to this user?

    a. Teams Service Administrator

    b. Teams Communications Support Specialist

    c. Teams Communications Support Engineer

    d. Reports reader

19. You need to ensure that users in the London office do not have the ability to record Teams meetings. You create a new custom meeting policy with the setting of **Allow cloud recording** set to **Off**. You assign this policy to the London office users and leave the Chicago and New York City office users assigned to the **Global (Org-wide default)** meeting policy. Does this achieve the objective?

    a. Yes.

    b. No.

20. A user deletes a team that she is an owner of. 2 months later, she asks you if the team can be restored. Is this possible?

    a. Yes.

    b. No.

16
Mock Exam Answers

In this chapter, we will review the mock exam from the previous chapter and provide the answers and explanations for each question.

Answers and explanations

1. B. `Grant-CsTeamsUpgradePolicy`, `SfBWithTeamsCollab`

   Explanation: `Grant-CsTeamsUpgradePolicy` is used for Skype for Business Online users, while `Set-CsTeamsUpgradePolicy` is specifically for Skype for Business 2019 (on-premises) deployments. `SfBWithTeamsCollab` co-existence mode will allow users to continue using Skype for calls, meetings, and chats but will allow channel collaboration in Teams.

   Reference: `https://docs.microsoft.com/en-us/powershell/module/skype/grant-csteamsupgradepolicy?view=skype-ps` and `https://docs.microsoft.com/en-us/microsoftteams/migration-interop-guidance-for-teams-with-skype#detailed-mode-descriptions`

2. A. Yes, users from other companies are able to join our meetings.

Explanation: Based on the information given, we can assume that users from other organizations are able to join our meetings as the meeting settings currently allow anonymous participants. We do not have information about blocked domains, and even if there were, users from those domains could still join meetings as anonymous individuals (they just wouldn't be able to collaborate in our teams and channels).

Reference: `https://docs.microsoft.com/en-us/microsoftteams/meeting-settings-in-teams#allow-anonymous-users-to-join-meetings`

3. B. 1,000 calling plan licenses, 5 Phone System – Virtual User licenses, 1,005 phone numbers

Explanation: Bots don't need calling plan licenses, as you use the free Phone System – Virtual User license for each of them instead. So, we only need 1,000 calling plan licenses for our human users and 5 of the free virtual user licenses. Each virtual bot (5 total queues and attendants) as well as each human user (1,000) will need a unique number, so we need 1,005 phone numbers.

Reference: `https://docs.microsoft.com/en-us/microsoftteams/plan-auto-attendant-call-queue` and `https://docs.microsoft.com/en-us/microsoftteams/setting-up-your-phone-system#step-2-buy-and-assign-phone-system-and-calling-plan-licenses`

4. B. Go to the Teams admin center, and under **Org-wide settings | Teams upgrade**, choose the option to download the Teams app in the background for Skype for Business users and set it to **On**.

Explanation: You should go to the Teams admin center, and under **Org-wide settings | Teams upgrade**, choose the option to download the Teams app in the background for Skype for Business users and set it to **On**. This will achieve the goal if the coexistence setting for the user is set to Teams only.

Reference: `https://docs.microsoft.com/en-us/microsoftteams/setting-your-coexistence-and-upgrade-settings`

5. B. No, configuration profiles may not be used with Teams Rooms devices.

Explanation: Configuration profiles may only be used with IP phones, collaboration bars, and Teams displays.

Reference: `https://docs.microsoft.com/en-us/microsoftteams/ devices/device-management#use-configuration-profiles-in- teams`

6. D. Call analytics dashboard

    Explanation: Call analytics can be used to troubleshoot poor call quality and grant the Teams communications support specialist role to those needing tier 1 support abilities (limited) and the Teams communications support engineer role to those needing tier 2 (full access) support abilities to per-user call analytics.

    Reference: `https://docs.microsoft.com/en-us/microsoftteams/ use-call-analytics-to-troubleshoot-poor-call-quality`

7. A. Create a call queue.

    Explanation: Call queues can ring any available user in the queue, or all users simultaneously depending on the configuration.

    Reference: `https://docs.microsoft.com/en-us/microsoftteams/ create-a-phone-system-call-queue`

8. B. Create an auto attendant.

    Explanation: Auto attendants can be configured to provide choices to callers and route calls based on callers' responses.

    Reference: `https://docs.microsoft.com/en-us/microsoftteams/ create-a-phone-system-auto-attendant`

9. B. Channel meeting

    Explanation: Channel meetings automatically invite all team members, and discussions and/or recordings are saved to the channel, making any shared resources or chats available to team members as well.

    Reference: `https://docs.microsoft.com/en-us/MicrosoftTeams/ tutorial-meetings-in-teams?tutorial-step=2`

10. D. Messaging policy

    Explanation: Chat and channel messaging features, such as GIF usage, can be limited via messaging policies.

    Reference: `https://docs.microsoft.com/en-us/microsoftteams/ messaging-policies-in-teams`

11. D. Teams settings

    Explanation: You can find the Teams settings under **Org-wide settings** in the Teams admin center. There is a section for files in which you can enable or disable certain cloud storage providers, such as Dropbox.

    Reference: `https://docs.microsoft.com/en-us/microsoftteams/enable-features-office-365#files`

12. A. App setup policy

    Explanation: App setup policies determine which apps appear in users' left-side navigation menus and in what order. They can be assigned to specific users and groups.

    Reference: `https://docs.microsoft.com/en-us/MicrosoftTeams/teams-app-setup-policies`

13. B and E. Purchase a calling plan for each user and assign the license to each along with a phone number.

    Explanation: A calling plan license and phone number will be required for each user in the voice pilot project.

    Reference: `https://docs.microsoft.com/en-us/microsoftteams/set-up-calling-plans#step-2-buy-and-assign-licenses`

14. B and C. Create an access review in the Azure Active Directory admin center and assign User1 a P2 license.

    Explanation: Any user performing an access review, User1 in this case, needs an Azure Active Directory Premium P2 license. Access reviews allow users to review group membership regularly and can be done by members themselves (if licensed appropriately) or by designated individuals (group owners or static chosen individuals).

    Reference: `https://docs.microsoft.com/en-us/azure/active-directory/governance/access-reviews-overview`

15. A. App permission policy

    Explanation: App permission policies control which apps (Microsoft, third-party, or custom) users are able to install. As with other policy types, you can assign these to specific individuals and groups. If a custom policy isn't assigned to a user, the global (org-wide default) policy will apply to them.

Reference: `https://docs.microsoft.com/en-us/microsoftteams/ teams-app-permission-policies`

16. D. Teams communications support specialist

Explanation: Teams communications support specialist is the most appropriate role for the user. The Teams communications support engineer role would grant the user advanced troubleshooting tools. The Teams device administrator role would allow the user to manage devices configured for use in Teams, and the Teams service administrator role grants access to all areas and features within the Teams admin center.

Reference: `https://docs.microsoft.com/en-us/microsoftteams/ using-admin-roles`

17. B. No

Explanation: The Skype for Business with Teams collaboration mode will not provide the meeting scheduling option. You should set the coexistence mode to Skype for Business with Teams collaboration and meetings.

Reference: `https://docs.microsoft.com/en-us/microsoftteams/ setting-your-coexistence-and-upgrade-settings`

18. C. Create a new security group and add the required users to the group.

Explanation: You need to create a new security group and add the required users. Then, you will use PowerShell to ensure that no one in your organization can create teams apart from members of this security group. Microsoft 365 groups, distribution groups, and dynamic distribution groups may not be used to configure these settings.

Reference: `https://docs.microsoft.com/en-us/microsoft-365/ solutions/manage-creation-of-groups?view=o365-worldwide`

19. B. No

Explanation: Guest access settings control whether people outside of your organization can be invited into your teams and channels. They do not control the ability to communicate with external users. You should instead navigate to **Org-wide settings | External access**.

Reference: `https://docs.microsoft.com/en-us/microsoftteams/ manage-external-access`

20. B. 2

    Explanation: 2 is the correct answer as Microsoft Teams retention policies must be created in a separate retention policy. All other Microsoft 365 workloads may coexist in a single policy, but Teams must be separate.

    Reference: `https://docs.microsoft.com/en-us/microsoftteams/retention-policies`

21. C. The user who created the team is a global administrator.

    Explanation: Global administrators are exempt from group naming policies, as are user administrators and partner support (tiers 1 and 2).

    Reference: `https://docs.microsoft.com/en-us/microsoft-365/solutions/groups-naming-policy?view=o365-worldwide#admin-override`

22. A. Yes

    Explanation: An alert policy allows you to select an administrator who can be notified of the new team creation.

    Reference: `https://docs.microsoft.com/en-us/microsoft-365/compliance/alert-policies?view=o365-worldwide`

23. D. Reports reader

    Explanation: The reports reader will provide the required access.

    Reference: `https://docs.microsoft.com/en-us/microsoftteams/teams-activity-reports`

24. A. Yes

    Explanation: The global (org-wide default) meeting policy will apply to all Teams users by default until you explicitly assign specific users to another policy.

    Reference: `https://docs.microsoft.com/en-us/microsoftteams/meeting-policies-in-teams`

25. B. No

    Explanation: Teams can only be restored for a 30-day period after they have been deleted. This is known as a soft delete.

    Reference: `https://docs.microsoft.com/en-us/microsoftteams/archive-or-delete-a-team#restore-a-deleted-team`

17
Assessments

In the following pages, we will review all the practice questions from each of the chapters in this book and provide the correct answers and explanations, where applicable.

Chapter 1 – Planning Your Migration to Microsoft Teams

1. C. Configure both hybrid connectivity and coexistence with Teams.

    Explanation: If you are running Skype for Business Online, then you will only need to complete a coexistence mode setup with Teams.

    If you are running Skype for Business on-premises, you need to both set up coexistence and establish hybrid connectivity with your Microsoft 365 environment. This is required because Skype for Business on-premises users must be moved to the cloud in order to function correctly during the subsequent coexistence mode setup: `https://docs.microsoft.com/en-us/MicrosoftTeams/upgrade-to-teams-execute-skypeforbusinessonline`.

2. D. Meeting Migration Service

    Explanation: You would use Meeting Migration Service to migrate users' meetings from Skype for Business to Microsoft Teams. The Skype for Business admin center and Microsoft Teams admin center do not include this feature. There is no such thing as the Meeting Migration tool: `https://docs.microsoft.com/en-us/skypeforbusiness/audio-conferencing-in-office-365/setting-up-the-meeting-migration-service-mms`.

3. B. False

    Explanation: Skype for Business internal users may not communicate with Microsoft Teams internal users when the coexistence mode is set to Islands as Skype for Business and Microsoft Teams are considered two separate solutions in Islands mode: `https://docs.microsoft.com/en-us/microsoftteams/teams-and-skypeforbusiness-coexistence-and-interoperability#islands-mode`.

4. C. `https://admin.teams.microsoft.com`

    Explanation: `https://admin.teams.microsoft.com` is the URL for the Microsoft Teams admin center. `https://teams.admin.microsoft.com` and `https://admin.teams.office.com` are not genuine URLs for any Microsoft service. `https://teams.microsoft.com` will open the Microsoft Teams web app: `https://docs.microsoft.com/en-us/microsoftteams/manage-teams-in-modern-portal`.

5. A. True

    Explanation: With the Skype for Business with Teams Collaboration coexistence mode, users will use mainly Skype for Business, but can use Teams for collaborating in Teams channels: `https://docs.microsoft.com/en-us/microsoftteams/teams-and-skypeforbusiness-coexistence-and-interoperability#skype-for-business-with-teams-collaboration`.

6. A. Lync with Teams collaboration

    Explanation: There is no such setting. The available coexistence modes are explained at `https://docs.microsoft.com/en-us/microsoftteams/teams-and-skypeforbusiness-coexistence-and-interoperability`.

7. B. **Org-wide settings | Teams upgrade**, and C. **Users**

   Explanation: Use **Org-wide settings | Teams upgrade** to set coexistence for the whole organization, and **Users** to set coexistence on a per-user basis: `https://docs.microsoft.com/en-us/microsoftteams/setting-your-coexistence-and-upgrade-settings#set-upgrade-options-for-all-users-in-your-organization` and `https://docs.microsoft.com/en-us/microsoftteams/setting-your-coexistence-and-upgrade-settings#set-upgrade-options-for-a-single-user-in-your-organization`.

8. A. True

   Explanation: The PowerShell command to trigger meeting migrations is `Start-CsExMeetingMigration`: `https://docs.microsoft.com/en-us/powershell/module/skype/start-csexmeetingmigration?view=skype-ps`.

9. D. Enable the SIP address space in your Microsoft 365 environment by using the Teams admin center.

   Explanation: Enabling the SIP address space is done by using Skype for Business Online PowerShell. It cannot be done from the Teams admin center: `https://docs.microsoft.com/en-us/skypeforbusiness/hybrid/configure-federation-with-skype-for-business-online#configure-your-on-premises-environment-to-enable-shared-sip-address-space-with-microsoft-365-or-office-365`.

10. A. True

    Explanation: In coexistence mode, when selecting the option to notify Skype for Business users that an upgrade to Teams is available, users will see a yellow banner in the Skype for Business app telling them that they will soon be upgraded to Teams: `https://docs.microsoft.com/en-us/microsoftteams/upgrade-to-teams-execute-skypeforbusinessonline#step-1-notify-the-users-of-the-change-optional`.

Chapter 2 – Assessing Your Network Readiness for a Microsoft Teams Deployment

1. D. `Install-Module -Name NetworkTestingCompanion`

    Explanation: The other three commands are incorrect.

2. D. `50060:50079`

    Explanation: The other listed port ranges are not relevant to Teams media types: `https://docs.microsoft.com/en-us/microsoft-365/enterprise/urls-and-ip-address-ranges?view=o365-worldwide#skype-for-business-online-and-microsoft-teams`.

3. A. True

    Explanation: Quality of Service in Microsoft Teams is designed to improve media performance during Teams meetings: `https://docs.microsoft.com/en-us/microsoftteams/qos-in-teams`.

4. D. Network Organization Chart

    Explanation: The available options are Report, Personas, Network Plans, and Network Sites: `https://docs.microsoft.com/en-us/microsoftteams/network-planner`.

5. A. True

    Explanation: When configuring QoS in the Teams admin center, selecting the option to automatically set the media ports will result in the ports from range `1024-65535` being used: `https://docs.microsoft.com/en-us/microsoftteams/qos-in-teams#choose-initial-port-ranges-for-each-media-type`.

6. D. Teams Chat

    Explanation: Teams Chat has no relation to Quality of Service settings within Microsoft Teams: `https://docs.microsoft.com/en-us/microsoftteams/monitor-call-quality-qos`.

7. C. **Meetings | Meeting settings**

   Explanation: The network settings for Quality of Service are configured from the Teams admin center under **Meetings | Meeting settings**: `https://docs.microsoft.com/en-us/microsoftteams/meeting-settings-in-teams#set-how-you-want-to-handle-real-time-media-traffic-for-teams-meetings`.

8. A. True

   Explanation: The Network Testing Companion must be configured using Windows PowerShell.

9. C. Firstline Worker

   Explanation: The Network Planner tool contains the following built-in personas: Teams Room system, office worker, and remote worker.

10. B. False

    Explanation: Custom personas can be created using the Teams Network Planner: `https://docs.microsoft.com/en-us/microsoftteams/network-planner#create-a-custom-persona`.

Chapter 3 – Planning and Implementing Governance and Life Cycle Settings within Microsoft Teams

1. A. Attribute, and C. String

   Explanation: Attribute and String are the possible options when configuring prefixes and suffixes for Microsoft 365 group naming policies: `https://docs.microsoft.com/en-us/microsoft-365/solutions/groups-naming-policy?view=o365-worldwide`.

2. B. False

   Explanation: Teams that have been archived may be restored/made active again: `https://docs.microsoft.com/en-us/microsoftteams/archive-or-delete-a-team#make-an-archived-team-active`.

3. B. 730 days

    Explanation: A group expiration policy may be set to 365 days, 180 days, or a custom setting. While you could set the custom option to 730 days, there is no specific option for this value as there is for 365 or 180: `https://docs.microsoft.com/en-us/microsoft-365/solutions/microsoft-365-groups-expiration-policy?view=o365-worldwide`.

4. A. True

    Explanation: Global administrators will not be bound by the Teams naming policy: `https://docs.microsoft.com/en-us/microsoft-365/solutions/groups-naming-policy?view=o365-worldwide`.

5. D. **Azure Active Directory | Groups**

    Explanation: Expiration policies relate to Azure AD/Microsoft 365 groups: `https://docs.microsoft.com/en-us/microsoft-365/solutions/microsoft-365-groups-expiration-policy?view=o365-worldwide`.

6. C. 30 days

    Explanation: An administrator may restore a deleted team up to 30 days after it has been deleted: `https://docs.microsoft.com/en-us/microsoftteams/archive-or-delete-a-team#restore-a-deleted-team`.

7. B. False

    Explanation: A security group is required to control who in an organization may create Microsoft 365 groups: `https://docs.microsoft.com/en-us/microsoft-365/solutions/manage-creation-of-groups?view=o365-worldwide`.

8. C. Pre-built Teams templates may be edited.

    Explanation: It is not possible to edit the pre-built Teams templates: `https://docs.microsoft.com/en-us/microsoftteams/get-started-with-teams-templates`.

9. A. True

    Explanation: A Microsoft 365 group is required when a new team is created in Microsoft Teams: `https://docs.microsoft.com/en-us/microsoftteams/get-started-with-teams-create-your-first-teams-and-channels`.

10. A. True

    Explanation: It is possible to create Teams templates from the Microsoft Teams admin center: `https://docs.microsoft.com/en-us/microsoftteams/get-started-with-teams-templates-in-the-admin-console`.

Chapter 4 – Configuring Guest Access in Microsoft Teams

1. B. Security group settings

   Explanation: Guest user access relating to Microsoft may be controlled by/from the Teams admin center, Microsoft 365 group settings, or the Azure portal. These settings may not controlled by security group settings: `https://docs.microsoft.com/en-us/microsoftteams/guest-access`.

2. B. Specific Guests

   Explanation: Specific Guests is not a valid option when choosing the settings for external sharing policies. Valid choices would be **Specific people**, **Only people in your organization**, and **Anyone with the link**: `https://docs.microsoft.com/en-us/microsoft-365/solutions/collaborate-with-people-outside-your-organization?view=o365-worldwide`.

3. A. True

   Explanation: Guest users who you invite into your organization must use an existing Microsoft 365 account or a personal email account such as `Outlook.com` or `Gmail.com`, which can be enabled as a Microsoft organizational account, or a **One-Time Passcode (OTP)**, for guest access: `https://docs.microsoft.com/en-us/microsoft-365/solutions/collaborate-with-people-outside-your-organization?view=o365-worldwide`.

4. B. Azure AD Access reviews

   Explanation: You can use Azure AD access reviews to review existing guest user permissions. You cannot review existing guest user permissions with Azure AD Identity Protection, Azure AD Privileged Identity Management, or Azure AD Conditional Access: `https://docs.microsoft.com/en-us/azure/active-directory/governance/access-reviews-overview`.

5. B. False

    Explanation: Azure AD access reviews may not be used with Azure AD
    Premium P1 licenses. Instead, an Azure AD Premium P2 license is required:
    `https://docs.microsoft.com/en-us/azure/active-directory/`
    `governance/access-reviews-overview#license-requirements.`

6. D. **Org-wide settings | Guest access**

    Explanation: Guest access settings may be configured in the Teams admin center
    under **Org-wide settings | Guest access**. The other options in this question do not
    exist: `https://docs.microsoft.com/en-us/microsoftteams/guest-`
    `access.`

7. C. Collaboration

    Explanation: Collaboration is not a valid option within guest access in the Teams
    admin center. Valid options are **Calling**, **Meeting**, and **Messaging**: `https://`
    `docs.microsoft.com/en-us/microsoftteams/guest-access.`

8. B. False

    Explanation: Azure AD guest accounts are not removed when a guest is removed
    from a team: `https://docs.microsoft.com/en-us/microsoftteams/`
    `guest-access.`

9. A. **External identities | Access reviews**, and C. **Identity Governance | Access
    reviews**

    Explanation: Access reviews may be viewed from either the **External Identities** or
    Identity Governance sections of the Azure portal. **Administrative Units** and **User
    Settings** are valid Azure AD sections, but don't contain any settings relating to
    Access reviews: `https://docs.microsoft.com/en-us/azure/active-`
    `directory/governance/create-access-review.`

10. A. True

    Explanation: Members of a group who are being reviewed under an Access review
    are able to complete the Access review themselves: `https://docs.microsoft.`
    `com/en-us/azure/active-directory/governance/create-access-`
    `review.`

Chapter 5 – Managing the Security and Compliance Settings for Microsoft Teams

1. D. Teams device support engineer

    Explanation: Teams device support engineer is not a valid role. Valid roles include **Teams Service Administrator**, **Teams Device Administrator**, and **Teams Communications Administrator**: `https://docs.microsoft.com/en-us/microsoftteams/using-admin-roles`.

2. A. True

    Explanation: The **Teams Service Administrator** role has access to all of the features available within the Teams admin center: `https://docs.microsoft.com/en-us/microsoftteams/using-admin-roles`.

3. C. The Security & Compliance Center

    Explanation: Alert policies must be set up from the Security & Compliance Center: `https://docs.microsoft.com/en-us/microsoft-365/compliance/alert-policies?view=o365-worldwide`.

4. B. False

    Explanation: It is possible to configure **sensitivity labels** for use in Microsoft Teams: `https://docs.microsoft.com/en-us/microsoft-365/compliance/sensitivity-labels-teams-groups-sites?view=o365-worldwide`.

5. C. Prevents users from communicating with other users by configuring information barrier segments

    Explanation: Information barriers are used to create segments internally between individuals or groups who should not be allowed to communicate with each other: `https://docs.microsoft.com/en-us/microsoftteams/information-barriers-in-teams`.

6. C. Delete after a dynamically determined time period

    Explanation: Delete after a dynamically determined time period is not a valid action option within a retention policy: `https://docs.microsoft.com/en-us/microsoftteams/retention-policies`.

7. B. False

    Explanation: Retention policies for Teams may not be set up in the same policy as other Microsoft 365 workloads. They must be configured in a separate policy: `https://docs.microsoft.com/en-us/microsoftteams/retention-policies`.

8. B. Download the report and export to Excel.

    Explanation: When running a report in the Teams admin center, it may be downloaded and exported into Excel. It may not be exported into Power BI, PDF, or a TXT file: `https://docs.microsoft.com/en-us/microsoftteams/teams-analytics-and-reports/teams-reporting-reference`.

9. B. False

    Explanation: Retention policies may not be applied to private channels within Teams: `https://docs.microsoft.com/en-us/microsoftteams/retention-policies`.

10. B. Teams Communication Administrator

    Explanation: The **Teams Communication Administrator** role is the minimum required from the listed roles that can be used to configure **Meeting policies** and **Meetings settings**: `https://docs.microsoft.com/en-us/microsoftteams/using-admin-roles`.

Chapter 6 – Managing Endpoint Devices in Microsoft Teams

1. B. Teams Rooms

    Explanation: Configuration profiles may not be used with **Teams Rooms**. They can be used with **Teams displays**, **collaboration bars**, and **IP phones**: `https://docs.microsoft.com/en-us/microsoftteams/devices/device-management#use-configuration-profiles-in-teams`.

2. D. 2

    Explanation: The two most recent versions of the Teams iOS app are supported by Microsoft: `https://docs.microsoft.com/en-us/microsoftteams/hardware-requirements-for-the-teams-app#hardware-requirements-for-teams-on-mobile-devices`.

3. A. True

    Explanation: The Teams app may be deployed to mobile devices using Intune app protection policies: `https://docs.microsoft.com/en-us/mem/intune/apps/app-protection-policy#app-protection-policies-on-devices`.

4. D. Recommended minimum of 2 GB of disk space available for each user profile.

    Explanation: This is not one of the minimum requirements for installing the Microsoft Teams app on Windows devices: `https://docs.microsoft.com/en-us/microsoftteams/hardware-requirements-for-the-teams-app#:~:text=Hardware%20requirements%20for%20Teams%20on%20a%20Windows%20PC,-Hardware%20requirements%20for&text-=Requires%202%2Dcore%20processor.,processor%20with%20AVX2%20instruction%20set`.

5. C. 4

    Explanation: The four most recent versions of the Teams Android app are supported by Microsoft: `https://docs.microsoft.com/en-us/microsoftteams/hardware-requirements-for-the-teams-app#hardware-requirements-for-teams-on-mobile-devices`.

6. C. More settings

    Explanation: More settings is not one of the available settings headings for configuration profiles for an IP phone in the Microsoft Teams admin center. The available options include **General**, **Device settings**, and **Network settings**: `https://docs.microsoft.com/en-us/microsoftteams/devices/phones-for-teams`.

7. A. True

    Explanation: It is possible to deploy Microsoft Teams to VDI environments: `https://docs.microsoft.com/en-us/microsoftteams/teams-for-vdi`.

8. C. Shared phones

    Explanation: Shared phones is not a description for a type of IP phone in the Microsoft Teams admin center. Types of IP phones available include **User phones**, **Common area phones**, and **Conference phones**: `https://docs.microsoft.com/en-us/microsoftteams/devices/phones-for-teams`.

9. A. True

   Explanation: Teams Rooms devices may be configured within hybrid environments: `https://docs.microsoft.com/en-us/microsoftteams/rooms/rooms-configure-accounts`.

10. B. User

    Explanation: In VDI mode, the Teams app should be deployed in user mode: `https://docs.microsoft.com/en-us/microsoftteams/teams-for-vdi#install-or-update-the-teams-desktop-app-on-vdi`.

Chapter 7 – Monitoring Usage within Microsoft Teams

1. C. Teams meeting usage

   Explanation: Teams meeting usage is not a valid option for an available report in the Microsoft Teams admin center. **Teams live events usage**, **Teams usage**, and **Teams user activity** are all valid reports that can be used: `https://docs.microsoft.com/en-us/microsoftteams/teams-analytics-and-reports/teams-reporting-reference`.

2. C. **Reports | Usage**

   Explanation: You would need to go to **Reports | Usage** in the Microsoft 365 admin center to view the available usage reports: `https://docs.microsoft.com/en-us/microsoft-365/admin/activity-reports/activity-reports?view=o365-worldwide`.

3. A. True

   Explanation: Call analytics dashboard activity may also be viewed in Power BI Desktop: `https://docs.microsoft.com/en-us/microsoftteams/cqd-power-bi-query-templates`.

4. A. `https://cqd.teams.microsoft.com`, and D. `https://admin.teams.microsoft.com`

   Explanation: Both URLs can be used to navigate to the call analytics dashboard: `https://docs.microsoft.com/en-us/microsoftteams/turning-on-and-using-call-quality-dashboard#:~:text=Open%20the%20Microsoft%20Call%20Quality,and%20select%20Call%20Quality%20Dashboard`.

5. A. True

    Explanation: Teams call and meeting quality may be monitored on a per-user basis from the Microsoft Teams admin center: `https://docs.microsoft.com/en-us/microsoftteams/teams-analytics-and-reports/user-activity-report`.

6. C. 60 days

    Explanation: The Teams user activity report may not be filtered and viewed on a 60-day range basis. It may be viewed over 7-day, 30-day, or 90-day periods: `https://docs.microsoft.com/en-us/microsoftteams/teams-analytics-and-reports/user-activity-report`.

7. A. **Users | Username | Call History**

    Explanation: To view per-user call analytics data, you would navigate to **Users | Username | Call History**. The other listed options will not navigate to this data: `https://docs.microsoft.com/en-us/microsoftteams/teams-analytics-and-reports/teams-reporting-reference`.

8. B. False

    Explanation: Power BI must be used in order to use Power BI to view the Call Quality Dashboard statistics: `https://docs.microsoft.com/en-us/microsoftteams/cqd-power-bi-query-templates`.

9. D. `[Documents]\Power BI Desktop\Custom Connectors`

    Explanation: The Power BI query templates must be downloaded to the **Custom Connectors** folder in order for the Call Quality Dashboard statistics to be successfully viewed in Power BI Desktop: `https://docs.microsoft.com/en-us/microsoftteams/cqd-power-bi-query-templates`.

10. A. True

    Explanation: Summary reports are an available feature in the Call Quality Dashboard: `https://docs.microsoft.com/en-us/microsoftteams/turning-on-and-using-call-quality-dashboard`.

Chapter 8 – Managing Collaboration and Chat within Microsoft Teams

1. B. Use the Teams admin center or PowerShell to reassign the global policy to affected users and then delete the policy that is not required.

   Explanation: Before you can delete a policy, no users can be assigned to it. We use the Teams admin center to reassign the users affected to the global/default policy, and then we're able to delete the policy that is not required.

   Reference: https://docs.microsoft.com/en-us/microsoftteams/ messaging-policies-in-teams#assign-a-custom-messaging- policy-to-users.

2. B. False

   Explanation: Users can only have one of each type of Teams policy assigned to them at once. In the event of membership in multiple groups that each have policies assigned to them, the group rank in the policy assignment settings determines which policy applies to the user.

   Reference: https://docs.microsoft.com/en-us/microsoftteams/ assign-policies.

3. A. True

   Explanation: As with the last question, users can have one policy of each type assigned at a time and group policy settings determine rankings for each group in case of conflicting assignments for users who are members of multiple groups.

   Reference: https://docs.microsoft.com/en-us/microsoftteams/ assign-policies.

4. B. No

   Explanation: Preventing users from messaging external users is configured in the **External access** settings.

   Reference: https://docs.microsoft.com/en-us/microsoftteams/ manage-external-access.

5. D. External access settings

   Explanation: The external access settings include domain-specific configurations such as this.

Reference: `https://docs.microsoft.com/en-us/microsoftteams/
manage-external-access`.

6. B. No

Explanation: Teams file content is stored in SharePoint. Managing access to it can be done in SharePoint's admin center.

Reference: `https://docs.microsoft.com/en-us/sharepoint/
external-sharing-overview`.

7. A. Yes

Explanation: Teams file content is stored in SharePoint. Managing access to it can be done in SharePoint's admin center.

Reference: `https://docs.microsoft.com/en-us/sharepoint/
external-sharing-overview`.

8. A. SharePoint Online admin center

Explanation: Teams file content is stored in SharePoint. Managing access to it can be done in SharePoint's admin center.

Reference: `https://docs.microsoft.com/en-us/sharepoint/
external-sharing-overview`.

9. C. Teams policy

Explanation: Private channel creation can be enabled or disabled for a group of users who are assigned a Teams policy that specifies as much.

Reference: `https://docs.microsoft.com/en-us/MicrosoftTeams/
teams-policies`.

10. D. All of the above

Explanation: All three are things that should be checked when messages aren't delivered as expected. The message could have too many attachments or images, the sender's domain could be blocked, or emailing channels might be blocked at the Team or tenant level.

Reference: `https://support.microsoft.com/en-us/office/send-
an-email-to-a-channel-in-teams-d91db004-d9d7-4a47-82e6-
fb1b16dfd51e`.

Chapter 9 – Managing Meetings and Live Events in Microsoft Teams

1. B and C. Create a meeting policy, and then apply the policy to the subset of users.

   Explanation: Camera usage in meetings can be restricted per user or group by creating a meeting policy and assigning it to users.

   Reference: `https://docs.microsoft.com/en-us/microsoftteams/meeting-policies-in-teams`.

2. B. No

   Explanation: There is no way of preventing a meeting invitee from inviting/forwarding to other potential attendees via a meeting policy.

   Reference: `https://docs.microsoft.com/en-us/microsoftteams/meeting-policies-in-teams`.

3. A. **Meetings | Meeting settings**

   Explanation: Help URLs are configured in the **Email invitation** section of the **Meeting settings** page.

   Reference: `https://docs.microsoft.com/en-US/microsoftteams/meeting-settings-in-teams`.

4. C. **Meetings | Live events settings**

   Explanation: The support URL can be specified in the **Support URL** section of the **Live events** settings page.

   Reference: `https://docs.microsoft.com/en-us/MicrosoftTeams/teams-live-events/configure-teams-live-events`.

5. C. **Meetings | Live events policies**

   Explanation: Live event recording can be never recorded, always recorded, or left to the organizer. The policy specifying it to be left to the organizer's discretion would then be applied to the group or users as appropriate.

   Reference: `https://docs.microsoft.com/en-US/microsoftteams/teams-live-events/set-up-for-teams-live-events`.

6. B. **Meetings | Meeting policies**

    Explanation: You can have users restricted to sharing none of their screen, one application at a time, or their entire screen by using meeting policies.

    Reference: `https://docs.microsoft.com/en-US/microsoftteams/meeting-policies-in-teams`.

7. D. **Meetings | Meeting settings**

    Explanation: This setting is a simple on/off toggle button that applies to your entire organization.

    Reference: `https://docs.microsoft.com/en-US/microsoftteams/meeting-settings-in-teams`.

8. B. Purchase third-party SDN/eCDN solutions.

    Explanation: Third-party SDN/eCDN solutions help lessen the bandwidth burden events and meetings place on your network. There are a few pre-integrated with Stream that you can choose to make it a simple process.

    Reference: `https://docs.microsoft.com/en-US/microsoftteams/teams-live-events/configure-teams-live-events#configure-a-third-party-video-distribution-provider`.

9. A. Vimeo Enterprise eCDN

    Explanation: Vimeo Enterprise eCDN is a real solution, but not one that is pre-integrated with Teams/Stream.

    Reference: `https://docs.microsoft.com/en-US/microsoftteams/teams-live-events/configure-teams-live-events#configure-a-third-party-video-distribution-provider`.

10. B. The user isn't licensed for audio conferencing.

    Explanation: If a user isn't licensed for audio conferencing, they'll be unable to use the conference bridge ability in their Team meeting invites. Users attending their meetings won't have the dial-in options available.

    Reference: `https://docs.microsoft.com/en-us/microsoftteams/set-up-audio-conferencing-in-teams`.

Chapter 10 – Managing Phone Numbers in Microsoft Teams

Question set 1

1. A. Calling plans

    Explanation: Calling plans are the simplest to implement.

    Reference: `https://docs.microsoft.com/en-us/microsoftteams/` `cloud-voice-landing-page`.

2. B. Direct routing

    Explanation: Using existing analog devices will require direct routing.

    Reference: `https://docs.microsoft.com/en-us/microsoftteams/` `cloud-voice-landing-page`.

3. B. Direct routing

    Explanation: Using existing numbers and on-premises PBX solutions requires direct routing.

    Reference: `https://docs.microsoft.com/en-us/microsoftteams/` `cloud-voice-landing-page`.

Question set 2

1. B. False

    Explanation: Users can only have one number assigned to them.

    Reference: `https://docs.microsoft.com/en-us/microsoftteams/` `assign-change-or-remove-a-phone-number-for-a-user`.

2. D. Add an emergency address for the office, and then update each phone number to use it.

    Explanation: Each phone number can have a different address, and it should be configured so that the location assigned to the number is the actual specific location where the user to whom it belongs is working.

    Reference: `https://docs.microsoft.com/en-us/MicrosoftTeams/` `add-change-remove-emergency-location-organization`.

3. D. Voice routing policy

   Explanation: Voice routing policies allow you to specify SBCs to be used for specific users when using direct routing.

   Reference: `https://docs.microsoft.com/en-us/microsoftteams/manage-voice-routing-policies`.

4. A. Dial plan

   Explanation: Dial plans enable the dial-by-extension capability within your organization.

   Reference: `https://docs.microsoft.com/en-us/microsoftteams/create-and-manage-dial-plans`.

5. A. True

   Explanation: Voicemail is automatically available when a user is licensed.

   Reference: `https://docs.microsoft.com/en-us/microsoftteams/set-up-phone-system-voicemail`.

6. B. False

   Explanation: Users can set up their own delegation settings via **Profile Picture | Settings | General | Delegation**.

   Reference: `https://support.microsoft.com/en-us/office/share-a-phone-line-with-a-delegate-16307929-a51f-43fc-8323-3b1bf115e5a8`.

7. B. Two locations with three places each

   Explanation: Each location can have multiple places. This would be most appropriate for adding separate buildings to a shared campus/address/location.

   Reference: `https://docs.microsoft.com/en-us/MicrosoftTeams/add-change-remove-emergency-place-organization`.

Chapter 11 – Managing Phone Systems in Microsoft Teams

1. A. True

   Explanation: Auto attendants' settings include a place to type a message rather than upload a recording. This typed text is then read aloud.

   Reference: `https://docs.microsoft.com/en-us/microsoftteams/create-a-phone-system-auto-attendant#call-flow`.

2. B, D, and E: You'll create a call queue assigned to a resource account and assign a service number to it.

   Explanation: All three (call queue assigned to a resource account with a service number) are required to solve the scenario.

   Reference: `https://docs.microsoft.com/en-us/microsoftteams/create-a-phone-system-call-queue`.

3. B. Call park policy

   Explanation: Call park is the process of placing a call on hold so that it can be transferred to other users.

   Reference: `https://docs.microsoft.com/en-us/microsoftteams/call-park-and-retrieve`.

4. C. Calling policy

   Explanation: Calling policies can include a setting for busy on busy that could provide a busy tone rather than permitting notification of another incoming call.

   Reference: `https://docs.microsoft.com/en-us/microsoftteams/teams-calling-policy`.

5. A. Caller ID policy

   Explanation: Caller ID policies can be used to replace a user's actual assigned number with a general line such as an auto attendant or receptionist.

   Reference: `https://docs.microsoft.com/en-us/microsoftteams/caller-id-policies`.

6.   C. Longest idle doesn't work with Skype for Business.

Explanation: Anything that involves presence reliance in Teams call queues won't work for agents using Skype.

Reference: `https://docs.microsoft.com/en-us/microsoftteams/business-voice/set-up-call-queues#call-routing`.

7.   A, B, and C: All routing methods except Longest idle work with Skype for Business.

Explanation: As with the previous question, anything involving presence reliance won't work for agents using Skype.

Reference: `https://docs.microsoft.com/en-us/microsoftteams/business-voice/set-up-call-queues#call-routing`.

8.   A, B, C, and D: All of the options are valid ways to specify call queue agent membership.

Explanation: Distribution lists, security groups, and M365 groups and (by extension) Teams' teams are all valid ways of specifying call queue agent membership.

Reference: `https://docs.microsoft.com/en-us/microsoftteams/business-voice/set-up-call-queues#call-agents`.

9.   B and C: Create a holiday, update the auto attendant's call flows during holiday settings to select the holiday, and then choose the auto attendant's behavior for it.

Explanation: First holidays are created in org-wide settings, and then they can be used in auto attendants' advanced options for holiday handling.

Reference: `https://docs.microsoft.com/en-us/microsoftteams/create-a-phone-system-auto-attendant#call-flows-during-holidays`.

10. A. Call queue

Explanation: Under the **Voice** node of the Microsoft Teams admin center, there are call park, caller ID, and calling policies, but call queues don't have policies – they are just queue configurations.

Reference: Check out the **Voice** node of your Microsoft Teams admin center at `https://admin.teams.microsoft.com/`.

Chapter 12 – Creating and Managing Teams

1. A. Private

    Explanation: Private teams cannot be joined by anyone unless they've been invited or added by a current member or owner (permissions allowing).

    Reference: `https://support.microsoft.com/en-us/office/make-a-public-team-private-in-teams-6f324fbc-6599-4612-8daa-ff5d35a746bf`.

2. B. Public

    Explanation: Public teams are searchable and can be joined by anyone without an invitation or request, but they aren't automatically added.

    Reference: `https://support.microsoft.com/en-us/office/make-a-public-team-private-in-teams-6f324fbc-6599-4612-8daa-ff5d35a746bf`.

3. C. Org-wide

    Explanation: Org-wide teams are available to organizations with 5,000 or fewer users and all users are automatically added.

    Reference: `https://docs.microsoft.com/en-us/microsoftteams/create-an-org-wide-team`.

4. C. <5,001 users and no more than 5 org-wide teams per tenant

    Explanation: Org-wide teams are limited to 5,000 members and only 5 org-wide teams can be created per organization.

    Reference: `https://docs.microsoft.com/en-us/microsoftteams/create-an-org-wide-team`.

5. D. You can create a team from Outlook.

    Explanation: You can create an M365 group from Outlook, but not a team directly. If you create an M365 group in Outlook, you can create a team by choosing the option to create a team from an existing M365 group.

    Reference: `https://support.microsoft.com/en-us/office/create-a-team-from-an-existing-group-24ec428e-40d7-4a1a-ab87-29be7d145865`.

6. C. Any private team can be made non-discoverable.

    Explanation: Public teams and org-wide teams are characteristically discoverable and will remain so. Private teams, however, can be made unsearchable.

    Reference: `https://support.microsoft.com/en-gb/office/make-a-public-team-private-in-teams-6f324fbc-6599-4612-8daa-ff5d35a746bf`.

7. B. False

    Explanation: Once a team is created for an M365 group, it can't be undone. You can delete a team and its associated SharePoint site, but you can't "undo" team creation.

    Reference: `https://docs.microsoft.com/en-us/microsoftteams/archive-or-delete-a-team`.

8. A. True

    Explanation: Yes, the `Set-Team` cmdlet with `-ShowInTeamsSearchAndSuggestions` as `$true` or `$false` will accomplish this.

    Reference: `https://docs.microsoft.com/en-us/powershell/module/teams/set-team?view=teams-ps`.

9. A. True

    Explanation: Public teams can be made private, and vice versa, by simply modifying the team's settings.

    Reference: `https://support.microsoft.com/en-us/office/make-a-public-team-private-in-teams-6f324fbc-6599-4612-8daa-ff5d35a746bf`.

10. A, C, and D.

    Explanation: Once you create a new team from scratch, you can still change the M365 group name, team name, and team privacy level without PowerShell. You won't be able to change the M365 group email, however, without PowerShell.

    Reference: `https://docs.microsoft.com/en-us/powershell/module/exchange/set-unifiedgroup?view=exchange-ps`.

Chapter 13 – Managing Team Membership Settings

Question set 1

1. Marketing (Universal security)

   B. Recreate the group as an O365 group.

   Explanation: Security groups cannot be upgraded to M365 groups.

   Reference: `https://docs.microsoft.com/en-us/microsoft-365/admin/manage/upgrade-distribution-lists?view=o365-worldwide`.

2. IT (Distribution)

   A. Change the group to an O365 group.

   Explanation: Distribution lists (non-nested) can be upgraded.

   Reference: `https://docs.microsoft.com/en-us/microsoft-365/admin/manage/upgrade-distribution-lists?view=o365-worldwide`.

3. HR – Benefits (Nested distribution list)

   B. Recreate the group as an O365 group.

   Explanation: You can only upgrade non-nested distribution lists.

   Reference: `https://docs.microsoft.com/en-us/microsoft-365/admin/manage/upgrade-distribution-lists?view=o365-worldwide`.

4. Sales (Global Security)

   B. Recreate the group as an O365 group.

   Explanation: Security groups cannot be upgraded to M365 groups.

   Reference: `https://docs.microsoft.com/en-us/microsoft-365/admin/manage/upgrade-distribution-lists?view=o365-worldwide`.

Question set 2

1. A. Access reviews in the Azure AD admin center

    Explanation: Azure AD access reviews can be used to perform regular reviews of group membership, whether by the individual members, group owners, or other designees who are appropriately licensed.

    Reference: `https://docs.microsoft.com/en-us/azure/active-directory/governance/access-reviews-overview`.

2. B. Access reviews in the Azure AD admin center

    Explanation: Azure AD access reviews can be used to annually (or at another frequency) email group members to confirm renewed interest in remaining part of the group, thereby making group membership more autonomous.

    Reference: `https://docs.microsoft.com/en-us/azure/active-directory/governance/access-reviews-overview`.

3. D. A guest user in HR that has the country attribute set to USA

    Explanation: The rule states that the user's department must be HR or IT *and* they must be in the US *and* the user type must be **Guest**.

    Reference: `https://docs.microsoft.com/en-us/azure/active-directory/enterprise-users/groups-create-rule`.

4. B. `Add-TeamUser -GroupId $team.GroupID -User bertha@natechamberlain.com -Role Owner`

    Explanation: Adding `-Role Owner` to the usual add user cmdlet assigns the owner role to new or existing members.

    Reference: `https://docs.microsoft.com/en-us/powershell/module/teams/add-teamuser?view=teams-ps#parameters`.

5. A. You aren't assigned an Azure Active Directory Premium P1 license.

    Explanation: You must have an Azure AD Premium P1 license in order to change a group from assigned to dynamic.

    Reference: `https://docs.microsoft.com/en-us/azure/active-directory/enterprise-users/groups-create-rule`.

6. A, B, and D.

    Explanation: If not a global or user administrator, a user must be assigned an Azure AD Premium P2 license in order to participate in access reviews. It is not required, however, if someone else is evaluating your membership – only those responsible for evaluating/reviewing require the P2 license.

    Reference: `https://docs.microsoft.com/en-us/azure/active-directory/governance/access-reviews-overview`.

Chapter 14 – Creating App Policies within Microsoft Teams

Question set 1

1. B. False

    Explanation: Third-party and custom apps are blocked, according to the screenshot.

    Reference: `https://docs.microsoft.com/en-us/microsoftteams/teams-app-permission-policies`.

2. B. False

    Explanation: Custom apps are blocked, according to the screenshot.

    Reference: `https://docs.microsoft.com/en-us/microsoftteams/teams-app-permission-policies`.

3. B. False

    Explanation: DocuSign is third-party and therefore blocked, according to the screenshot.

    Reference: `https://docs.microsoft.com/en-us/microsoftteams/teams-app-permission-policies`.

4. A. True

    Explanation: Power Virtual Agents is one of the explicitly allowed Microsoft apps in the screenshot.

    Reference: `https://docs.microsoft.com/en-us/microsoftteams/teams-app-permission-policies`.

Question set 2

1. B. App setup policy

    Explanation: App setup policies can be used to specify which apps appear in the left-hand navigation menu of Teams for certain users and groups and in what order.

    Reference: `https://docs.microsoft.com/en-us/microsoftteams/ teams-app-setup-policies`.

2. C. Create an app setup policy and assign it to specific users.

    Explanation: App setup policies can be used to specify which apps appear in the left-hand navigation menu of Teams for certain users and groups and in what order.

    Reference: `https://docs.microsoft.com/en-us/microsoftteams/ teams-app-setup-policies`.

3. A. An app permission policy assigned to a subset of users

    Reference: `https://docs.microsoft.com/en-us/microsoftteams/ teams-app-permission-policies`.

4. A. An app permission policy assigned to a subset of users

    Explanation: App permission policies specify who can install certain apps within Teams.

    Reference: `https://docs.microsoft.com/en-us/microsoftteams/ teams-app-permission-policies`.

5. C. Adjust the Global (Org-wide default) app setup policy

    Explanation: App setup policies can be used to specify which apps appear in the left-hand navigation menu of Teams for certain users and groups and in what order.

    Reference: `https://docs.microsoft.com/en-us/microsoftteams/ teams-app-setup-policies`.

6. B. Uploaded apps

    Explanation: App permission policies include Microsoft, Custom, and Third-Party setting sections.

    Reference: `https://docs.microsoft.com/en-us/microsoftteams/ teams-app-permission-policies`.

Other Books You May Enjoy

If you enjoyed this book, you may be interested in these other books by Packt:

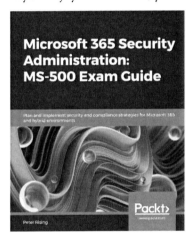

Microsoft 365 Security Administration: MS-500 Exam Guide

Peter Rising

ISBN: 978-1-83898-312-3

- Get up to speed with implementing and managing identity and access
- Understand how to employ and manage threat protection
- Get to grips with managing governance and compliance features in Microsoft 365
- Explore best practices for effective configuration and deployment
- Implement and manage information protection
- Prepare to pass the Microsoft exam and achieve certification with the help of self-assessment questions and a mock exam

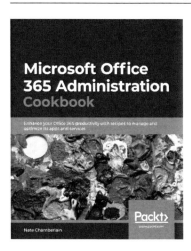

Microsoft Office 365 Administration Cookbook

Nate Chamberlain

ISBN: 978-1-83855-123-0

- Get to grips with basic Office 365 setup and routine administration tasks

- Manage Office 365 identities and groups efficiently and securely

- Harness the capabilities of PowerShell to automate common administrative tasks

- Configure and manage core Office 365 services such as Exchange Online, SharePoint, and OneDrive

- Configure and administer fast-evolving services such as Microsoft Search, Power Platform, Microsoft Teams, and Azure AD

- Get up and running with advanced threat protection features provided by the Microsoft 365 Security & Compliance Center

- Protect your organization's sensitive data with Office 365 Data Loss Prevention

- Monitor activities and behaviors across all Office 365 services

Packt>

`Packt.com`

Subscribe to our online digital library for full access to over 7,000 books and videos, as well as industry leading tools to help you plan your personal development and advance your career. For more information, please visit our website.

Why subscribe?

- Spend less time learning and more time coding with practical eBooks and Videos from over 4,000 industry professionals

- Improve your learning with Skill Plans built especially for you

- Get a free eBook or video every month

- Fully searchable for easy access to vital information

- Copy and paste, print, and bookmark content

Did you know that Packt offers eBook versions of every book published, with PDF and ePub files available? You can upgrade to the eBook version at `packt.com` and as a print book customer, you are entitled to a discount on the eBook copy. Get in touch with us at `customercare@packtpub.com` for more details.

At `www.packt.com`, you can also read a collection of free technical articles, sign up for a range of free newsletters, and receive exclusive discounts and offers on Packt books and eBooks.

Leave a review - let other readers know what you think

Please share your thoughts on this book with others by leaving a review on the site that you bought it from. If you purchased the book from Amazon, please leave us an honest review on this book's Amazon page. This is vital so that other potential readers can see and use your unbiased opinion to make purchasing decisions, we can understand what our customers think about our products, and our authors can see your feedback on the title that they have worked with Packt to create. It will only take a few minutes of your time, but is valuable to other potential customers, our authors, and Packt. Thank you!

Index

Made in United States
North Haven, CT
02 February 2022

15534836R00248